DEVELOPING EMPLOYEE RELATIONS

Developing Employee Relations

PETER WARR, STEPHEN FINEMAN, NIGEL NICHOLSON, ROY PAYNE
MRC Social and Applied Psychology Unit, The University of Sheffield

 SAXON HOUSE/GOWER PRESS

Published by
Saxon House in association with Gower Press, Teakfield Limited, Westmead, Farnborough, Hants, England.

  British Library Cataloguing in Publication Data

Tinsley Park Employee Relations Project
Developing employee relations.
1. Tinsley Park Employee Relations Project
I. Title II. Warr, Peter Bryan
331'.046'9106542821   HD6976.I52G7

ISBN 0-566-00209-4

ISBN 0 566 00209 4

Printed in Great Britain by Biddles Limited, Guildford, Surrey

Contents

Figure

Table

Foreword

by Derrick Canham,
Manager, Industrial Relations,
British Steel Corporation Sheffield Division

Trade unionists and managers are frequently embarrassed by the allegation that they spend more time 'fire fighting' than they do 'organising to prevent' fires. However, the number and variety of developments in the industrial relations scene has recently been such that the parties can scarcely avoid a preoccupation with immediate events. Scant resources are of necessity directed towards the limited aim of understanding the causes of particular disputes and dealing with the pressing problems they create.

Both groups might naturally look towards the increasing number of academic researchers in this field to provide them with a framework to interpret their experience in a constructive way. However, many managers and union representatives who have sought help from the writings of organisational theorists will have found that the general theories which are available, even when they are comprehensible to them, have limited applicability to shop-floor problems in a unionised works; they refer mainly to professional and managerial workgroups.

Increases in the rate of technological change are being matched by changes of a social and political nature. The growing aspirations of employees, for instance, towards an increased involvement in the management of companies create a need for the development of new forms of organisation and management styles which can accommodate these whilst maintaining or improving the effectiveness of the business. Enormous advantages could arise, in such areas, from the right kind of collaboration between industry and academic researchers. This book documents an exercise in which the parties set out through a mutually productive association to improve employee relations in a British Steel Corporation works. It describes how they succeeded to a large measure, outlining frankly and readably the problems encountered in setting up the Project, agreeing its terms of reference, and maintaining its momentum to the end. Some useful lessons are drawn, and the later part of the book sets these into a wider industrial relations context.

The Project described here grew from a need felt by management and trade unions alike to examine and discuss the industrial relations climate at Tinsley Park Works in a more structured and constructive way than had previously been possible. In this case, however, a team of psychologists spent more than two years getting to know the people and the plant, as they applied their specialist knowledge to helping all parties to improve their understanding of this particular industrial relations scene.

From the outset, it was made clear that primary responsibility for implementing change would rest with management, trade unions and workpeople. Having helped to set up the social machinery of the Project the academics deliberately confined their role to providing information, feeding it back to joint discussion groups, acting as a resource to those groups, coaching individuals who found the general process baffling and, wherever possible, encouraging the participants to take action and make changes when agreement was reached and resources were available.

For many people on the works the Project did not have an end, in that the institutions and habits created continued after the researchers had left the plant. It has been suggested that the Project should be regarded as a novel form of in-plant training and this is how it worked. No-one expected its evaluation in objective terms to be easy, and all parties approached the venture with the kind of moderate expectation appropriate to planned organisational change. However, this particular Project included a systematic attempt to measure its own effectiveness, and several different assessments were undertaken. In a more general sense one major value of projects like this one is to try out and learn from new ideas; we need to experiment with new possibilities and we will not necessarily 'get it right' first time. In this case we learned much which is of practical value and the book sets out to explain how companies could be still more successful next time.

In the event, the Project met with its fair share of problems. Not all managers nor all trade unionists were able to share the enthusiasm which the Project engendered in others. The high rate of management turnover created special difficulties, and, for completely external reasons, a long and difficult strike occurred during the Project. It is interesting to note, however, that the degree of reported improvement following the Project has been strongly correlated with the degree of commitment and enthusiasm to the Project contributed by the various interests.

What follows describes a fruitful collaboration between management and employees at all levels of a steelworks and a team of psychologists from the MRC Social and Applied Psychology Unit at Sheffield University. The book contains significant contributions to academic knowledge about employee relations and organisational design but it is written in a non-technical way and without jargon. Many line managers and personnel specialists will recognise the problems described and most of them will benefit from the sensible but imaginative way in which they are gradually set into an explanatory theoretical context. The message comes through, however, that the collaboration was not about testing academic theories. It was a piece of 'action research' and, as such, dedicated to making useful changes which in themselves might improve theory and subsequent practice. A sufficient number of changes were made to ensure the good reputation of the Project even among participants whose interest was confined to an early practical outcome.

British Steel Corporation employees of Tinsley Park Works would wish to place on record their lasting appreciation of the sustained effort and patient help contributed by the authors of this book.

Preface

As the pace of social and technological change increases, there is growing collaboration between industry and academic researchers. The goal is to assist each to build upon the knowledge and ideas of the other and from this process to develop new understanding and practical applications.

Some of the most fruitful collaborative ventures of this kind have concerned the problems of change itself. Projects under the umbrella labels 'organisation development' and 'action research' have helped industrial, commercial and public organisations to mobilise their own resources to initiate and cope with change, to learn from these processes, and to increase long-term effectiveness.

Researchers in this field come from several academic disciplines, amongst which psychology is increasingly represented. Many organisations now employ psychologists or seek their assistance in the fields of human factors, training, and personnel, and for projects concerned with employee relations, communication, and decision-making. The British Steel Corporation is one such organisation, and this book is based upon one such project.

For two and a half years we worked closely with the managers and workpeople of Tinsley Park Works, a modern and successful British Steel Corporation plant on the outskirts of Sheffield. Our brief was to apply social psychological knowledge to the benefit of employee relations. A project of this kind makes additional demands upon many already busy people, and we wish to preface this book with a statement of our respect and gratitude to the management, unions and workpeople who had the confidence and openmindedness to create what became known as the 'Tinsley Park Employee Relations Project'.

How this Project came about and its implications for change programmes elsewhere are described throughout the book. It will be clear from our account that the plant is not untypical. It has had its share of problems, most of them common to manufacturing units of large corporations, but it has naturally been shaped by particular local features and individual personalities. Contacts at a personal level with members of the plant were among the most fruitful and enjoyable elements of our relationship with the works. We would not like to spoil this relationship by being quoted out of context and leaving the false impression that Tinsley Park Works was 'a problem plant'. On the contrary, its underlying strength and confidence is evidenced through the initiation of the Employee Relations Project and the publication of this book.

The book itself is in two parts, each preceded by a brief introduction. Part One contains the narrative of events making up the Employee Relations Project and its evaluation, and Part Two is a more general treatment of issues and themes relating to employee relations and the introduction and maintenance of change. This second part draws upon the events and experiences described in Part One but goes beyond them to utilise other research findings and theories. We have attempted to do this in a non-technical way, to avoid the use of jargon, and to keep supplementary notes and literature citations to a minimum. Our aim is to say something useful to line managers and personnel specialists as well as to teachers and researchers, and we hope that the presentation of material in Part One will attract the reader to the more analytical treatment of problems and procedures to be found in Part Two.

PART ONE

Introduction to Part One

Part One of the book is made up of eight chapters detailing the history of the Employee Relations Project. Chapter 1 introduces ourselves and the kind of work we do, and examines how the Project took shape during discussions with the works manager and his senior colleagues. Chapter 2 contains a description of the plant at the time of the Project, and presents details of production processes, number and type of employees and the industrial relations climate at the time.

Chapter 3 takes us onto the initial stage of the Project and describes its principle objectives and procedures. The most important mechanism was a network of 'project groups', and the operation of these is described in some detail in chapter 4. The issues raised and the manner in which they were handled at each level of the works are illustrated throughout that chapter.

Chapter 5 presents an account of a large-scale survey investigation, which tapped opinions about major themes identified through the project groups and 'fed back' the results for examination by members of the works. In the following chapter we describe the Interlinked Phase, a more specialised inquiry into the industrial relations climate on the works as seen by shop stewards and management and as reflected in their formal dealings with each other. This chapter also describes our Interim Report, in which we set down an analysis of major employee relations issues and our recommendations for further action.

Chapter 7 takes a look at differences between the departments participating in the Project, and illustrates how a different pattern of events and attitudes in each department contributed to varying progress and effectiveness. Finally, in chapter 8, we describe some ways in which the Project was evaluated. At that point we examine the scope and number of changes introduced through the mechanisms of the Project and review the measures which were taken of changing attitudes and opinions. Details of trends in the level of industrial disputes and information about the cost of the Project are also presented.

The events described in these eight chapters took place over a duration of two and a half years, although the period of major activity was only half that time. The principal dates were as follows:

Major events in the Employee Relations Project

August 1973	Discussions between ourselves and British Steel Corporation senior managers about the possibility of a study.
September 1973	Our outline proposals accepted by senior managers.
November 1973	Discussions with management and shop stewards on site, leading to agreement to proceed with an Employee Relations Project, and the establishment (in January 1974) of a union-

	management Steering Committee.
February 1974	Briefing sessions for foremen and others, followed by training for project group leaders.
March 1974	Level one project group commences (works manager and department managers). Publication of the first issue of *Focus*, the Project Bulletin. Completion of the Before questionnaire, establishing a baseline for later evaluation. Level two project groups commence (department managers and section managers and their equivalent).
April 1974	Level three project groups commence (section managers and foremen and supervisory staff).
May 1974	Level four project groups commence (foremen or shop stewards and shop-floor operatives and non-supervisory staff).
June 1974	*Focus*, issue number 2.
August 1974	*Focus*, issue number 3, including the Project questionnaire. (Project group meetings continue up to February 1975.)
September to November 1974	Interviews and questionnaires for the Interlinked Phase.
November 1974	*Focus*, issue number 4, including results of the Project questionnaire.
February 1975	Interim Report to the works.
March 1975	Discussions commence about the Interim Report, involving management at group and works level, the Section Council, departmental Joint Consultative Committees, and individual management teams.
April 1975	*Focus*, issue number 5, including a summary of problems raised and actions taken and a statement by the works manager on longer-term issues.
June 1975	After questionnaire to gather additional data for evaluating the Project. (Discussions about the Interim Report continue up to February 1976.)
February 1976	Second Report to the works, presenting evaluation material and describing some factors likely to affect the success of future programmes.

Throughout the chapters of Part One we pay only limited attention to questions of interpretation and generalisation. Our aim is to present an informative, readable and complete account of the Project as a whole. A more general treatment of theoretical and practical issues will be found in Part Two.

1 The Employee Relations Project takes shape

Industrial organisations are always in a state of change, but occasionally it is desirable for a deliberate attempt to be made to shape and assist this process. The Employee Relations Project was one such programme of assisted change carried out in a large and modern Sheffield steelworks. Tinsley Park Works is a unit of the British Steel Corporation, employing at the time of the Project some 1,250 people in the melting, rolling, finishing, and transportation of high grade steel. It had fulfilled these functions efficiently and profitably, but in the years up to 1974 some people within the Corporation had increasingly felt that Tinsley Park's industrial relations and communications compared unfavourably with other works, principally its 'sister' plant at Stocksbridge. A number of senior managers had come to believe that some form of change programme was needed to help the works achieve a more harmonious and effective climate of employee relations.

This book describes and interprets the steps taken towards that goal and our own involvement in them. We are four psychologists engaged in full-time research and development into the psychology of work. We are employed by the Medical Research Council at the Social and Applied Psychology Unit in the University of Sheffield.* This Unit is unique in the UK, employing more than twenty full-time researchers on continuing projects in the areas of organisational change and effectiveness, occupational stress and well-being, training, employee participation, job redesign, communication systems, union—management relations, man—computer interaction and related fields. The Unit is government-financed, so that we are not in any way paid consultants for management or another interest group. We are very much aware that managers, workers and subgroups of each are sensitive to the balance of power between them, and while in particular situations we may sometimes express opinions more to the liking of one side than the other, we are avowedly non-partisan.

Our projects in industrial and other organisations are varied, but underlying them all are four basic features:

1 Our long-term purpose is to increase understanding through the systematic acquisition of knowledge, although on the way to this goal we may become engaged with many specific questions of immediate practical importance.
2 Our assistance in these practical problem-solving activities is without financial charge. This ensures that our longer-term perspective is preserved and that we retain our independence.

---

* Stephen Fineman is now at the School of Management at the University of Bath.

3

3 We try to ensure that both management and shop floor are kept informed at all stages of a joint venture. This means that our research proposals, progress reports and recommendations are made widely available throughout the organisations in which we work.

4 We consult fully in advance with all parties on the use to be made of information obtained and we maintain strict confidentiality about the facts and opinions we gather. In the present case, for instance, drafts of this book have been made available to management and shop-floor representatives of Tinsley Park Works.

The initiation of research projects in collaboration with industry or public authorities can take many forms. Sometimes we design a study of importance to ourselves and then seek organisations who are willing to assist us. On other occasions firms approach us with questions for discussion and possible investigation. In most cases there ensues a dialogue between us and the firm, in which our research objectives and the firm's problem-solving goals are compared, aligned and accepted, so that both sets of interests will be served by undertaking a joint project. This was how the Tinsley Park Employee Relations Project came into being.

Origins of the Project

The Unit had undertaken a number of investigations with the steel industry in Sheffield and Rotherham before the Employee Relations Project was launched. Over a period of years we had carried out studies of foremen's training needs, the evaluation of training, communication to crane drivers, readership analysis of a works newspaper, employee participation in decision-making and several other investigations. During the spring and summer of 1973 contacts between the Unit and senior British Steel Corporation management were developing in two principal ways. On the one hand we had been assisting with an Accident Prevention Seminar organised through Divisional Head Office; during this we had emphasised the need to bridge the communication gap between management and shop floor through face-to-face meetings. On the other hand we had been discussing with the management of several local works a possible investigation into the job training needs of shop stewards.

Out of these activities and our previous collaborative work came a suggestion from senior British Steel Corporation management that the Unit might be interested in the industrial relations situation at Tinsley Park. This works had been opened ten years previously and despite its technological similarity with its 'sister' plant, the older Stocksbridge Works, its industrial relations climate had been quite different. Stocksbridge Works had been founded in 1842 as Samuel Fox and Company and had subsequently become part of the United Steel Companies until nationalisation in 1967. Tinsley Park Works had opened in 1963 and had belonged to the English Steel Corporation. After nationalisation the two works were brought

together into one unit, and this had naturally required administrative and managerial changes. There was general agreement that these changes had been more
substantial in Tinsley Park than in Stocksbridge.

The Stocksbridge plant was described to us in 1973 as a stable and traditional
works in a mainly rural setting. A relatively harmonious spirit, based upon a local
community life, was said to cut across organisational levels and functional divisions.
This meant that the day-to-day business of employee and industrial relations was
conducted in a reasonable spirit of trust. The image conveyed to us of Tinsley Park
Works at that time was in sharp contrast: a new plant, lacking the same sort of
community base, and located more firmly in an urban environment with a workforce drawn from a wide range of other industries. Senior management felt that
the mechanisms for daily problem-solving, whether those of informal relations or
established custom and practice, could not be relied upon. An atmosphere of
mistrust was described as underlying the promotion of sectional interests without
regard for their wider impact. This was partly substantiated by our analysis of
disputes data, which showed that the level of conflict at Tinsley Park had regularly
exceeded by a considerable amount the level at Stocksbridge over the previous
three years.

However, we soon discovered that such a view was not universally held among the
Tinsley Park workforce. Although many people recognised that in some sections of
the works relations between management and shop floor were undoubtedly strained,
others held the opinion that on balance the Tinsley Park industrial relations climate
was no worse than that at Stocksbridge. Many resentments were focussed outside
the works, and some people, particularly shop-floor representatives, felt that there
was too much dependence on and interference from Stocksbridge. This perspective
arose partly from the pre-nationalisation rivalries which had existed between the
two plants, but also from the problems of communication and centralised decision-
making which are familiar to members of any large corporation.

At the time of writing the picture has changed in several ways. Revisions to the
British Steel Corporation structure were introduced in April 1976 and these
included some realignments within Stocksbridge and Tinsley Park Works. Secondly,
long-range plans to expand production on the spacious Tinsley Park site have
moved forward, whereas no comparable changes have been initiated at Stocksbridge. Thirdly, a number of local administrative changes have eased the
relationship between the plants. Finally, there was the Employee Relations
Project which took place during 1974 and 1975 and which we believe helped to
develop relationships between the two plants and to improve the effectiveness of
Tinsley Park Works.

This Project involved the employees of the main production and ancillary
departments of the plant. The aim was to assist the members of the works to look
afresh at the problems facing them and the manner in which they were being
handled, and to rouse and utilise the interest and skills of a broad spread of the
workforce towards their solution.

The first serious exploratory meetings between ourselves and senior management took place during June and July 1973, at which a wide variety of the above mentioned issues were discussed. At this stage our main contacts were with the divisional director of personnel, the general manager and group personnel manager (both of whom had responsibility for the joint Stocksbridge and Tinsley Park Works), and the works manager of Tinsley Park itself. At the early meetings to discuss what might be done at Tinsley Park these managers drew our attention to a survey that had recently been conducted at the Corporation's Ravenscraig and Gartcosh Works by a team from Chicago University together with Gallup Poll (UK). We subsequently looked closely at the Ravenscraig Survey, and it played an important part in the design and development of the Employee Relations Project. For this reason its main features will be outlined here.

The Ravenscraig Survey

The Ravenscraig Survey had comprised three main stages. The first stage was the voluntary completion by the workforce of a lengthy and wide-ranging question-naire. The information derived from this not only showed how people felt about important issues in their work setting, but also allowed comparisons to be made between the attitudes and opinions of different sections and work groups. The second stage consisted of 'feedback' of these results to the workforce. Each group discussed its own results in relation to those of the rest of the works, and developed action recommendations out of them. This process was guided by 'feedback leaders', junior managers from elsewhere in the works, who were under instruction to be as 'participative' as possible. In the third stage groups' recommendations were noted upon special 'Feedback Forms' and the forms were passed to appropriate members of management to decide whether action was to be taken. The manage-ment decision was subsequently entered on the form and a copy returned to the Feedback Group, for display on a noticeboard of their choice.

The British Steel Corporation report of the Ravenscraig Survey indicates that managerial opinions about it were mixed. Department and assistant department managers were keen, as was the works director, but intermediate level management were more doubtful. The official trade union view was neutral. In terms of action developments, half of the Feedback Form recommendations were positively received by management and a sample check suggested that about half of this proportion were followed by changes on the works.

The Ravenscraig Survey was clearly an important attempt to involve a broad spread of a workforce in the exploration and solution of day-to-day problems. Like all first attempts it could be improved upon, and as we considered in autumn 1973 its lessons for a project in Tinsley Park Works our aim was to overcome its limitations and to expand its clearly beneficial features. The BSC Manpower Planning, Research and Statistics Section, who had supervised the Survey, readily recognised two of the major difficulties:

1   The Survey was seen largely as a Head Office exercise, and local managers did
    not identify themselves with its success or failure. Too little effort was made
    to encourage personal commitment before and during the Survey.
2   Feedback Leaders were sometimes ineffective, perhaps because they were
    inadequately trained. The fact that Feedback Leaders were unconnected with
    a workgroup was also thought to be undesirable, as they were not in touch
    with many of the issues discussed.

Principles of the Project

As we worked upon the design of what was to become the Employee Relations
Project, with the shortcomings of the Ravenscraig Survey in mind, we believed that
the main interest and momentum would have to come from within the works
itself; this meant active union and shop-floor involvement, as well as commitment
from several levels of management. We also wanted to establish continuing face-to-
face discussions among people who shared day-to-day working problems; this
probably meant that a group's immediate boss should be their group leader. We
argued that a greater emphasis on continuing group meetings and decision-making
(rather than on a single questionnaire) was vital to encourage interested participation, and that some personal contact with people higher in the organisation to
discuss action recommendations would also be necessary. Another theme was that
special discussions within management would be as important as those between
management and manual workers.

Because of this concern beyond a narrow definition of industrial relations, the
programme was to be referred to as an Employee Relations Project. In later
introductions of the Project to the works we emphasised how 'employee relations'
were to do with the way people of all levels and functions worked together across
a wide range of issues; the Project went beyond merely union—management
relations. The deliberate use of the word 'project' rather than 'survey' was
symbolically important to emphasise the active nature of the problem-solving
process and to stress its relevance to employees at all levels.

We thus viewed the Project as building upon the experience of the Ravenscraig
Survey to get people together to examine and talk through their mutual problems
and their customary ways of tackling the issues that divided them. Our early
deliberations on how to accomplish this focussed on two principal mechanisms:

1   'Project groups' would be set up at all levels of the works to raise problems and
    seek solutions. The Problem Record Form idea from the Ravenscraig Survey
    could be used to assist the 'unfreezing' of orthodox communication channels
    and to enable individuals and groups to raise issues and make requests in areas
    they would otherwise be unable to reach.
2   A form of 'survey feedback' was considered in order to channel back to the
    works information from a questionnaire study on the current state of opinion

about problems and issues. The goal here was to provide additional impetus for change through the publication and discussion of information which was not normally gathered in a systematic way.

We were especially aware of how important it was that these mechanisms should not undermine existing and accepted managerial authority, and project groups were not envisaged as having formal authority. The idea was that an early managerial commitment to the Project, coupled with the momentum for change brought about by its operation, would ensure that serious consideration was given to recommendations arising from each group. We were also confident that this effect would be enhanced by the inherent good sense in many of the proposals.

This kind of approach can be viewed within the recent growth of 'organisation development' exercises, though departing from approaches that examine inter-personal relations away from the work situation, such as one finds in T-group meetings or some more structured management training exercises. Instead, we chose a mechanism that aimed to enhance operational effectiveness by focussing on practical changes within the works itself, and which would draw its strength from the extent that people saw it as desirable to make use of the mechanism. Through early success with local changes in working practices and equipment we hoped to create confidence in the mechanism so that it would later be used to tackle problems of interpersonal attitudes and behaviour between groups and individuals. The unfolding of this general plan is described throughout the book, and a broader perspective together with our conclusions about its potential application in other settings is presented in Part Two.

At this point it is appropriate to summarise in terms of three issues: the nature of the initial problem; our underlying assumptions in approaching the problem; and what we sought to achieve through the Employee Relations Project.

It was clear from our initial contacts that senior management regarded Tinsley Park as a 'difficult' works, reflected in the ready use of sanctions to win disputes and the frequent breakdown of agreements and custom and practice rules of conduct. At the outset we did not allow ourselves to be convinced that this was the whole story, for others might see it differently. We argued that making known the major different interpretations and generating constructive face-to-face discussion about them would be a significant step towards action.

This strategy assumes that 'reality' is many-sided, a matter for agreement, dis-agreement, and even negotiation. Part of our job is to help people to achieve consensus where consensus is possible and otherwise to help them to examine the nature of their conflicting views and the issues that divide them. This process not only aids problem diagnosis but also indicates the areas where there may be room for movement to greater agreement and understanding. Working through and exploring conflicts can often teach the parties something important that can fruitfully be used to improve future decision-making. Of course, there are also divisive issues where conflict will always be present and on which no 'solution' will satisfy everyone. It would be a serious mistake to argue that the discussion of

8

problems will inevitably lead to their solution, yet there are many organisations where discussion has been replaced by habitual stereotyped and prejudiced assumptions and the scope for 'unfreezing' these habitual reactions is often considerable.

Much research has now accumulated which suggests an approach to change which contains four main ideas about relationships and decision-making at work:

1   When people have a say in decisions that affect them it often results in better decisions.
2   When people have been involved in this decision-making their commitment to action is generally increased and their fear of harmful consequences reduced.
3   More creative and innovative solutions to problems are likely when people strive to work in an atmosphere of openness, trust and informal cooperation, than when the mode is formal and polarised into 'us' versus 'them'.
4   When an organisation accepts the need to improve its effectiveness then a procedure based upon the three points above is likely to be useful.

This outlook is not uncontroversial, since it reflects a system of values that cannot claim to be definitive. However they appeared to be useful guidelines that were appropriate to the needs of Tinsley Park Works in 1973. The major problem was how to apply the guidelines in practice to a busy industrial organisation, and the vehicle created for this was the Employee Relations Project. The Project sought to achieve its goal of more effective relationships between people and groups by:

1   Providing time for people to meet.
2   Improving the quality of communication between them when they did meet.
3   Identifying problems which could affect employee relations of all kinds.
4   Committing people to spend time, money, and other resources to solve the problems.
5   Monitoring the progress made and learning from the information gathered.

The focus of improvement was intended to be as broad as possible: aimed not just at people and problems within their own 'patch' (e.g. relations between the shop floor and management within a particular department), but also between sections and departments at all levels (e.g. between management and other staff groupings), as well as between people at Tinsley Park Works and elsewhere in the British Steel Corporation.

A secondary though extremely important aim was evaluation. From the outset we regarded it as essential to build in procedures for systematically evaluating the Project. This was necessary not only for our long-term goals as research workers, but also for the British Steel Corporation and others to be able to assess the effects of the Project and to reach informed decisions about the desirability of similar projects elsewhere.

How plans for the Project and its evaluation evolved during the course of our early contacts is described in chapter 3, but first we should set the scene by describing the works, its history and climate.

2   The works and its climate

Tinsley Park Works is situated on a large flat expanse of land bounded by a dual-carriageway road leading to the London to Leeds motorway on the north side of Sheffield. Large modern rectangular buildings are widely spaced over an area of approximately one square mile, interlaced with railway tracks and roads. The open spaces that are not given over to stockyards and piles of scrap metal are grass-covered and trimmed. There is a misleading appearance of inactivity as you travel along the road from the security gate-house to the central office complex, for the trains are often immobile, the roads are empty apart from the occasional car or lorry, and there are few people to be seen. Entering any one of the buildings quickly dispels the illusion of quiet: making, rolling and finishing steel demands large scale and precise coordination of men and machines.

It is helpful to think of the works as carrying out a single integrated and linear process, from right to left in Figure 2.1. The raw material, mainly scrap metal and chemical materials, is melted and cast into ingots, about the size of a large man. The ingots are rolled into billets and blooms (long rectangular bars of steel), dressed (scraped clean and tested), and transported to other works. The steel produced at Tinsley Park Works is of high quality and cost, and it is used where special-purpose material is required in the car, aircraft and engineering industries.

The Melting Shop, seat of the primary process in the sequence, is an imposingly large and clean-cut building, appropriately unique in standing on the only elevated part of the site. The interior is a massive cathedral to man's power over materials: a dark vaulted chamber whose centre-piece is the concentrated fire of the twin electric arc furnaces. These provide a uniquely clean and smokeless means of melting metal. Approximately every 4½ hours each of them is charged with 120 tons of scrap, brought to its doors by locomotives.

Once the furnace has completed its task and is ready for tapping, the load is initially transferred to the vacuum degassing plant, a fully automated process whereby every part of the steel is three times treated for the removal of gaseous impurities. Next the molten steel is poured into ingot moulds, which are mounted on bogies drawn by locomotives operated by men of the Traffic section. Tapping a furnace is spectacular, and there are few sights in industry more awe-inspiring than the stream of white, yellow, and red molten metal tumbling into the ingot moulds. Most of this process is supervised remotely from modern control rooms, though men wearing dark goggles and heavily protective clothing stand watching from the surrounding raised walkways and gantries.

The Bloom and Billet Mill impresses in a different way: less volcanic and more self-evidently a manufacturing process. Rollered tracks run parallel along the 400 yard shop, punctuated by the towering arched structures that house the great

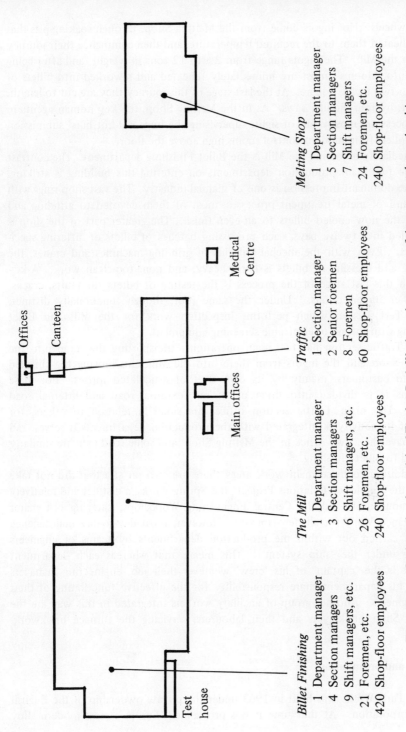

Billet Finishing

1	Department manager
4	Section managers
9	Shift managers, etc.
21	Foremen, etc.
420	Shop-floor employees

The Mill

1	Department manager
3	Section managers
6	Shift managers, etc.
26	Foremen, etc.
240	Shop-floor employees

Traffic

1	Section manager
2	Senior foremen
8	Foremen
60	Shop-floor employees

Melting Shop

1	Department manager
5	Section managers
7	Shift managers
24	Foremen, etc.
240	Shop-floor employees

Offices

Canteen

Medical Centre

Main offices

Test house

Figure 2.1   Outline plan (to scale) of Tinsley Park Works and summary of departmental membership (Further details are in the text. The distance between the outer edges of Billet Finishing and the Melting Shop is about 1000 yards.)

11

rolling wheels. Hot ingots come from the Melting Shop, through soaking pits that have reheated them to the required temperature, and then commence their journey through the Mill. The ingots range from 2½ to 12 tons in weight, and after being rolled into 'blooms', most are immediately reheated and reworked into billets of down to two inches square. At the last stage of this journey they are cut to length, still hot, by four circular saws. As in the Melting Shop, the key human agents in this process are mostly out of sight, supervising the huge red-hot bars' submission to the rollers from modern control rooms high above the floor.

Immediately adjoining the Mill is the Billet Finishing department. The contrast with the two main production departments on entering this building is striking. Here the dominant impression is one of manual industry. The vast shop rings with the sound of metal treatment processes, most of them devoted to grinding and shaving the now cooled billets to an even finish. The greater part of the shop is subdivided into twelve bays, each processing batches of billets of differing speci-fications. Even with the mechanical aids of grinding machines and cranes, the stacking and dressing of billets is hard, heavy, and none-too-clean work. A key phase in this last stage of the process is the testing of billets for faults, cracks, and other imperfections. Under the same roof, though functionally distinct, is the Test House, which performs inspection work for the Mill and Billet Finishing with the aid of electronic screening equipment.

The Traffic section has two main operations: transporting the scrap into the Melting Shop and the ingots from there into the Mill; and moving the finished billets to customers, mainly by its own fleet of articulated lorries. For these functions it is divided into three parts: rail, external road and internal road traffic. The main Traffic section offices are small in relation to others, for much of its activity is integrated with the production departments it serves: rail traffic have their own office in the Melting Shop, and some road men are similarly attached to Billet Finishing.

In addition to these main work areas there are two on site that did not take part in the Employee Relations Project: the Spring Works, a distinct and relatively autonomous unit, and the Central Engineering Workshops, carrying out major maintenance work for all departments. However, most day-to-day maintenance work is carried out within the production departments by teams of engineers working under the 'ship system'. This means that whereas each department manager is the 'captain' of his 'crew' whatever their job, engineering managers outside his department share responsibility for the effective functioning of their own engineers. Another group of ancillary workers integrated in this way are the Melting Shop bricklayers and their labourers, servicing the furnace brickwork.

History and organisation

Tinsley Park Works was built in 1963 under the private ownership of the English Steel Corporation. At that time it was proclaimed 'Europe's most modern alloy steel plant'. Since nationalisation into the British Steel Corporation in 1967 the plant had been a unit of the Corporation's Special Steels Division. Examples of other divisions within BSC were Heavy Steels, Tubes, etc., although this structure was altered in April 1976 so that, for example, Stocksbridge and Tinsley Park Works became part of the Sheffield Manufacturing Division. Before this reorganisation each product division was subdivided into groups, Tinsley Park being a member of the Alloy and Stainless Steels Group. Within this group the Tinsley Park plant was a component of the joint Stocksbridge and Tinsley Park Works. We described in chapter 1 how the plant at Stocksbridge, a small rural town some ten miles north-west of Sheffield, is older and larger than the Tinsley plant, although carrying out many of the same functions. At the time of nationalisation the English Steel Corporation plant at Tinsley Park and the Samuel Fox plant at Stocksbridge were combined to form a single, although geographically separated, works unit. This amalgamation increased operational flexibility and enabled the two plants to share managerial and service functions.

One feature of the amalgamation was the siting of most senior managers in offices at Stocksbridge. While Tinsley Park had its own works manager, and department managers for the main production areas, the joint Tinsley Park and Stocksbridge Traffic department and the Inspection department both had bosses located at Stocksbridge. Similarly, Tinsley Park had its own senior industrial relations officer and a personnel services officer for normal day-to-day working, but major issues involved their superiors at Stocksbridge. The general manager, with responsibility for the full Stocksbridge and Tinsley Park Works, was himself based at Stocksbridge.

The top executive body for the joint works was the Works Management Committee, headed by the general manager and comprising the works manager of each plant, the industrial relations manager and functional heads of equivalent status, such as the chief engineer. This group met regularly at Stocksbridge, but the main responsibility for day-to-day operations was left in the hands of each plant and its management.

Within the production departments of Tinsley Park Works the organisation was broadly as follows.

Melting Shop

Under the department manager were 5 men of section manager status with responsibility for steelmaking, raw materials and stocks, mould preparation and casting, engineering, and quality control. The 7 managers at the next level were shift managers, senior foremen, senior inspectors or section engineers, and at the lowest level of management were 16 foremen (mainly on shifts), 3 shift steelmakers, 3 shift metallurgists, and 2 inspectors. The shop floor was made up of approximately 135 shift production men, 8 day production men, 28 shift maintenance men, 8 day maintenance men, approximately 50 bricklayers and mates, and a few apprentices; a total of around 240.

The Mill

The department manager was the immediate boss to 3 men of section manager status responsible for production, engineering, and quality control respectively. Six men at the next rung on the ladder were designated shift managers, section engineers, and training officer, and the next level was occupied by 18 foremen and 8 quality control assistants and shift production controllers. The shop floor total of approximately 240 men was made up of about 140 shift production workers, the remainder being maintenance men (electricians, fitters, etc.).

Billet Finishing

Under the department manager were 4 section managers covering production, quality control, planning, and engineering. The next level contained 9 men with the job titles of shift manager, shift quality controller, senior inspector, day metallurgist, and training officer. Under them, the 21 supervisors were mainly shift foremen with various others holding responsibility for inspection and supervision of billet testing. This, the largest of the main departments, had a shop-floor complement of over 420. Apart from a small number of shift and day maintenance men and day production men these were all shift production workers employed as slingers, grinders, crane drivers and so on.

Traffic

The department manager for the joint Tinsley Park and Stocksbridge Traffic Department was located at the latter site, while operational control at Tinsley Park was in the hands of a section manager. Under him were 2 senior foremen, 1 each responsible for road and rail transport, and beneath them a total of 8 foremen. The shop floor totalled approximately 60, roughly evenly divided between rail traffic employees, internal road drivers and weighmen, and external road drivers.

Hours of work, pay and amenities

In all the main production areas most men worked what in effect was a three-shift weekly rotation system, that is, five days a week on either 06.00—14.00, 14.00—22.00, 22.00—06.00, with shift changes occurring after the weekend. Amounts of overtime varied across departments, most regular weekend working taking place in the Melting Shop, where the pressure for production was greatest. The reason for this was that the entire plant's output was governed by the capacity of the Melting Shop, since the secondary production stages of the Mill and Billet Finishing had spare capacity beyond the limits set by the Melting Shop. Most junior managers and foremen similarly worked shifts, although there was a small number of 'days regular' production workers. The works manager, the heads of the production departments and people of section manager status also worked days. The only employees working a scheduled round-the-clock continuous shift system were the maintenance men, most of whom worked a 'continental' rotation system, a complex rapid-change system consisting of a seven-shift cycle made up of 2-2-3 day changes.

The system of grades and pay rates was inevitably complicated. In outline, the organisation of work in the Melting Shop and Mill was on a team basis, with a system of interlocking jobs, hierarchically graded. Progress to top positions in a team was by seniority within the works, such that men from outside or from other steelworks were recruited at the bottom of the ladder. This system naturally gives parts of the steel industry an unusually stable direct workforce. In the Melting Shop and Mill wages were generally high by local industrial standards. They were determined by basic job grade (twenty-four of them in the Mill), overtime pay, additional job allowances (e.g. shift premiums) and a shop bonus (under the 'ship system' this also accrued to maintenance men). Billet Finishing had a similar hierarchy of jobs and grades (eighteen in all), with associated overtime rates, but all bonus earnings were on an individual basis. Payment systems in Traffic differed for road and rail, the former group's earnings being through an individual bonus system, while railmen's earnings were topped up by group tonnage-based bonuses.

Steelmaking is generally acknowledged to be a dangerous business, and, in recognition of this fact, safety-consciousness and the provision of medical facilities and protection gear were of a high order. Continuous monitoring of plant safety was in the hands of a full-time safety officer, and safety matters were regularly considered by departmental Joint Consultative Committees. The Works Medical Centre was staffed on a 24-hour basis. The three main departments had their own Amenity Blocks, equipped with washrooms, rest rooms, and locker space. Automatic vending machines were sited in all the main working areas, providing hot food and drink at all times of day and night. The central canteen provided meals in the daytime for staff status employees only. Housed in a single block, the canteen facilities were threefold: a large self-service canteen serving staff below section manager level, a room containing four tables providing a waitress service for staff of section manager status, and more opulent single table in a small adjoining room serving the works manager and department managers. Our indeterminate status within this hierarchy meant that we all at various times ate in all the canteens!

Organisational and industrial relations climate

Before the Project was underway, we undertook a number of enquiries into past and present personnel and industrial relations statistics. For example, the calculation of age distributions showed the workforce to have an average age around forty-one. Comparing the three main production departments, there were fewest young and most older workers in Billet Finishing, the Mill having the highest proportion

15

of workers under thirty, with the Melting Shop intermediate. However, these differences were not large. The stability of the employee population was reflected in turnover data, approximately three per cent per annum on average, with highest levels in Billet Finishing and lowest in the Melting Shop with the Mill again intermediate. The overall turnover level compared favourably with that of Stocksbridge. Labour statistics also indicated lower overall absenteeism rates at Tinsley Park than at Stocksbridge, highest rates within the plant occurring in Billet Finishing, Traffic and service sections, lowest rates in the Mill, and intermediate levels in the Melting Shop. (The range of total time-lost absence was between four and ten per cent.) Accident statistics revealed that the number of shifts lost in Billet Finishing exceeded those in other departments by up to a factor of six, no doubt because of the more extensive manual handling of materials in that department. However, *absolute* levels were generally low.

The favourable comparisons with Stocksbridge did not extend to statistics for strikes and industrial disputes. In the thirty-four months up to the end of 1973 there had been a mere two instances of disputes resulting in industrial action at Stocksbridge but a total of thirty-one at Tinsley Park. Disputes occurred in all areas of the plant, with most in Billet Finishing and among the maintenance sections and fewest in the Mill. They centred on a wide range of issues to do with pay grades, bonus rates, working conditions, manning, demarcation, and discipline.

Industrial action had often taken the form of the embargo (going slow, working to rule, blacking jobs, etc.), although 14 of 31 disputes had been walk-outs or strikes. Seventeen of the 31 led to recorded losses of production, and in 12 cases full-time union officials had been called in. The records painted a picture of rapid escalation of grievances with early application of industrial sanctions.

Unionisation

Finally in this chapter we should describe the pattern of unionisation on the works. The main shop floor union in the industry is the Iron and Steel Trades Confederation (ISTC, the successor to what was formerly known as BISAKTA). This union represented all the production workers in the Melting Shop and Mill and roughly half the men in Billet Finishing. Being an 'industrial' union (i.e. based on a single industry), organisation into branches is within the boundaries of plants. Thus there were separate ISTC branches within each of the three production departments. Each had lay officers elected by the branch membership to the jobs of branch chairman, secretary, and committee members, the total committee usually numbering about seven.

The second largest blue-collar union for the areas covered by the Employee Relations Project was the Transport and General Workers' Union, organising the other half of Billet Finishing's production workers and the workforce of the Traffic section. The TGWU differs from ISTC in operating a shop steward system, with the fourteen or so union representatives on site forming a single branch, headed by a

16

convenor, a chairman, and a secretary. Craft and maintenance unions accounted for the remainder of the blue-collar workforce, union membership on site being 100 per cent for blue-collar workers. The largest of these was the Amalgamated Union of Engineering Workers, with substantial membership in all departments, but drawing its main strength from the Central Engineering Workshops. Branch organisation in the AUEW is geographical, encompassing all the membership of several plants in an area. This means that the AUEW tends to organise informal grouping within plants, and on site at Tinsley Park the eight or so stewards elected one of their number as convenor. The Union of Construction and Allied Trades Technicians organised the group of bricklayers in the Melting Shop, with two elected representatives on site; and a small number of men across the site were members of the Electrical, Electronic and Telecommunications Union/Plumbing Trade Union and of the Boilermakers' Union.

Membership divisions were less neat for white-collar staff. ISTC had three branches: one for clerical staff, one for the foremen of Billet Finishing, Traffic and the Mill, and one for all the white-collar staff of the Melting Shop. Operating in the same grades and areas, and in open competition for membership, was the Association of Scientific, Technical and Managerial Staff, organised into a single site branch. Finally, middle managers had in increasing numbers been seeking union membership for themselves, and at the time of the Project they were organised in a branch of the Steel Industry Management Association. However, the refusal of the other unions to recognise SIMA meant that it was excluded from any inter-union bargaining or agreements, and indeed from explicit membership of joint representative bodies.

The pattern of pay bargaining in almost all these unions was a two-stage process of nationally agreed basic rates and grades, and locally determined additional pay rates and conditions of employment. This tended to result in somewhat fragmented and sectional bargaining. Grievance and disputes procedures were informal up to the highest in-plant level, and then followed a strictly laid-down sequence of events. Non-substantive issues were mainly the province of the joint consultative system, comprising an interlocking series of committees. The Works Council represented Stocksbridge and Tinsley Park together, Section Councils covered each of the two plants, and departmental Joint Consultative Committees existed within each production department. We shall review the operation of these committees later in the book.

3 Introducing the Project to the works

We have described in chapter 1 how plans for the Tinsley Park Employee Relations Project took shape during the autumn of 1973. The objective would be to help improve relations through a systematic exploration of the attitudes, problems and difficulties experienced by people at all levels of the works, and where possible by getting people to use this information to formulate direct action plans for change. As we then envisaged it, the Project was to be a comprehensive one across the whole site, taking place over a period of between twelve and eighteen months.

The outline plan

Our thoughts gradually crystallised into proposals for a four-stage* project along the following lines:

Stage one: Finding out the major problems
A sample of work groups at all levels (project groups) meet to define the problems; each group has two or more meetings. In the second meeting problems are classified in three ways:
1   Problems that can be dealt with within the group
2   Problems that need to go to higher management
3   Problems that should go on to stages 2 to 4 for wider views.
Stage two: Peoples' views about the problems
People are invited to complete a simple questionnaire on their views about the problem areas found from stage 1; all responses are anonymous.
Stage three: Turning problems into action
Project groups meet again to discuss questionnaire results, and to formulate action plans which are passed on to senior management.
Stage four: Results of action
Work groups meet to be informed of what is being done about the action plans. If no action has occurred, management explains why, and further discussion takes place.
Interlinked phase
An interview study to find out how trade union and management representatives feel about the way industrial relations procedures work at Tinsley Park.

Proposals of this kind were presented to the Works Management Committee in

---

* In practice, the separate stages described here tended to merge into each other, in ways described in subsequent chapters.

September 1973. We suggested that the Project might commence at the beginning of 1974 and continue actively for twelve months, after which there would be a phase of follow-up assessment. We emphasised that the decision to proceed must be taken by employees and management of Tinsley Park themselves, and that the Project should be seen throughout as a Tinsley Park activity. It was up to the members of the works to identify and rectify their problems, and the Project and ourselves should be viewed as resources to assist the works itself to reach that goal. We would not be participating as consultants providing solutions, but acting as catalysts in a process involving the members of the works themselves.

The members of the Works Management Committee present at this early meeting were broadly in favour of the Project. There was some disquiet at the duration envisaged, while one or two managers attempted to cast us in a prescriptive consultancy role: 'How soon will you be able to come up with some answers?' We sought to disclaim that intention (as we had to do periodically throughout the Project), and stressed that the people directly involved were competent to resolve their own problems; our job was to set up and help run a mechanism which would assist their own problem-solving process. In practice, the developing course of the Project drew attention to a number of difficulties arising from the structure of the organisation and some of its administrative practices, and we subsequently agreed to make known our views about these and other issues outside the action range of the Project's mechanisms. We did this in the form of an Interim Report presented to the works after the main stages of the Project had been completed in February 1975. The Interim Report is described in chapter 6.

In submitting a report of that kind we did become consultants offering advice, but throughout the Project this role was deliberately minimised to encourage the participants to take responsibility for initiating those changes which they themselves thought were both desirable and practicable. One suggested means of emphasising this joint responsibility for the Project was the institution of a Project Steering Committee of union and management members to guide the development of the programme within the works.

Following senior management's acceptance in principle, steps had next to be taken to present the proposals for discussion on site at Tinsley Park. Before we could do this it was necessary to plan more details of the Project's administration. The logistics were complex: with four of us to be engaged part-time on the Project throughout its duration (we each had additional and separate research obligations elsewhere) we had to think strategically about its scope and our divison of labour. These and other issues were discussed in a series of internal meetings and a number of decisions were taken.

We agreed that the Project should aim to cover the main production and service areas, but exclude the relatively autonomous Spring Works. The engineering unions had chosen not to take part, so that the Central Engineering Workshop would not be included. Each of us would be attached to one of the main participating departments, allowing a continuous relationship with and detailed knowledge of the people and events in each area. Other commitments would be as appropriate at the time, in terms of who was available for meetings and other required activities. The principal instrument for decision-making, feedback and scheduling of the Project's progress would be the Steering Committee of union and management representatives, although some additional coordinating and administrative work would be needed on site. As the Project evolved this latter office of project coordinator was filled on a part-time basis by a junior manager in the Technical Department.

One of the principal sources of documentation would be the main questionnaire survey of stage 2, but additional material would be needed to trace the Project's progress. Three strategies were devised for this purpose:

1 'Before' and 'After' questionnaire surveys.
2 The use of 'Problem Record Forms'.
3 The documented assessment of what occurred in project groups.

First, we envisaged questionnaire studies of employee opinions about the climate of relations on the plant to take place at the start and end of the Project. These would enable us to show what changes, if any, had taken place over the period.

Second, we decided to develop from the Ravenscraig Survey (see chapter 1) the use of Problem Record Forms, to show what problems had been raised in each group and to record what was done about them. These modifications of the earlier survey's Feedback Form were to be headed 'Tinsley Park Works Employee Relations Project' and would have three principal columns for Problem Definition, Action on Problem, and Outcome. An additional feature subsequently incorporated was space for the classification of problems in terms of priority (high, medium, or low) and time span for action (long, medium, or short). The forms would be completed in project group discussion meetings and copies (on no-carbon-required sheets) would be held by the group leaders, by a member of the group, and by the member of our team attached to that group. Thus each problem item would be documented and could easily be reviewed as the Project proceeded. The intention that copies should be held by several people was in order to ensure that items did not become 'lost' in the course of time. Action recommendations, relevant communications and eventual outcomes would all be recorded on the forms, using a single form for each problem item.

Third, we wanted project groups to review their own progress by recording their opinions about each meeting. The idea here was that at the end of a meeting members would anonymously record their views about its conduct and success. We would later summarise the recorded reaction and feed back average opinions at the beginning of the next meeting for comment and discussion. The 'Meeting Assessment Forms' designed for this purpose included space for free comments about the meeting, as well as five-point rating scales to summarise opinions about the leader's and members' contributions and the value of the meeting. In practice the Meeting Assessment Forms were only used in early meetings, and more informal feedback of opinion sufficed on later occasions. However, the four of us kept notes at every meeting, and immediately afterwards wrote up our impressions of each to maintain a record of what had taken place. Much of the present account has been drawn from these records.

Two important aspects of the Project's mechanisms for change were also discussed and further refined in our internal meetings in late 1973. First, we had to decide on the composition of project groups, and after discussion we settled for groups of people working in some contact with each other to be led by their boss or sometimes by their shop steward. We would attempt to achieve full coverage of employees above shop-floor level, but believed that a representative proportion of shop-floor workers would be adequate. We also decided that some training for group leaders would be necessary.

Another issue on which we deliberated before presenting plans for the Project to the works was the role of the Interlinked Phase. We realised that much of the Project's impact would be outside the conduct of more formal union—management relations. The Interlinked Phase was to be a more conventional inquiry into the opinions of principal union and management representatives about the procedures and mechanisms for consultation, grievance handling and bargaining. This would be a separate interview and questionnaire investigation, the form of which would evolve as the Project got underway and we became familiar with the central issues. Its results would be fed back into the Project as a stimulus for further action and change.

Finally, some mention should be made of the nature of our 'contract' with the British Steel Corporation. This was always relatively informal and it was recognised that either party could request termination if it wished. On our side this was said to be likely only if we felt that employees' commitment to the Project was inadequate. The agreement in principle reached at the meeting described above was however confirmed in an exchange of letters between ourselves and the general manager of Stocksbridge and Tinsley Park Works in October 1973. Our letter reviewed the plans so far prepared, and drew attention to our wish to subsequently publish reports of the Project. We made these promises: 'We shall not identify the Corporation or the works without your prior permission. Any proposed publication will be submitted to you for comment, and we promise to take your views into serious consideration'. These undertakings were accepted in the Corporation's reply.

The exchange of letters of October 1973 also formalised the financial arrangements for the Project. Our financial independence was retained, and we received no fees from BSC. It was however agreed that our travel expenses should be reimbursed, and costs of printing and postage were also to be met. Furthermore, the works provided many a tasty lunch!

Presenting the Project to the works

Our early contacts with the plant were through the works manager and the senior industrial relations officer. The latter's superior (the industrial relations manager), although based at Stocksbridge, spent a proportion of his time at Tinsley Park Works, and was often present at the initial discussions about administrative and procedural arrangements.

Our first formal presentation of the Project to members of the works itself was at the beginning of November 1973. A special meeting of managers was convened to hear and discuss our proposals. The works manager acted as chairman, and he was accompanied by the three production department managers, the section manager in charge of Traffic, three service and engineering managers and the senior industrial relations officer. The group personnel manager was also present.

Several of the managers were suspicious, cool and sceptical, with some either denying the need for change at Tinsley Park or attributing blame for their present climate to forces over which they had no control. The outcome of this meeting was not outright rejection, but neither were we given a firm commitment to proceed. We were conscious that the managers felt under some pressure from their superiors to participate, and that they had some anxieties about what it would entail for them. We assured them that there was no intention of imposing the Project on anyone and that they could withdraw later if they did not like the way it was going. The meeting ended by our suggesting that the managers should think things over for a time, while we explored the unions' attitudes to the venture, and that we would consult with them again before any decision was taken.

The meeting with the trade unionists was attended by eight shop stewards and two district full-time officials, representing staff and shop-floor interests. The works manager introduced us to the group and then left us to discuss the Project. The atmosphere was in marked contrast to that of the management meeting. Everyone responded with interest, though the conversation was dominated by two or three individuals. The general tenor of opinion was encouraging, and the discussion was both friendly and relaxed. The dominant view seemed to be: it can do no harm and only possible good by providing another vehicle for tackling problems and grievances. Most of the union representatives appeared to greet the Project in a positive spirit, although the enthusiasm of some did seem to be at least partly based on the belief that it would provide them with ammunition to fire at management.

Two procedural issues raised at this meeting were worries that foremen leading shop-floor project groups would stifle opinion, and reservations about the questionnaire. In the former case we noted that some shop-floor groups might be led by shop stewards and we pointed out that the training of leaders and our presence at all meetings should help ensure that views were freely aired. On the latter issue, we agreed that the project questionnaire should not be taken as the final word about people's true feelings. It would be designed around the issues that people had raised in project groups, and throughout the Project we would gather information on attitudes from the more direct sources of project group discussions and our informal contact with people on site. The main disappointment in our consultation with the unions occurred some time afterwards, when the AUEW stewards, who had been unrepresented at the discussion, reported that they had held a meeting at which it had been decided not to take part in the Project. Most AUEW members were employed in the Central Engineering Workshop, but the decision did also

22

mean that maintenance engineers in the production departments would not join in the project group discussions. This undoubtedly led to some reduction in the groups' effectiveness, since maintenance issues loomed large in many later discussions.

Four weeks after our first meeting with plant management we met them again, this time with the knowledge that the unions in the three production departments and the Traffic section had given the Project their blessing to go ahead. This second meeting was intentionally not attended by the works manager and the discussion turned out to be a lot more free and open than it had been on the previous occasion. The managers asked many more detailed questions about plans for the Project and were more willing to express their anxieties. It turned out that no real persuasion on our part was necessary, since they had met in the interim period and had reached a collective view that they were willing to go ahead and would like to get moving as soon as possible. Some managers offered the opinion that in practice they felt they had no real option, but others were more positive and echoed the view expressed in our meeting with trade union officials that nothing but good could come out of the Project.

We assumed now that the Employee Relations Project would probably get underway, so we extended our communication meetings to cover section managers, shift managers, and foremen. All were asked to attend one of a series of meetings at specified times. Six of these took place during December 1973 and January 1974. Although attendance varied, the discussions were lively and the principles of the Project were well debated. At all these meetings handouts showing the intended stages of the Project (as summarised at the beginning of this chapter) were distributed, and it was emphasised that these sessions were for the informal exchange of information and opinion; the final formal decision to go ahead lay in the hands of a forthcoming special meeting of the Section Council, the highest consultative body within the Tinsley Park site.

This meeting took place in the Tinsley Park main conference room in January 1974, and was attended by about thirty managerial, staff and shop-floor representatives. Discussion was animated, and attitudes varied from the very enthusiastic ('This is a good chance to sort out the blockages in communication which we all know exist') to the totally negative ('I am completely opposed to calling outside bodies to deal with our problems: it's up to unions and management here to put them right'). Several shop stewards expressed doubt that any changes were possible, since management had in their view repeatedly failed to follow up issues in need of attention. Others noted that assistance from people unconnected with the works could shed fresh light on difficult problems, and the view of a senior steward was apparently widely accepted: 'It's a sorry state of affairs when a third party has to be called in. But if the Project can reduce the friction which exists on the works then it will be worthwhile'.

When the Council chairman (the works manager) called for a vote, there was majority approval for the proposals, with three votes against and one abstention. The latter was an engineering shop steward, who had yet to consult his colleagues.

Two of those who opposed the idea were in favour of it in principle, but voted against it at this time on the grounds that they wanted the engineering union to be included from the start. The third person who voted against the Project was simply against it.

Over the course of these introductory meetings we had become aware that there were indeed some difficult problems in the area of employee relations at Tinsley Park. Whilst we had not been looking for 'one big happy family', we were a little surprised at the fragmentation of interests and mutual mistrust on site. For example, the members of some trade union groups in certain areas viewed both management and other unions with deep distrust, as did some middle managers view both their superiors and the shop floor. We were becoming inclined to accept the opinion of the industrial relations manager that the atmosphere in the works was indeed an especially 'prickly' one.

The Steering Committee and *Focus*

The Section Council meeting which sanctioned the Project also went on to discuss the question of a Project Steering Committee. This was designated a subcommittee of the Section Council, and was to have a membership broadly representative of the works as a whole but excluding the engineering workers who had opted out of the Project. Its composition is shown in Table 3.1.

Table 3.1
Composition of the Project Steering Committee

	Managers	Foreman and staff	Shop stewards
Melting Shop		1	1
Mill			1
Billet Finishing and Test House	1	1	2
Traffic	1		1
Works Services			2

The foreman and staff members of the Committee were also union representatives. As well as the eleven people referred to above, the works manager and the industrial relations manager were appointed to the Committee, as was the part-time project coordinator. The latter acted as Committee secretary as well as undertaking other work for the Project such as arranging meetings and passing information between individuals and groups. Two or more of us attended each meeting of the Committee.

The Project Steering Committee held nine meetings between February 1974 and March 1975. In the early stages it planned the steps to be taken and discussed details of questionnaire construction and administration. It reviewed progress in each department and suggested ways to overcome obstacles as they arose. The

Steering Committee was a principal recipient of our Interim Report in February 1975, and its members held special meetings to discuss the contents. In general terms the Committee was a generator of ideas, a means of communication and a source of bipartisan approval for the Project and its procedures. It did not suggest any major deviations from the initial plans and it tended to adopt a rather reactive stance, assuming that we would submit proposals for its consideration.

An important decision taken at the first meeting of the Project Steering Committee was that there should be a special bulletin circulated to all members of the works as the Project proceeded. This was felt to be essential if interest was to be generated and maintained across a large plant with three-shift operation. This bulletin was produced by journalists housed at Stocksbridge on the basis of material which we provided and sometimes altered in the light of recommendations from the Steering Committee. It emerged under the title of *Tinsley Park Focus*, in broadsheet style, attractively printed with a red banner and containing all major news about the Project. Five issues of *Focus* were produced, as follows:

Issue 1, in March 1974, was a two-page, four-sided bulletin which introduced the Project to the works. The opening headline was 'Employee Relations Project Under Way' and the text commenced thus: 'The Tinsley Park Employee Relations Project is a joint venture between management, unions and Sheffield University. Its aim is to bring to light as many problems as possible, to give them a full and free airing and to work together to solve them.' It went on to describe the plans and to inform readers about the Steering Committee and its membership. Photographs of the committee members were on an inside page and our pictures were on the back page.

Issue 2, in June 1974, was introduced as 'the latest progress report' about the Project. It contained a photograph of the Steering Committee in session, described the developments so far, and included photographs of all the leaders of shop-floor project groups together with the names of people in their groups.

Issue 3, in August 1974, had the opening headline 'Now *You* Give Us The Answers'. It contained the four-page project questionnaire described in chapter 5 inserted loosely within a two-page issue of *Focus*. The outer two pages described actions and achievements so far and contained photographs and opinions from shop-floor workers.

Issue 4, in November 1974, contained the results of the project questionnaire survey. It also gave some illustrative comments from people who had completed the questionnaire, and the front cover introduced the views of the new works manager under his exhortation 'Let's see it through together'.

Issue 5, in April 1975, was a larger edition of five tabloid pages. It introduced 'Just Three Vital Jobs Left To Do' in terms of a review of progress to date, a campaign to tackle wider issues, and a final follow-up questionnaire to assess attitudes after the Project. Much of this edition was devoted to a complete list of topics raised and actions undertaken in each of the principal departments. These lists were enlivened with photographs and the use of different type-faces. The final page contained a

review by the works manager of the major issues referred to him and gave his reaction to these issues.

Focus was undoubtedly an important method of communicating ideas and information about the Project. It was well received by those who took the time to study it, but there is always some doubt about how many people will read this kind of organisational bulletin. One encouraging sign was provided by the fact that eighty-five per cent of shop floor and non-supervisory staff replied positively to the item in the project questionnaire: 'Having a Tinsley Park newspaper along the lines of *Focus* would greatly help communications within the works'. On the other hand, there were some members of the works who commented later that *Focus* was an unnecessarily expensive production. Our general conclusion is that it played a major part in the development of the Project, being especially important in the earlier stages to publicise the Project and to gain the interest of the works.

Project groups

The Steering Committee also finally determined the number and composition of project groups which were to meet in stage one and stage three of the original plan. These were constituted at four levels of the works, and were timed to start in a 'cascading' fashion. First to commence would be the works manager's project group, made up of department managers and others of similar status. After experience in the first group, the department managers would themselves initiate project groups made up of their section managers and equivalent. Then the section managers would lead groups of foremen, and finally the shop floor groups would commence their meetings. As each lower group began work, the higher-level groups continued their series of meetings, progressing their own action items as well as responding to items from lower groups.

Through the works as a whole there were twenty-four project groups, as detailed in Table 3.2. Seven of the level-four groups (with shop-floor participants) were led by their own foremen and six were led by a shop steward from amongst them. The decision that some shop stewards should act as group leaders was partly in response to anxiety expressed earlier by union representatives that shop-floor workers might feel unable to speak frankly of their problems in front of their foremen. It was also argued that a foreman might be less willing to push hard for action on a group's recommendations than would their shop steward. Subsequent experience suggested that neither of these fears was warranted. It turned out that the major difference was in terms of the personality, ability and enthusiasm of the group leader, irrespective of whether he was a foreman or a shop steward.

The project groups covered entirely the line and staff employees above shop-floor level. At shop-floor level (level four in the classification) a twenty per cent coverage was attained in each department. Although meetings were not always

Table 3.2

Number of project groups and meetings

Level	Date of commencement	Group leader	Number of groups	Total number of meetings
One	March 1974	Works manager	1	9
Two	March 1974	Department managers	3*	22
Three	April 1974	Section managers	7	34
Four	May 1974	Foremen or shop stewards	13	39
		(Overall)	(24)	(104)

* The Traffic Department on the site was headed by a section manager. His meetings are therefore included with those at level three.

fully attended, the average number of people allotted to each group was fifteen, so that approximately 360 employees were actively involved through project groups. The duration of meetings varied from time to time and from group to group, but the average length was around two and a half hours.

Training the group leaders

It was widely agreed that training for group leaders was desirable before meetings began, and in conjunction with members of the Training Department we evolved a brief training programme. This had three principal objectives:

1   To ensure that all group leaders understood the nature, scope and content of the Employee Relations Project.
2   To ensure that they could communicate this to their colleagues and project group.
3   To ensure that they had the necessary knowledge and skills for effective group leadership to encourage participation, openness and creative problem-solving.

A more general intention of the training was to encourage group leaders to have positive attitudes about the Project and its progress.

The training was undertaken separately in a single one-day session for foremen and shop stewards and in one half-day session for managers. It was conducted by two of us in collaboration with a member of the Works Training Department. The works manager received no structured training because of his established knowledge of the Project and his experience in discussion leading; however, one of us did spend two hours with him in an individual briefing.

The training sessions covered information about the Employee Relations Project and its goals. The Problem Record Forms and the Meeting Assessment Forms were introduced and illustrated, and the kinds of action which a project group could initiate were described. We stressed how project groups would be free to approach anyone they chose with their recommended actions about problems which they had identified. People could be contacted either personally or in writing and they could be invited to attend a group meeting to explore a problem and its possible solution. We emphasised that management and others were committed to making the Project a success by responding promptly to requests from project groups.

The second part of the training for group leaders concentrated upon the style of leadership they should adopt. We began with a discussion of some issues about group behaviour and attitude change. The leaders of shop-floor groups (but not the managers) then viewed and discussed a film-strip with sound commentary about discussion-leading, and all trainees next saw and debated a twenty-minute case study film. The training was completed by presentation and discussion of a duplicated summary sheet on the techniques of discussion leading.

The training seemed to be most useful in reassuring people about the Project and in allowing further discussion about its aims. It was more difficult to assess whether it had any significant impact upon styles of discussion-leading. Some of the shop-floor group leaders made it clear that they found certain of our ideas hard to grasp, and we had to assure them that one of us would always be on hand during group meetings to help them in case of need. The management group leaders were more used to the role and in general appeared more confident. However, it was clear that not all of them appreciated the participative style which the training was advocating, and several of those who did favour the approach expressed doubts about the adequacy of their own skill in using it.

When the training for group leaders was completed, at the end of February 1974, the Employee Relations Project was ready to commence. The events described so far have taken us from the initial planning of the Project, through senior management acceptance, approval by the works, briefing for foremen and shop stewards, establishment of a Steering Committee and training for group leaders. What happened within the project groups is the subject-matter of the next chapter.

4 The project groups

In this chapter we describe the development of the project groups. These were intended as the principal means of concentrating attention on work problems and their potential solution, and as the main method of examining and possibly changing attitudes. Most project group activity took place between April and July 1974, although groups continued meeting up to February 1975.

One of us attended each meeting and subsequently prepared a record of what had taken place. The meetings of the works manager's group are particularly important to convey the flavour of what was attempted and achieved among a group of managers, and we therefore start by looking in detail at this group. We then go on to consider the achievements and problems of lower-level groups, and in chapter 10 we will take a broader look at the operation of this part of the Project.

The works manager's project group

The works manager's project group met on nine occasions between April 1974 and January 1975. Its members were those managers reporting to the works manager with production or service responsibility on the site. In addition to the department managers from the Melting Shop, Mill, and Billet Finishing and the section manager from Traffic, the rolling mills development manager and the senior industrial relations officer were present. So too was the latter's superior, the industrial relations manager, who (as we have noted) was based at Stocksbridge and had responsibility for both Tinsley Park and Stocksbridge sites. Finally, the group included four other managers in charge of maintenance, construction, engineering workshops and quality control respectively. The works manager had been a keen advocate of the Project during the early discussions and he retained his strong interest throughout his period in office. He had always been clear that the project groups would present some problems for management but argued that facing these problems would be of great value.

Project group principles

For all project groups we were particularly concerned with these principles:

1   The goals of a meeting should be clear to all participants.
2   Adequate preparation should have been made.
3   Participants should listen to each other and when in doubt check that they understand what another person was intending.
4   The leader should summarise at appropriate times to ensure agreed

understanding of progress so far.

5   The leader should not dominate the meeting whilst being responsible for its effectiveness.
6   Participants should be clear when decisions had been reached by the group and records should be kept.
7   Participants should be clear who was given responsibility for carrying out an agreed action, and how and when this action would be monitored by the group.
8   The group should be able frankly to discuss its own effectiveness and to consider improvements where these were deemed necessary.

Of course, these principles are easier to state than to practice, and quite often one is, as it were, walking on a tight-rope: when does a leader's control become domination, for instance, or how much time is left to reach decisions if everyone is allowed to speak as frequently as they wish? The ideal group process is thus extremely difficult to attain, but there is little doubt that the early meetings of the works manager's group were less than entirely successful. In part this was because of the abstract nature of the issues raised at this level; for example, 'management philosophies' were examined in an early meeting and such a diffuse topic is difficult to summarise and to form the basis of agreed action plans.

In part also the difficulties arose from our own uncertainty about procedures. The intention stated at the outset was to work systematically through three separate stages:

1   Examine problems facing the group in its work and draw up a list of major issues; attempts at solution were thought to be undesirable at this stage.
2   Classify each of these issues in terms of its priority for action.
3   Discuss possible solutions to the high priority items, moving on later to those of lower priority.

It transpired that this procedure was not easily followed, and early discussions were somewhat disorganised. We and the managers did learn from these difficulties, however, and after three meetings of the top group of managers we drew up a checklist for group leaders which was used with greater success in other groups. For example, the third phase identified above was broken down into six steps:

1   Outline the agreed problem.
2   Identify differing views about possible solutions.
3   Decide on a solution.
4   Make someone responsible for action.
5   Set a time for reporting back to the group.
6   Complete a Problem Record Form (see chapter 3).

As the works manager had predicted, the first meetings of his project group were sometimes difficult. He was an energetic and forthright man, and his style in the first meeting sustained the uncertainty with which some of his colleagues still viewed the Project. Furthermore, we felt it necessary to illustrate our role in project group meetings, for example, by pointing out to the leader that he had allowed the group to move into problem *solving* when they were supposed to be first *identifying* problems. We also had to bring out the effects of his forceful approach, and these interpersonal issues combined with the problems of learning a new procedure to make the early meetings uneasy experiences for the participants.

The member of our team associated with the level one group drew attention (both in and out of meetings) to areas where he believed that improvements were possible. During the second meeting he temporarily took over the role of leader to illustrate the process which we were advocating of first defining the full range of problems before moving on to set priorities and to examine possible solutions. The works manager and several of his colleagues themselves commented that the way the meetings had been conducted was reducing their effectiveness, and this lead to issues of interpersonal style being examined throughout the series. The works manager's insistence was that everyone should be 'brutally frank if necessary'.

For the first three meetings examination of the processes of discussion was associated with completion of the Meeting Assessment Form (see chapter 3), in which ratings of interaction procedures and meeting effectiveness were recorded and members were asked to write down any additional comments they wished to make. The Meeting Assessment Form caused much dismay, partly because our design had not yet successfully avoided ambiguity and partly because many members (but not all) felt that the meetings were not going well. This awareness was reinforced through statements during the meetings, such as the group leader's exclamation from time to time that 'it's much harder to run these groups than I anticipated' or that 'I'm making a bloody mess of this job'. Some members openly disagreed with him about that and felt he was doing a difficult job quite well, but others shared his own view. After three meetings the group decided to discontinue the Meeting Assessment Forms, a decision which we shall see repeated in later groups.

Whilst such a formal mechanism as the Meeting Assessment Form may be a cumbersome way of repeatedly monitoring the effectiveness of discussion groups or meetings, this process of examining the group's performance is an important one which is too easily dismissed. People are likely to reject evaluation because it makes them uncomfortable. This is not only because it opens up conflict, but because people recognise the difficulty of doing anything about many of the problems which they feel are rooted in personality or established styles of behaviour. Despite our belief in the value of feedback in learning we did not find a generally acceptable way of dealing with these issues.

Before turning to the content of the works manager's project group meetings, the subsequent development of their style should be noted. We have stated that, because of the difficulty of the topic, our own inexperience at this stage, and the actions of the participants, the early meetings were somewhat ineffective. However, we believe that from these experiences several members learned new and useful ways of behaving in managerial meetings. A number of the managers volunteered their opinion on several occasions that from the project group meetings they had acquired a different approach to problem-solving, group decision-making and action follow-up. We certainly felt that these changes were taking place and we see considerable merit in these groups as a method of learning as well as for the actions which they can generate.

Level one issues

The first meeting of the level one project group covered a lot of issues in outline, and these were well summarised by the works manager. His written summary listed eight general areas, usually in the form of questions. The first two sections of his paper are given here to illustrate its content:

1 *Are the operatives too suspicious of management motives?*
   If so, why?
   Is this linked to the 'poor relation' situation *vis-à-vis* Stocksbridge?
   How does one break it down?
2 *Problems of information flow both from managers and to managers*
   Do the trade unions have a better/faster information flow?
   How much is our own fault, e.g. do we make proper use of foremen?
   Is there a manager—foreman gap?
   How much is the works manager's fault?
   How much is caused simply by the 'bigness' of BSC?
   How can we make present Joint Consultative Committee procedures more effective?

These questions were further discussed in the next few meetings and more specific issues were entered upon Problem Record Forms with priority classifications and recommended actions. Some of the actions involved department managers (to bring foremen more into the centre of negotiations and other meetings, for example), and others were somewhat optimistic assertions about personnel outside the group itself whose commitment to the decision had not been determined; for example, one action item was: 'general manager to encourage more inter-works transfers'.

Several significant changes were made through the project group to the pattern of management meetings and in communication channels of several kinds, and many of the items raised found their way into discussions throughout the works in subsequent months. A number of recommendations were in terms of action to be taken by the works manager at a later date. For example, the question of defining limits of authority and responsibility was tackled in this way: 'works manager to arrange a further meeting within three months to clarify and identify action items'.

It is here that we come upon a major limiting factor to the success of this group and indeed of the Project as a whole. During the early months of the Project several important managerial changes took place. In May 1974 the Melting Shop manager was promoted to a post in another plant, and the same month saw changes in the quality control structure. The Mill manager was ill during May and June and his place was taken intermittently by one of his section managers; the Mill manager himself was expecting to leave his position, and plans for his transfer were being made during the period of the Project. Furthermore, the works manager was himself promoted to be general manager of another works during July.

Discontinuities of this kind put a severe brake on the progress within a managerial team. Apart from the obvious difficulty in maintaining continuity of style and in carrying forward necessary action, newly appointed managers naturally have their own priorities in learning about their job and tackling matters of immediate concern to themselves. These features undoubtedly influenced the activities of the works manager's project group.

The group had a number of clear successes in terms of significant action developments and the acquisition of new behaviour styles, but there were two areas in which we were particularly sad to see little progress made. The first was to do with working relationships within the group of managers themselves. This matter emerged strongly in early discussions, and the industrial relations manager and the works manager were two people who were keen for the group to explore the ways they each helped and hindered the others. However, these matters were dropped due to the works manager's promotion and the lower level of enthusiasm for explicit examination of relations within the group on the part of the new works manager and some of the other department managers. The second area which was not explored in much depth was the possibility of loosening some of the constraints from elsewhere in the Corporation. It became accepted early in the discussions that nothing substantial could be achieved in relation to the organisation structure outside the works. Such a conclusion might indeed have been realistic, but the history of the Project as a whole came to show that larger issues of this kind need to be agreed as legitimate agenda items right at the outset, even if nothing is likely to be done about them. The discussion that they provoke at least clarifies the nature of the contraints.

Department managers' project groups

As the works manager's project group progressed through its series of meetings, groups commenced activity throughout the lower levels of the works. Next to start (in March 1974) were those led by department managers, and meetings at this second level were held on six, seven and nine occasions in the Melting Shop, Mill and Billet Finishing Department respectively. We will here look briefly at the main themes arising at this level, and will save until chapter 7 an account of how progress differed from department to department.

The group leaders at this second level had themselves attended the works manager's project group. They had also received training about the Project and its goals. This experience led to considerable early progress in Billet Finishing and the Melting Shop. Meetings were held every ten days or so, and substantial inventories of departmental and more general problems were drawn up. Action recommendations were agreed and group members were asked to pursue these and then to report back. The usual sequence was for fairly frequent meetings to take place during March and April 1974, with a first follow-up meeting in June 1974 and (in two departments) further action and review meetings in November and December 1974.

By the start of the department managers' meetings attempts had been made to ensure that the Employee Relations Project was widely publicised throughout the works. In addition to the briefing meetings with section managers and foremen held earlier in the year, the first edition of the Project newspaper, *Focus*, appeared in March, describing the plans for the Project and introducing the Steering Committee and ourselves.

March 1974 had also seen the distribution of the 'Before' questionnaire. This was required to obtain a snapshot of opinions and attitudes before the Project got underway; the same questions were to be asked on two further occasions during the next fifteen months. Both the Before questionnaire and *Focus* were distributed with wages slips on a single payday in March, and we collected the completed questionnaires through ballot boxes placed throughout the works. It was emphasised that no-one would be identifiable from their questionnaire answers and that all analyses would be carried out by ourselves. Further details of the Before questonnaire and the results of the analyses will be presented in chapters 7 and 8.

Level two issues

Each department manager's project group contained section managers and shift managers as well as those of similar status responsible for quality control, maintenance or clerical functions. It will come as no surprise that questions of communication loomed large in the discussions, and many of the problems raised under this heading were immediately soluble within the authority of the group. For example, one department instituted fortnightly meetings between managers and foremen, another increased membership of its morning meetings to include quality control staff and attempted to change the emphasis from backward-looking fault-finding to the development of future plans.

We should note that most of the discussions and actions brought about by the project groups could in different circumstances have arisen from other types of decision-making meetings. The key feature of the Project was its establishment of a large-scale operation with built-in procedures and disciplines. The operation created time and resources for looking at problems which may have been present for some time. As one member of a level two group exclaimed: 'This is what the ERP is all about — sorting out things that should have been settled a long time ago. There are a lot of old problems to take a fresh look at, so it's going to take quite a while.'

By this time (April 1974) the Project had become part of the local jargon and acquired the label of 'the ERP' (pronounced as a three-letter word rather than as three initial letters). This allowed all sorts of allusions from Wyatt Earp to burp! The references were mainly in a friendly spirit, for the ERP was widely seen as a novel activity which could be potentially very rewarding. During one department manager's group meeting the leader rejected an incoming telephone call with a cheerful: 'I'm busy. This is ERP, the next best thing to sex.' In more serious vein at another meeting it was proclaimed: 'We've made a lot of shout and ERP has been the vehicle. It gives me new hope for the future.'

Because so many issues within a department could be dealt with effectively by the managers assembled in a level two project group, there were many successful innovations at this level. Further illustrations include decisions to invite attendance at union—management negotiating meetings of those foremen likely to be closely affected, and the development within one department of plans for redecoration and extension of office facilities. One department introduced substantial and successful changes into the training and working conditions of shift clerks, a group which had previously been marked out by problems of high absenteeism and labour turnover.

Some problems were less readily solved. All departments were troubled by the inadequacy of their joint consultation system and this became a particular focus of the Project's Interlinked Phase (see chapter 6). Each group of managers spent much time lamenting the supposedly inferior status of Tinsley Park Works relative to Stocksbridge Works. Some Tinsley Park managers claimed that senior management were biased towards Stocksbridge, and the presence there of several important service functions was symbolic of this status difference as well as causing communication difficulties. Others pointed out that this could too easily be an excuse for not tackling their own problems, and that their difficulties as members of a large organisation were no greater than in other works. Not surpsingly this was an area where consensus and practical recommendations were not easily reached. Relations between the two plants were discussed repeatedly at all levels of the Project. As a result of this some improvements in mutual understanding occurred, but these cannot be attributed to any one decision or action: rather to the steady process of clarification and argument arising from the frequent expressions of concern at project group meetings.

The ways in which the level two project groups raised their recommendations at higher levels were of special interest. There was an initial tendency for the group leader (in this case the department manager) to assume that he should represent the group in the higher reaches of the organisation. This worked well in some cases, but it was apparent that if all action were to be through the group leader then he could become overloaded while others would be reluctant to accept responsibility for the group's progress. We therefore emphasised that tasks should be shared around the group, so that a junior member could approach other members of the organisation with the authority delegated to him from the group. This caused some anxiety at first, but was soon accepted enthusiastically as good practice by several of the groups.

Questions of interpersonal style and the handling of meetings were examined in a number of ways in level two groups. The Meeting Assessment Form was anonymously filled in during the early meetings, and the one of us present with the group collected the completed forms and prepared a summary for the next meeting. As with the level one group, this summary indicated how many people had ticked each of the boxes on each of the scales and also listed the written comments which had been offered. The routine was for these summaries to be presented at the beginning of the following meeting for interpretation and discussion.

For the first few meetings of the department managers' groups this worked quite well. Attention became focussed upon the pattern of contributions, the leader's style, people's confidence and willingness to test that they understood what other members were intending to say. Table 4.1 is an illustrative set of anonymous comments from the third meeting of one group, classified roughly from A to C into favourable, neutral or ambiguous, and unfavourable reactions.

Table 4.1
Meeting Assessment Form comments

A   Starting to make headway.
Very useful meeting.
Lengthy and at times hard-going, but a very useful meeting with considerable progress on this one subject.
Reasonably happy with this meeting.
Quite a good meeting.
A joint effort on the whole, with everyone contributing.
Started to result in hard positive action; this is an encouragement.
I enjoyed the discussions which were very honest.
Length of the meeting was about right.
I personally have learnt something from this meeting.

B   The group leader started by dominating but remembered training.
If no results, time better spent meeting order book requirements.
Took rather longer than anticipated because of different difficulties of each section.
Meeting tended to be sectionalised into different interests.
The problems tend to overlap.

C   3 hours is the maximum meeting duration.
A little long.
Have doubt whether we have tackled too many problems at this meeting.
A tendency to stray a little from the factual point under discussion.

However the Meeting Assessment Form procedure increasingly came to appear unnecessary after a few meetings. People's views had by then become established, and in many cases the style of meeting had been discussed and accepted. For example, one group made it clear that they had learned what was required and members felt free to comment directly whenever that was appropriate. Another group had discussed their leader's unwillingness to delegate and, in the face of his stated preference and intention to carry on in his usual style, they had agreed that this was acceptable.

So the Meeting Assessment Forms were discarded by level two groups by the end of April. Throughout the series of meetings we continued to attempt to find suitable opportunities to draw attention to interpersonal processes. For example, one group leader tended initially to see himself as separate from the other members; when summarising what had been discussed he would start: 'What they are saying is . . . ' Once this had been pointed out to him he adjusted his language to: 'What we are saying is . . . ' – a change which was loudly approved by the group.

As was noted previously, the department managers' project groups held most of their meetings between March and June 1974. Problem Record Forms were completed systematically throughout this period, so that details of issues, recommendations and actions were always available to group members. Subsequent review meetings took place towards the end of the year when the overall pattern of actions from the groups as a whole was visible. We shall catch up again with the level two groups in chapter 6.

Section managers' project groups

The groups at level three were led by section managers (who had themselves taken part in level two groups), and each group contained foremen and their staff equivalents. This meant that quality control staff, section engineers, clerical supervisors and chemists were involved as well as production foremen. Seven groups were established and these met on a total of thirty-four occasions between April 1974 and January 1975.

It was not customary for this mixture of people to sit down together to discuss their problems. Although the members all worked in contact with each other in a single department, their different functional specialisation meant that they had rarely examined work issues together as a group. On a number of occasions it was this varied composition of project groups that led to valuable exchange of information and the development of greater understanding of each others' problems. For instance, the more isolated role of the quality control inspectors gave them only a limited appreciation of the day-to-day industrial relations problems faced by their production colleagues, and discussion in level three groups helped them gain a better appreciation of the difficulties. In return some foremen's suspicion that quality control staff 'spied' on their work section was examined and agreement was reached about how they would be more open about what was happening within the production schedule. A second example came from the Traffic department, where road and rail traffic foremen were now able to look together at their overlapping problems. This had not previously happened in such a systematic way.

Five major themes emerged at this level: communication between departments, shop-floor industrial relations, equipment maintenance, British Steel Corporation staff policies, and the structure of Stocksbridge and Tinsley Park Works. Let us look at each of these in turn.

Communication between departments

It became apparent that one of the principal difficulties facing foremen and their colleagues was relatively poor liaison between departments. It is at foreman level that the operational difficulties arising from poor liaison tend to be most pressing and, although the project groups at levels one and two had referred to problems between departments, they had not given them the emphasis or the urgency that was expressed at level three.

Not surprisingly in view of their work role, members of the Traffic department expressed particular frustration here. Their project group examined problems about the links between themselves and Billet Finishing and the Melting Shop. They felt that they received inadequate loading information and that they were often given too little prior notice of work to be done. As a result of these points being raised in a project group, meetings were held between the departments and changes in administration and communication were introduced to the satisfaction of all three departments. The Traffic department and the Mill were both concerned about the information they received from the Planning department, and project groups set up meetings with planning staff to seek improvements. Success here was more limited, as the Planning department was reluctant to acknowledge the problems presented by the others, and in the long run the situation remained largely unchanged.

More substantial progress was made by a joint working party of Mill and Billet Finishing members. Level three project groups in both departments had raised the problem of coordination between them, and several meetings between foremen and section managers were held, leading to the establishment of the joint working party. This working party identified eleven main areas of friction and recommended solutions in nine cases. Some of the problems will be familiar in many large organisations. Here is an excerpt from the minutes of one of the meetings:

> The Mill continued rolling into mealbreaks without any prior notification (to Billet Finishing). Although it was appreciated that it was sometimes necessary for this to happen, the fact that no prior notification was given created ill-feeling. The Mill Shift Manager agreed to ensure that in future 6 and 8 Bay (in Billet Finishing) would be informed of any extended rolling times.

It would be unrealistic to claim that all ill-feeling between the departments was permanently removed by the joint working party, though the record in the minutes did state that 'all members agreed that the meeting was both constructive and worthwhile and that progress had definitely been made in certain areas'. The point to be made here is that the project groups had provided a mechanism to air this issue within a solution-seeking framework and that joint discussion between the

39

two departments is the only possible way to tackle such interface problems. Furthermore, by encouraging the creation of a working party whose members spanned several levels of both departments the project brought together the people who were themselves directly involved with the problem. This is often more effective than a discussion between, say, the department managers alone.

Shop-floor industrial relations

Questions of industrial relations also loomed large in the early discussions of level three groups. Many foremen were worried that shop-floor militancy had been shown to pay off in recent years (nationally as well as locally). This was at the height of the wages/inflation spiral in 1974/75. Grievances tended to be taken past the foremen as quickly as possible as a prelude to rapid militant action. Some procedural changes were achieved through the project groups (including the attendance of foremen in negotiations affecting them), but the broader issues offered no clear solution. For example, draft Works Rules had been prepared by management for joint discussion, but examination of these in the Works Council had come to a halt some time ago. The foremen were unhappy about this, but their project groups could do little more than send requests to the trade unions, the Works Council and senior management that progress should be resumed. These requests had no immediately visible effect. We expressed the hope that the Interlinked Phase might identify possible improvements in industrial relations procedures and that the Project might create desired increases in collaborative problem-solving. Not surprisingly, these vague hopes did little to relieve the pessimism.

Equipment maintenance

The third major theme was also difficult to influence; most level three groups spent much time lamenting their equipment maintenance problems. As was described earlier, the shop-floor engineering unions had declined to take part in the Project, and the scope for joint action was thus limited. Engineering staff members were however active in level three groups and some discussion did take place. As might be expected, production foremen tended to bring up criticisms which they expected the engineering staff to answer, and there were times when fruitless mutual recrimination ensued.

For example, a foreman in one group complained that he had been obliged to wait three days for a replacement crane brake shoe which resulted in his whole section being without work. The engineer replied that he was overwhelmed with jobs, that shop-floor people did not look after their equipment properly, there was not the cash available to hold a stock of all possible spares, and that anyway there were long delays on deliveries. Another group produced something which could have been straight out of Joseph Heller's 'Catch 22': 'Why does it take so long for our mobile equipment to get repaired?' asked the shop-floor group of the engineer they had requested to attend their meeting. 'Because we have to wait for spares' he replied, 'and our policy is to have a spare vehicle as standby rather than maintaining large stocks of spares.' 'It's broken too', the man howled. 'Ah yes, but we've not got the right spares, you see', the engineer, blushingly, replied. No easy answers were possible although some progress was made by focussing attention on the recent situation rather than allowing much capital to be made out of isolated incidents which had happened years ago.

Two kinds of attempt at constructive decision-making were made. Some groups prepared papers about their maintenance situation which were dispatched to senior engineering managers with a request for follow-up meetings with the project group leader. These meetings cleared the air a little and led to minor working changes (for example, in stock levels or in ordering procedures), but relations continued to be somewhat strained.

A second action recommendation was for senior engineering managers to be asked to attend a project group to discuss the problems which faced them. Several such meetings took place, and they were undoubtedly of value at the time. The works engineer was clearly no stranger to the criticisms which were raised and he was fluent and persuasive in his replies. Some local changes were agreed, but friction between production and maintenance is a potential problem in all industries and it remained an issue throughout the Project, particularly after the engineers were asked to reduce costs and cease using contract labour.

Corporate staff policies

The fourth major theme in the section managers' project groups was of direct personal significance to the members at this level — the status and career position of staff employees. Most groups raised the point that the relative standing of staff and shop floor had been changing and that staff benefits in terms of salaries, holidays, pensions and so on were now matched by the shop floor. Feelings ran deep on these issues and there was frustration that no positive action seemed possible. One project group raised a number of related anxieties of this kind in a letter to the general manager. He replied in the following terms:

> The first three items are questions which often crop up in discussion groups with foremen and junior management throughout the Corporation and they clearly involve a discussion of the management style of large corporations with special reference to the history of the steel industry. I could not recommend making changes in the staff salary structure or in staff conditions without reference to the wider subject of BSC employment policy. As you know from a letter that I recently circulated, all staff are currently committed to take part in a major revamping of the salary structure by using job evaluation. The introduction of incentive bonuses at this stage would prejudice the concept of job evaluation.
>
> Referring to the second question in particular, the complaint seems to be not so much that staff conditions have deteriorated but that the conditions for manual grade employees have improved, and thus 'differentials' have been eroded. Once again, this has been clear BSC policy.

Perhaps you would pass on my thanks to the Group for raising these important questions and, apart from the comments I have made, please assure them that they will be fed to the Divisional Personnel Director for consideration when long-term employment policy is being formulated.

In seeking possible actions here the general manager may well have been under constraints as severe as those on his subordinates, and his letter was carefully and politely worded. However, it merely increased the group's frustration and feelings that little could be done about their real problems, either with the Project or without it: 'there's no hope of changing the system, it's like pushing against a big lump of rubber'.

The structure of the works

The final major theme identified earlier (the structure of Stocksbridge and Tinsley Park Works) was also of this kind. Once again it was level three who particularly experienced frustrations here. The higher level groups had noted the problems but clearly felt less strongly about them: partly because their greater contact with Stocksbridge gave them a more benign view of the situation and partly because they were more influenced by the management policy of emphasising that the two works were in fact a single unit whose differences should not be exaggerated.

The foremen and other members of level three project groups had a fund of stories which were told during the initial meetings. One trouble was said to go back to the wage slips used just after amalgamation of the two units which were headed 'Samuel Fox and Company', the previous owners of Stocksbridge Works. Another common story was of a manager arriving from Stocksbridge to advise on problems while sporting his Samuel Fox tie. On the Tinsley Park side men still wore their safety helmets with ESC (English Steel Company) emblazoned across the front. Many foremen quoted other instances of how Stocksbridge practices had been introduced as replacements for Tinsley Park procedures; whilst agreeing that this was a necessary consequence of amalgamation, there was a feeling that the process had been too much a one-way development. More recently, some had claimed that Stocksbridge had been receiving better raw materials and the more profitable orders; as far as we could tell these were prejudices rather than facts. Another group member 'knew a girl who had worked in the kitchens both at Stocksbridge and at Tinsley Park', who had told him that the culinary standards were much higher at Stocksbridge — the evidence was indirect but readily accepted.

The widespread mistrust of Stocksbridge was particularly strong amongst the junior managers and staff represented in the level three project group. Many service functions (engineering, planning, quality control, training, traffic, clerical etc.) had their base at Stocksbridge and the impression had become firmly established that if these were moved to Tinsley Park then operational efficiency would increase. (By the same token Stocksbridge would suffer; but that was 'their' problem.) As one foremen put it: 'You don't feel proud to work at Tinsley Park, you're just an offshoot of Stocksbridge.'

The complex and wide ranging nature of this question made it a difficult one to get to grips with in the project groups. Specific attempts were made by asking staff managers based at Stocksbridge to attend meetings to discuss the difficulties which members were experiencing. In anticipation of one such meeting a foreman sarcastically asked the group leader to 'leave the first half an hour for introductions', because their manager did not know either their names or faces. Attendance at group meetings by traffic, management development and industrial relations managers allowed people to raise in discussion the problems that they thought were limiting work effectiveness and in some cases this led to promises which were attractive to group members. Unfortunately not all of these were carried out and the overall feeling of separation remained. We will take up this issue again later, but note here the developing opinion during later group meetings that the Project could not come to grips with the really major issues.

With more localised problems, however, there were a number of clear successes at this level. For example, foremen in one department were particularly concerned that the authority of chargehands needed enlarging and defining. From their project group emerged the recommendation to establish a working party to examine this issue, and a written specification was subsequently drawn up to everyone's satisfaction. Another group identified as a major problem the pattern of communications between themselves and their boss (the group leader). This led to useful discussions about management style and the administration of the department. Office and other facilities formed the focus of some action plans in another department, and significant and obvious improvements were achieved through the project groups. Similarly, the training of operatives within departments caused concern to some groups, and recommended improvements were successfully carried out.

In broad summary, it was the level three project groups that were generally least able to develop enthusiasm for the Employee Relations Project. This was partly due to their general feeling of being 'hard done by' in relation to the shop floor; they wanted some obvious improvements in their standing before they would be satisfied. Related to that was the observation that the level four groups (with shop-floor members) were raising a lot of issues which involved foremen and section managers in extra work: they wondered why they should work hard to tackle their subordinates' complaints when their own superiors were not responding positively to their requests. In fact many localised issues were resolved to everyone's satisfaction at level three, but it remains true that the five major themes at this level were particularly hard to tackle. Senior managers were able to offer little in the way of changes, and it may be that we had ourselves failed to recognise in our design of the Project that the boundaries of what was readily attainable would soon be reached. This aspect of the design of future projects is examined throughout Part Two.

Shop floor project groups

There were more project groups at shop-floor than at other levels: thirteen groups were established, meeting the goal of twenty per cent shop-floor involvement. They met on a total of thirty-nine occasions between May and November 1974 concurrently with the meetings at other levels, and one of us was again always present. Since we were each principally attached to a single department we were able to coordinate issues from different groups and pass information about action plans and outcomes from group to group. When it was felt appropriate to do so we also accepted responsibility for conveying items from the lower levels to meetings at higher levels, principally the department managers' and works manager's project groups.

The group leaders at the fourth level were either foremen or shop stewards, and at the outset most of them expressed anxiety about their role. The shop steward leaders were initially least clear about how to proceed, since unlike the foremen they had not had the advantage of prior membership of level three groups. In practice therefore it fell to us to ensure that the goals of the meetings and the suggested manner of proceeding were described and followed. We also assisted more at this level with secretarial work, suggesting appropriate forms of words to frame problems and actions, and summarising issues and action plans on display charts and on Problem Record Forms.

By the second meeting, however, the majority of group leaders had found their feet and progress was generally good. The leaders had learned from experience, assisted by our guidance in private discussions between meetings when we talked about their style and possible changes.

We requested that the Meeting Assessment Form be completed in only a few of the initial meetings. By this time we had largely stopped using the Meeting Assessment Form with higher level groups, and our experience with it at this fourth level was not encouraging. Many of the shop floor employees were ill at ease with the concepts and procedures for answering, and a small number were unable to read. It also became apparent that when groups did use the Meeting Assessment Form they showed marked reluctance to say anything critical of their leader or their colleagues. In one or two cases a useful discussion of style did take place, but by and large the feedback at this level was of only limited value.

Just as the management groups had been inclined to see many problems arising from the attitudes of shop-floor employees, so did the shop-floor groups attribute many of their difficulties to management. Despite this obvious difference of emphasis, the problem lists generated at each level had considerable overlap. Relationships with Stocksbridge were often discussed at level four, as was the need to give more authority to foremen. Liaison between departments and departmental training and personnel policies were also prominent issues.

Shop-floor militancy was examined in some of the groups. The atmosphere was one of regret rather than enthusiasm for the militant postures which had been adopted in some parts of the works. There was general agreement that 'as soon as we walk out our point gets conceded' and that 'the only way to get any progress in negotiations is to threaten to strike'. The assumption behind these discussions was a somewhat simple one, that if management would only concede earlier, then progress would be more rapid. Such a view was of course unrealistic from management's position, and lasting solutions would surely require rather more complicated changes in working relationships.

In passing, we should note that some new negotiating styles were developing in certain sections of the works. During July 1974 a dispute over payment for ancillary workers within one of the departments was handled in a different and successful way. Stress was laid on tackling the dispute along the lines of the Employee Relations Project and on involving foremen from the start. Furthermore, a strong emphasis was placed on the identification and recording of specific problems and possible actions and on communicating what was happening to others in the department. Following the ERP model a working party was established and agreement reached quite swiftly. Management and shop stewards commented that the atmosphere was quite different from that in earlier disputes: 'A year ago we would have been completely at each others' throats, and a lot of mud would have been thrown around.'

All was not sweetness and light, however, for during the autumn of 1974 a small number of employees brought the whole works production to a halt for several weeks. The fifty-six Melting Shop bricklayers were adamant that their earnings position had dropped too much relative to other groups, and they wished it to be restored. In practice they were still among the highest paid bricklayers in the Corporation, with earnings considerably above those at Stocksbridge. Their strike extended through most of September and October 1974, and effectively halted Melting Shop production. For part of this period the rest of the workforce received the average earnings guaranteed by national agreement and were employed on housekeeping duties within the plant. Attitudes towards the bricklayers were unsympathetic, but they maintained a solid opposition to returning to work. The issue was ultimately resolved through a reference to the recently-established Arbitration Conciliation and Advisory Service.

The bricklayers' strike undoubtedly coloured people's views of the Employee Relations Project. Some middle managers were particularly scathing, observing once more that the workers were only interested in themselves and that the welfare of the works and their colleagues meant nothing to them. However, the bricklayers retained an interest in the Project and apparently saw no inconsistency between the strike and their participation in it. They were keen to complete the Project questionnaire (see the next chapter) and to continue their involvement on the Project Steering Committee. Indeed, it was a measure of our good standing that we were accepted as possible mediators in the dispute and invited to attend several meetings with their negotiating team, though our conciliatory impact was extremely limited.

Most meetings of the level four project groups had taken place before the bricklayers' strike commenced. The meetings generated many dozen issues, and substantial changes were introduced in some areas. Many of these issues concerned safety, equipment and local operational procedures; further details are given in chapter 8. Two groups identified as a problem the limited managerial abilities of their foreman and shift manager respectively. In one case, 'he's a smashing feller but a terrible foreman', the shop steward group leader undertook to have private dicussions with him. In the second case the shift manager was alleged to be too reluctant to take decisions, lacking trust in his foremen, and unwilling to push for his men. The shop steward group leader and two members of the group had extensive discussions with him over this. They were not optimistic that major changes would follow, but the open communication and discussion of mutual problems was thought to have been valuable.

Communication with management

This aspect of the Project is the principal theme to be illustrated in our account of the level four groups. Once the problem lists had been drawn up in initial meetings, action recommendations almost inevitably involved some communication with management. This might be a visit from designated group members to their department or section manager, or a visit or letter to managers of staff departments elsewhere in Tinsley Park or Stocksbridge. In many cases the manager in question attended a subsequent group meeting to discuss the issues troubling shop-floor members. For example, the personnel services officer attended one group to describe and discuss the policy on clocking in and the prospects of staff status for shop floor employees. This discussion had no direct action implication, but it was greatly appreciated by the members.

Also appreciated was the visit to another group by the works manager to discuss the distribution of work between Stocksbridge and Tinsley Park. This occurred soon after he had taken up his post (in July 1974), so that it provided an opportunit for him to become better known at shop-floor level. His previous position at Stocksbridge allowed him to talk with authority about the position there, and he emphasised how Stocksbridge people often thought that it was Tinsley Park who had the better deal. This theme, that Stocksbridge had many problems of the same kind as Tinsley Park, was one which he emphasised on many occasions in the subsequent months.

Almost every level four group met with one or more members of management to discuss problems which they had raised. Particularly interesting were some discussions with their department managers. These provided ready information and allowed quick decisions about local issues, they gave the managers a chance to raise their own problems and to request action and cooperation of certain kinds, and they were an indication that the department manager was willing to devote his time to exchanging views with the shop floor.

The meetings regularly found their way into areas where the common interest of management and shop-floor was greater than had previously seemed likely. This was particularly noticeable in groups whose leaders were shop stewards and who sometimes tended to give a consistently negative picture of management's concern for the workforce. In these groups the opportunity to meet management face-to-face undoubtedly changed some level four members' and leaders' views of their department.

Many of the discussions that evolved between a department manager and his level four groups centred on working difficulties within the department. The goal of more effective operation was embraced by all parties, and shop-floor interest in greater effectiveness seemed to be quite genuine. In addition to these specific questions, more general discussions about relationships between management and shop floor also took place, in which such notions as 'trust', 'respect', 'pride' and 'friendship' were informally and openly discussed. An atmosphere of warm feeling between management and men characterised some of these meetings, though how far that warmth was carried over into operational decisions and industrial relations meetings is of course the crucial question; we look further into this in chapter 8.

The flavour of these meetings can best be given through a sample of quotations recorded at the time. These are excerpts and should not be read as a continuous dialogue.

Shop-floor employee to manager: 'There's a widespread feeling that managers don't respect the men. They won't treat us as human beings. You storm through the plant without taking any notice of anyone. You just look through us as though we're not there ... When you do come through the department, there's nothing better for a workman than feeling that his manager is bothered about what he thinks about the job, he wants to know that you're valuing his opinions and knowledge ... Some plain silly decisions have been made around here because you wouldn't speak to the men.'

Shop-floor employee to manager: 'Management treat workmen as a set of morons. There's a lack of discussion, you won't answer questions. We have no trust in management ... it's all master and serf around here.'

Manager to shop-floor employees: 'I'm not going to make straight concessions in the face of claims. Like everyone else, I've got a job to do. I've got to run this department and make a profit. And I've got to be fair. It's only human nature to ask for a bit more than you would settle for. You can't distrust people for not giving in to you like that.' The reply was one of agreement: 'It's management's job to manage. We don't mind them saying "no" as long as they keep to their word and take our views seriously.'

Manager to shop-floor employees: 'How far should I go in asking for views? You don't always agree yourselves, and someone has to make a decision. We can't please everyone all the time. A stronger JCC is one way of getting what we all want.'

Shop-floor employee to manager: 'Things have been changing since the Project started. You've started talking to people now. You stopped next to someone last week. He was so surprised that you talked to him that he nearly fell over backwards.'

Manager to shop-floor employees: 'We have had problems. We've all had bad times, but we are trying to improve. This is what the ERP is all about, trying to break down that feeling of distrust. I can assure you that management are trying to build up a team . . . It'll be a long job but we're trying . . . We'll get people proud to say they work at Tinsley Park.'

Manager to shop-floor employees: 'Managers are no longer jumping in to cause trouble. In the atmosphere we had twelve months ago that was happening all the time.'
To which came the quick reply: 'In the atmosphere we had twelve months ago we'd never had seen management and men sitting together around a table like this.'

In these ways the level four meetings between management and shop floor undoubtedly increased mutual understanding. However, it was also the case that some of the promises entered into during the discussions were not carried out subsequently. This was partly because of practical difficulties, lack of time, opposition from colleagues and so on, but the reasons for inaction were not always reported back to the group, so that distrust over promises not kept was far from completely eradicated.

Other benefits of the level four groups were in terms of straightforward information transmission, and there were very many instances of this. Group leaders and visiting managers could provide facts about the works suggestion scheme, trade union policies and practices, the new job evaluation scheme for clerks, the availability of protective clothing, plans for new equipment, the procedures for machine inspection, maintenance, service and supply. The works medical officer explained the operation and facilities of the works first-aid system and gave useful advice on accident prevention and treatment. The works manager described the relationships between Tinsley Park and other parts of British Steel Corporation, providing information about the rationale behind the structure.

In any large organisation there are innumerable opportunities for rumour and factual misunderstanding. The project groups at all levels provided opportunities for widespread learning and informal instruction, as well as being the vehicle for action planning which was their primary purpose.

Limitations on action

However, the success of the level four groups in initiating action was limited by a number of significant factors. Although dozens of improvements were introduced, many recommended changes would have been very costly and had to be shelved. This was increasingly the tendency as 1974 wore on and the deepening recession gripped the steel industry with its accompanying need for cost reduction and general economies. Other action recommendations required months of investigation and long delays whilst items were ordered and installed. Progress was in this way not always visible to those who had initiated the item, and attitudes were sometimes coloured by this apparent lack of success.

Another limitation on action was in terms of management's feeling that they were under too much pressure from below. In general, the response to visits and requests from level four groups was cordial; but there were certainly times when department and section managers felt that the scale of demands was unreasonable and unrealistic. Management's difficulties were sometimes compounded by major operational problems or the installation of extensive new pieces of plant, and they realistically believed that these important jobs should receive priority. Their attitudes were undoubtedly influenced by their view that the shop floor had a duty within the spirit of the Project to cooperate more with requests from management for relaxation of restrictive practices and a greater willingness to meet targets. Such cooperation was not always forthcoming.

The level four project groups revealed an approach to participation in decision-making which also limited their effectiveness. There was a tendency to act as though once the issue had been raised it was no longer the responsibility of the group which had raised it. Whereas subordinate members of groups at higher levels had often accepted responsibility to pursue problems on behalf of the group, the shop-floor members at level four tended towards an 'over to you' stance: once the item was raised it was up to management, not them, to do something about it. If success was not achieved, then management were blamed for the failure.

Another factor limiting the success of the level four project groups was turnover of key group members. One group leader left the works after two meetings, another was ill for long periods, and several group members charged to follow up action items also left before their tasks were completed. The problem of discontinuity among management groups has already been noted, and the general difficulty is clearly one which has to be borne in mind when assessing the maximum likely success of organisational programmes of this kind; it has to be accepted that some 'slippage' is inevitable.

5 The project questionnaire

Stage two of the initial project design was a questionnaire survey of opinions across the works. The separate stages laid down in the original plan came in fact to merge into each other, so that the project group meetings of stages one and three described in chapter 3 tended to be continuous across much of the Project. The questionnaire survey of stage two therefore took place when several project group meetings had been completed at each level. The groups had identified issues, attempted to get action on them and received feedback about what managers and colleagues thought. In one sense this pre-empted the survey feed-back data to be provided through the questionnaire, but the project groups naturally involved only a proportion of people and of issues. A major aim of the questionnaire survey was to obtain information from a large sample of the work-force in order to paint as accurate a picture as possible.

The intention was to make public the opinions of separate groups of employees about the major issues on the works. By feeding back the results of the survey to participants in the Project, people would be able further to explore what action recommendations were desirable. Furthermore, the results would also allow a check on the generality of opinions which had been expressed in project groups: were the issues raised there in fact of significance to the workforce as a whole?

During the summer of 1974 we and the Steering Committee designed the questionnaire so that it closely reflected the issues raised in the project groups. We took care that the items were expressed through the language in which they had been raised in discussion. Since the balance of issues varied across departments separate versions were printed for each of the four departments taking part in the Project, and the questionnaires distributed as 'pull-out supplements' with the third issue of *Focus*. The material was in three parts: items on works-wide issues; items on departmental issues common to all departments; and items specific to a particular department and completed only by members of that department. A final page gave space for 'any comments you would like to make about issues raised in this Project or about the questionnaire itself'. This meant there were four departmental questionnaires for shop-floor and non-supervisory staff which were complemented by four other versions for foremen and managers. The latter contained the sixty-seven items of the shop-floor versions (including the nine which varied between departments) together with nine other items for foremen and managers only. An example of these is: 'The system of management meetings in this works needs improvement.'

The project questionnaire was administered in August 1974, two weeks after the annual holiday shutdown. Shop-floor workers were asked to complete it anonymously in supervised sessions during working time. Non-supervisory staff, foremen and managers received their copies personally from the project coordinator, and they returned them directly to him. It was emphasised that completion was voluntary, and in practice the amount of management encouragement varied between departments; we will look further at these differences in chapters 7 and 11.

The completion rate was a high one, eighty-three per cent of the employees of those departments taking part in the Project. Table 5.1 shows how this overall figure was made up.

Table 5.1
Response rate to the project questionnaire

	Melting Shop	Mill	Billet Finishing and Test House	Traffic	Overall
Shop floor and non-supervisory staff	95 (64%)	127 (84%)	361 (98%)	53 (67%)	636 (85%)
Foremen and managers	19 (49%)	26 (77%)	34 (89%)	10 (100%)	81 (74%)
Overall	114 (61%)	153 (82%)	395 (97%)	63 (71%)	725 (83%)

This high response rate was important, since it allowed us to have confidence that the results reflected the opinions of the works as a whole.

Answers to each question were in terms of 'Yes, that is true', 'I'm not sure', or 'No, that is not true', and 'Not applicable'. Opinions were expressed by placing a tick in one of four boxes, although in practice the 'Not applicable' box was (as we had hoped) only infrequently used. Our own statistical analyses of the results made use of all the responses, looking for example at the complete set of answers to each question across Yes, Don't Know and No. In feedback to the works simplicity and comprehensibility were required, and we relied upon the percentage of people answering Yes to each question.

Some results of the project questionnaire

Before turning to the ways in which the results of the project questionnaire were fed back, some of the central findings deserve mention. The percentage of people answering Yes to twelve of the questions can serve to illustrate how opinions expressed through project groups were indeed fair reflections of attitudes throughout the works. Some differences and similarities between shop floor and management are also worth noting. These are illustrated in Table 5.2.

The separate items for each department also presented a picture that was consistent with opinions expressed in the project groups. For example, one of the issues raised in both the Mill and Billet Finishing questionnaires was: 'More attention should be paid to improving working procedures between Billet Finishing and the Mill.' Some ninety per cent of shop floor and non-supervisory staff respondents

Table 5.2
Illustrative questionnaire items and responses

Question	Percentage Yes	
	Shop floor and non-supervisory staff %	Foremen and managers %
Managers at Stocksbridge with responsibility for a department at Tinsley Park just don't know what is going on here	62	74
Too many people at Tinsley Park blame Stocksbridge when it is really up to employees here to solve our own problems	51	63
Managers on this works are changed around too often for them to be able to do a good job	47	65
Industrial relations would be better if managers in my department were given more freedom to settle issues within the department	79	82
More decisions in my department should be taken by foremen without them having to refer to their managers	86	82
There should be more meetings in my department between foremen and work-people to discuss problems affecting the job	89	68
A lot of industrial relations problems in my department are caused by shop-floor people not being aware of agreed disputes procedures and national agreements	66	75
Shop-floor workers in my department are good at making complaints, but not so good at making positive suggestions	58	75
I would like to know more about what goes on at Section Council meetings	89	73
There needs to be better training for people who have to operate new equipment in my department	85	68
There should be more small items of stores available in my department	85	71
Canteen arrangements for shiftworkers are very bad	86	80

in both departments agreed with this.

The comments made in the space at the end of the questionnaire were varied, with a small number clearly negative being outnumbered by a variety of more favourable reactions: about thirteen per cent of people completing the questionnaire wrote in one or more comments. Typical positive reactions were these:

> 'Keep going along these lines and something should be achieved.'
> 'There's nothing to lose and all to gain.'

More embittered comments were of this kind:

> 'I think that filling in any questionnaire is a complete waste of time as nothing will be done. Just a flash in the pan to find jobs for some people until somebody thinks of a better job for them to do.'
> 'A load of tripe.'

And, as a salutory warning:

> 'I hope something will come of this Project, because if it doesn't it will make matters a lot worse than they are already.'

We have already indicated in our account of the project groups that something was indeed being done, but that progress was not uniform. Differences between parts of the works and an overall evaluation of the Project's success will be presented in chapters 7 and 8.

Feedback of the questionnaire results

The opinions reflected in the questionnaire results were made available for discussion in several ways. The main vehicle was the fourth issue of *Focus* at the beginning of November 1974. This had an introduction from the new works manager (who had taken up his post in July), pledging his support for the Project which had, of course, been initiated in the time of his predecessor. Quotations and photographs of project group leaders were also included, together with a statement of how project groups, the Steering Committee and senior management would follow through the questionnaire results. The results themselves took up most space, being presented in a separate eight-page supplement for each of the four departments.

Each questionnaire item was accompanied by four sets of percentage figures: those for the works as a whole, broken down for shop floor and non-supervisory staff versus managers and foremen, and those for the departments in question with the same breakdown. This layout was designed so that readers could easily compare the results for their own department and those of the whole works, as well as those between managers and the shop floor. As with earlier issues of *Focus*, copies were made available to everyone on the works.

A second form of feedback was more detailed. Readers of *Focus* were advised that separate breakdowns of figures on a job by job basis were available on request from the project coordinator. This level of detail was only requested by three managers who wanted to know the exact spread of opinion across groups in their department. No shop stewards or other workpeople asked for additional material.

The Project Steering Committee held two meetings in November and December to discuss possible actions arising from the survey results. For these we prepared lists that grouped questionnaire items according to the amount of agreement between the opinions of managers and their subordinates. Complete summaries of the four departments' results were also provided. The first meeting concentrated upon opinions about relations between Tinsley Park and Stocksbridge. The works manager (who was Chairman of the Steering Committee) emphasised how matters were improving all the time and drew attention to a questionnaire item suggesting that too many people at Tinsley Park used Stocksbridge as an excuse when it was really up to them to tackle their own problems.

Discussion settled upon industrial relations procedures on the works, and a number of recommendations were made. For example, it was agreed that department managers should chair negotiations in their department (rather than the senior industrial relations officer) and that negotiations should take place within departments rather than in the offices of the Industrial Relations Department. These changes were part of a developing emphasis on tackling problems as close as possible to their point of origin.

The second meeting of the Steering Committee discussed the works manager's views of the wide-ranging issues which had been brought up by project groups and the questionnaire results. He worked through twelve major areas, developing the themes that matters could be a lot worse (and he knew of places where they were worse) and that most problems were the inevitable by-product of membership of a large organisation; he stressed that such membership itself brought benefits which far outweighed the disadvantages. For example, concern that Stocksbridge procedures had been imposed on the works was misplaced: nationalisation had meant that all works had to introduce standard procedures, and it just happened that some of these were originally developed at Stocksbridge. Furthermore, before amalgamation with Stocksbridge Tinsley Park wages had initially been lower than those at Stocksbridge, so that one advantage to Tinsley Park of being part of a single unit was a gradual increase in wage levels.

The general tone of these discussions was one of 'we're all in it together and things aren't as bad as in some other works'. There may well have been some validity in this view, but it had the effect of bringing to a halt any attempts at questioning the present system. It thus seemed that many issues raised in the project groups were likely to be returned to them without any prospect of action. However, the works manager clearly recognised his responsibility to explain the situation as fully as he could and he took several steps in this direction. These will be summarised in the next chapter.

A separate discussion of the questionnaire results took place between the two meetings of the Steering Committee. This was at a meeting of the Works Management Committee, chaired by the general manager and including the works manager and senior managers from personnel, metallurgy, engineering and accounting functions. The general manager was keen to initiate immediate action at his level about several issues highlighted by the questionnaire. However, he wanted an overall analysis of the problems which the Employee Relations Project had raised, and we described our plans for an Interim Report early in 1975. This would present our interpretations and include recommendations for further action. In the meantime it was agreed that the general manager would attend future project groups when they requested him to do so.

The project groups themselves had the opportunity to use the questionnaire feedback as a basis for discussion, and we made several attempts to encourage examination of why a particular department's results were markedly different from the works as a whole. In general, we were disappointed that the feedback procedures generated little enthusiasm. This might have been because the issues were by then well known, because the material was too bulky and confusing, because it needed more interpretation and emphasis, or because people were increasingly of the opinion that few major changes were possible, especially in view of growing financial stringency enforced by the national economic recession. For whatever reason the survey feedback process was less helpful than it has sometimes been in other organisations, and we shall look further into its general value in chapter 11.

We took one further opportunity to draw attention to important aspects of the questionnaire results in our Interim Report presented later to the works. One section of this identified a number of questionnaire items which still deserved detailed consideration, and several of these items subsequently found their way into decision-making discussions based on the Interim Report. These discussions are summarised in the next chapter.

6 The Interlinked Phase and Interim Report

In this chapter we continue our narrative to describe the events leading up to our Interim Report to the works, which was submitted in February 1975. The content of the report will be summarised together with actions flowing from it.

By late autumn 1974 the project groups at all four levels had been meeting for several months. The considerable enthusiasm that had existed at the outset in many parts of the works was still high in several sections. Many local improvements had been introduced and others were still in the pipeline. But there was also a growing feeling that things were moving too slowly, and that many larger issues would remain untouched.

We had originally argued for a slow and steady unfolding of the Project, in order to let decisions and actions be fitted in with the day-to-day running of the plant and to give time for new equipment or procedures to be installed. However, we shared the view of many people on the works that by the autumn progress was not rapid enough to maintain widespread interest.

A common difficulty that besets many programmes of organisational change is the turnover of staff which occurs in most large corporations, and this was a serious impediment to the continuity of the Employee Relations Project. We have already noted that the works manager was promoted and transferred from the works in July 1974. He had been an especially keen advocate of the Project and was closely identified with its progress and success. The new works manager was unfailingly polite about the Project, but we felt he was less at ease with its style and less convinced of its possible benefits and priorities when he was adapting to a new job in a new works. His project group (level one) was well into its meetings before he arrived, and it was naturally difficult for him to pick up the threads sewn by someone else.

Another change was at the next higher managerial level. The general manager (another initiator of the Project) had also been promoted in mid-1974, and his successor's outlook was similar to that of the new works manager. Understandably, both these senior managers wanted to devote time to putting their personal stamp on their new jobs, and the Employee Relations Project was inevitably somewhat peripheral to this. Consequently, it probably received less impetus from these senior levels than it would have done if the previous works manager and general manager had remained in post.

Other significant managerial changes took place in the Melting Shop and the Mill, and we will look at these in the next chapter. Furthermore, three group leaders at level four were replaced or were ill from time to time, and across the shop floor as a whole there were naturally people leaving and arriving over the many months of the Project. This had the overall effect of diluting interest in the Project and reducing understanding of its goals.

The bricklayers' strike in September and October 1974 (see chapter 4) created a number of operational problems as work schedules were adjusted and steel from elsewhere was brought in for rolling and finishing. These problems were associated with minor grievances about special payments and administrative changes, and the tense atmosphere once again focussed managers' attention on the attitudes of the shop floor. Other unions on the site had attempted to persuade the bricklayers to continue working, but a general distrust of the shop floor was increasingly common among management at this time. During October these tensions crystallised into a strong opposition to the Employee Relations Project among a group of section managers.

This organised opposition was of considerable significance in that it had always been accepted that a group of employees could at any time withdraw from the Project if they wished. The central position of the section managers, both as decision-makers and as opinion leaders, meant that their withdrawal would have effectively brought the Project to an end. We therefore spent some time attempting to persuade them to choose to continue.

Two meetings between the group of section managers and ourselves took place. The first was an informal discussion over lunch in their dining room, in which a small number of them initiated a conversation about the Project and its goals. It was claimed that 'the shop floor are only interested in themselves. They forget we work here as well and that we've got a job to do.' The opinion of some managers present was that the Project was naïve and misguided, and merely playing into the hands of shop floor interests; 'they have no interest in this plant, just in themselves'. We agreed that self-interest would motivate the actions of many people in the Project, but that coupled with this there was also plenty of evidence that workpeople wanted an efficient and friendly plant. One section manager urged a tighter military style discipline to tackle the works' problems rather than 'expensive' projects like the Employee Relations Project. On the latter point we reminded him that we were receiving no pay from the Corporation.

This informal discussion led to the scheduling of a second meeting ten days later for the section managers to exchange their opinions and to decide whether they wished to continue with the Project. This was attended by nine managers and three of us. The meeting commenced with a listing of objections to the Project. These included a belief that it was 'simply a management bashing exercise, pandering to the shop floor'. 'The shop floor want expensive changes and they want them immediately.' 'Management is no longer able to manage − that's in the hands of the trade unions − so why bother anyway?' 'There'll be no real progress because top management won't give any support.'

These views were not universally held, and other section managers defended the Project for its obvious achievements. They felt that important steps had been taken in their departments, though they did share some doubts about the likelihood of action on some of the wider issues. We were also at pains to emphasise the achievements of the Project in some departments, and pointed out that the ERP would tend to succeed in direct proportion to the commitment which people like them put into it; it was a communication and decision-making mechanism which was set up to deal with their problems as well as anyone else's. We put the question to them, 'Why not use it to express *your* opinions and recommendations?'

This view carried the day, and the meeting agreed to continue to support the remaining stages of the Project. These involved further project group meetings and the collation and publication of all problems raised and actions taken.

The progress of project groups has been summarised in chapter 4, though two additional comments are appropriate here. First, mention should be made of visits from the works manager to express his views about issues referred to his level. These were appreciated as occasions to meet the new boss in face-to-face discussion, but despite his reassurances there were some expressions of 'I told you so. We needn't have bothered to bring it up, because nothing is going to change anyway.' The second point has been noted in the previous chapter: the availability of the questionnaire results in later project group meetings had little apparent influence on their deliberations or actions.

Publication of results

Between November 1974 and February 1975 attention was directed to summarising the outcomes of the Project. In the initial design we had emphasised that complete information about problems raised and actions initiated must be available to everyone when the Project was drawing to a formal conclusion (that is, in stage four of the schedule laid out at the beginning of chapter 3). This was thought to be desirable for three principal reasons:

1 To satisfy project groups that items would not get 'lost' after they had been raised.
2 To provide opportunity for groups to take an overall look at their progress, perhaps initiating some further action.
3 To give management another opportunity to explain why certain recommendations were not practicable.

The assessment of actions arising from the Project was also an important means of evaluating whether it had been worthwhile (we look at this aspect of evaluation in chapter 8).

As well as project group meetings for this purpose, special group leaders' meetings were held in each department to draw up summaries of what had occurred. A single issue had sometimes been entered on the Problem Record Forms of several project groups so that agreement had to be reached between them about the outcomes of their recommendations. Out of these meetings came the material for the fifth and final issue of *Focus*, which was published at the beginning of April 1975. This was a substantial ten-page edition summarising all problems and their outcomes or reasons why no action had been taken.

A total of 337 problems had been raised for action within departments, and approximately 260 of these had apparently resulted in progress towards their solution. An enlarged edition of *Focus* detailed all these problems and actions for the four departments, and the final page contained the works manager's responses to the wider issues which had been passed to him. His comments developed out of decisions taken by the Works Management Committee in their consideration of the Project's implications, and were in effect explanations of why the situation was as it was, with no commitment to major action.

The Interlinked Phase

Our narrative has at this point run ahead of the calendar, and we should move back slightly to describe the Interlinked Phase which took place between October and December 1974. This had been built into the Project's outline design as a questionnaire and interview inquiry into the industrial relations situation on the works. It was restricted to the main parties in the consultative and negotiating network, shop stewards and those managers who met formally and informally with them.

The consultative system was a comprehensive structure with a detailed written constitution, stating the objectives of joint consultation as follows:

(a) to foster and increase the cooperation between management and all other employees of the Corporation,

(b) to provide a forum for the frank discussion of matters affecting the efficient operation of the works and the welfare and safety of all concerned.

We had ample evidence from project groups, the questionnaire survey and from informal discussions that few members of the works saw these objectives as being met. Those people who were members of consultative committees complained loudly about them, and people who were not members had little knowledge of their activities and even less about any successes. As was reported in the last chapter, eighty-nine per cent of shop-floor and seventy-three per cent of management respondents recorded in the August 1974 questionnaire survey that they 'would like to know more about what goes on at Section Council meetings'. Furthermore, in a special section of the Before questionnaire (March 1974) restricted to shop stewards, foremen and managers, only forty-two per cent expressed satisfaction with 'the way the joint consultative machinery is used'.

We examined the workings of this machinery in three ways, by observation, questionnaire and interview. Throughout the study we were seeking information and opinion which would lead to recommendations for its improvement, and these were included in our Interim Report of February 1975.

Observation

The consultative network has three levels. At the top is the Works Council, which covers the whole of Stocksbridge and Tinsley Park Works. At the next level are Section Councils, one of which covers Tinsley Park itself, and below them are Joint Consultative Committees (JCCs) in each department. We first studied these levels by sitting in on meetings and observing the proceedings.

The Works Council. This was chaired by one of the senior trade union representatives from Tinsley Park and was almost parliamentary in its attention to procedure and wideranging subject matter. This tended to give meetings a rather ponderous atmosphere, accentuated by the fact that because the Council had such a diverse membership, most topics discussed were of minority interest. A lot of time was taken up with formal reports and exchanges of information, and much business was referred to outside agencies for further attention.

The Tinsley Park Section Council. The membership of this was naturally narrower and thus provided more opportunity for discussion of matters of common works interest. In practice the lengthy formal exchanges of information appeared to create boredom, and discussion commonly followed a pattern of 'grumble and defence'. Little genuine consultation was instigated by either side, and no clear-cut action recommendations emerged in any of the meetings we attended.

The Joint Consultative Committees. These dealt with localised questions within departments in a more unstructured and informal manner. Usually no agenda was worked to, and all items were effectively 'matters arising' from the Chairman's Report (the department manager in each case). These were commonly production or safety issues, and in many instances the JCCs could almost be described as functioning as production and safety committees.

Questionnaire

The second method of studying the consultative committees was through a special questionnaire survey of Tinsley Park Section Council and JCC members. Of the fifty or so respondents to this (just over half the possible number), the majority made clear their dissatisfaction with consultation. When opinions about different facets of the system were examined, it was revealed that most dissatisfaction centred on the outcomes of consultation. There was a widespread feeling that consultative meetings were often no more than 'talking shops' in which no progress toward real decision-making was made. Related to this dissatisfaction with the quality of discussion was a common feeling that the agenda usually were not conducive to good consultation, and that committees lacked the necessary powers to fulfil a useful function. This latter criticism was especially strongly expressed by trade union members. On the other hand people were generally less dissatisfied with the composition of the committees, chairmanship, the frequency and duration of meetings, and other arrangements such as the choice of meeting-place and payments for attendance by off-shift members.

In terms of the subject-matter of consultation, opinions differed from issue to issue. There was a fairly widespread feeling that only minor and trivial issues were successfully dealt with, and that major issues of policy, future developments, and allocation of resources were never seriously broached. The effect of this was to produce inappropriate polarisation on certain issues, to reduce the level of some debates to bickering, and to induce a fatalistic apathy among members that JCCs were a waste of time.

Interviews

Our third source of information about the consultative system was through interviews with shop stewards and managers. These also covered other aspects of industrial relations, described in the next paragraph. As far as the consultative machinery was concerned, they confirmed that dissatisfaction was widespread, and moreover that it was equally common among shop stewards and managers and extended to those who were not themselves JCC members. All these findings were fed back to the people concerned in summary reports early in 1975, and detailed recommendations for improvement were included in our Interim Report.

The second major part of the Interlinked Phase consisted of a series of structured interviews with twenty-four trade union and twenty-three management representatives from all parts and levels of the works. The aim of these was to find out what characterised the 'industrial relations climate' of different departments, by finding out which types of problems and grievances were most prevalent, and where union–management interactions were most problematic. Of the types of problem reported to cause friction, quality of maintenance emerged as the single most frequent and unwelcome source of difficulty, to both stewards and managers. Looking across departments, it was possible to rank order them in terms of severity of problems dealt with (computed by taking account of both the frequency of problems and how difficult people found them to handle). Traffic and Billet Finishing emerged as the most troubled areas by this method, with the Mill and Melting Shop reporting least difficulties.

When face-to-face dealings between shop stewards and managers were examined, differences between departments vanished. In short, there was revealed a generally good climate of relationships between individual stewards, both 'junior' and 'senior' and their managerial counterparts from foremen right up to works manager level. It should be added that stewards tended to have a somewhat 'rosier' view of relations than did the managers. Thus the industrial relations climate at Tinsley Park could be described as problem-centred rather than person-centred, with more dissatisfaction about the way issues were handled than about the people handling them.

Trade union and line managers' representatives held strongly critical opinions about the links with the industrial relations function, especially those outside the plant. The problem was again not one of personalities but to do with the authority attached to roles and the effectiveness of the communication channels which were available.

In common with other areas of decision-making, people at Tinsley Park express-ed frustration at their lack of autonomy and authority to handle their domestic industrial relations, and they showed resentment towards the external controls at Stocksbridge and beyond. There was a common feeling that the industrial relations function at Tinsley Park was little more than an information channel, and further-more that the people with the real decision-making powers did not understand local problems on the plant. Senior management's view of this was framed in terms of the restrictions imposed by membership of a large organisation and the need to build in checks against trade unions' exploitation of inequities. It was contended that the unions' objective is often to create such inequities for subsequent exploita-tion, and that careful monitoring by the industrial relations function was therefore essential; on some occasions this process would lead to senior management counter-manding proposals acceptable at departmental or works level.

A related pressure towards centralisation was apparent in the use of grievance procedures. Inside Tinsley Park Works informality in pursuing grievances was the general rule, although the constraints of wider Corporation policy were of course observed. Within the plant people consulted and negotiated with whomever, and in whatever ways, they felt appropriate up to works manager level; once this point had been reached formal procedure and external agents came into action. As a result of this, many believed that in order to get an important decision made it was necessary to make a lot of noise at ground level by threatening industrial action or otherwise by-passing lower parts of the system.

This kind of thinking was apparent in the major union—management conflict which occurred during the Project. The bricklayers' strike in September and October 1974 has already been mentioned, and the union's wish to raise this dispute quickly to senior management levels by refusing to undertake their allotted work was clear. One of their shop stewards subsequently expressed satisfaction to his colleagues on the Project Steering Committee that his grievance technique was the best one: he would march straight to the Industrial Relations Department, informing line management *en route* that he was going. Such a step simply by-passed departmental foremen and managers. (In practice one of the recommended changes from the Project was that this procedure should no longer be acceptable.)

A couple of months after the bricklayers' strike the same approach was apparent when a longstanding parity problem between Rail Traffic and the Melting Shop came to a head. The Traffic stewards, without warning, and some said following the bricklayers' earlier lead, expressed their intention to strike to narrow the differential between their pay and that of the men they worked along-side in the Melting Shop. This was averted by a sudden settlement on terms which management had hitherto ruled out as impossible.

It was clear that some open forum for discussion of the problems could be helpful and one of the Interim Report suggestions was for an Industrial Relations Seminar on the works. This duly took place at the beginning of 1976 and enabled the issues of procedure, decision-making, and internal and external powers to be thrashed out by Tinsley Park management and unions together with senior industrial relations management from Stocksbridge. The seminar also considered other key issues, such as industrial relations training, industrial democracy, and white-collar union representation. Although no concrete decisions were made at the time, there was general satisfaction that it had allowed important problems to be aired, and enabled some barriers of misunderstanding to be removed.

Finally, it should be re-emphasised that the Interlinked Phase only extended what was already central to the Project's activities. In almost all project groups industrial relations issues were raised and discussed. For example, problems of job evaluation, disciplinary procedures and union representation were of widespread concern. Indeed, on the latter issue, a special series of union—management discussions took place in one department, resulting in the re-allocation of stewards across shifts so that there were fewer gaps in the local decision-making network. The links between 'industrial relations' and 'employee relations' will be further examined in chapter 13.

The Interim Report

We have described how the Employee Relations Project aimed to draw upon the abilities, experience and interest of members of the works to develop their own recommendations. Our own views and suggestions as outside observers were however formally expressed in two principal documents. Apart from our report arising from the Interlinked Phase, we submitted a broad-ranging Interim Report in February 1975. In this we were acting more in the traditional consultant's role, suggesting areas in which we thought improvements were possible.

The Interim Report was initially submitted to the Project Steering Committee, but it was subsequently made much more widely available. Approximately 110 copies were distributed among trade unionists and managers, and a further 20 were sent to union district officials and to British Steel Corporation management outside the works.

The report itself was a series of detailed suggestions requiring twenty-two A4 pages of single-space typing. Our analyses and recommendations covered ten main areas:

1   Communications.
2   Management styles.
3   Relations between Stocksbridge and Tinsley Park.
4   Training.
5   Safety.
6   The personnel function.

7   The consultative system.
8   The industrial relations system.
9   The working environment.
10 The questionnaire survey.

Throughout the report we were striving to identify new operational procedures and communication structures which could continue to exist once the Project was formally concluded. Many of the improvements brought about through the project groups were one-off developments, to put right something which had gone wrong. These were important but the major goal was to introduce new procedures and strengthen the existing ones on a lasting basis. Could the patterns of communication, joint problem-solving and styles of employee relations advocated during the Project be continued on the works through standard procedures and routine organisational structures?

The flavour of our thinking can be illustrated through some excerpts from the Interim Report. Better information transmission between departments was one of the themes of our examination of communication networks, as follows:

> At present there is a certain 'them and us' attitude between different departments, only a limited appreciation of each others' problems, and a tendency to reject in advance any initiative from another department towards better relations. Working parties of management, foremen and shop-floor employees from departments in operational contact with each other could helpfully meet approximately twice a year. They should review problems of working relationships and procedures and agree upon changes. It is also important that they monitor the operation of those agreements reached at their last meeting.

Not surprisingly, several proposals flowed from repeated evidence from the project groups and the Interlinked Phase that the joint consultative committees were not felt to be working effectively. As described further in chapter 13, we offered a number of suggestions here, to do with publicity, membership, training, union representation, frequency and duration of meetings, minute taking, the initiation of discussions and so on. Particular emphasis was given to the need for discussions and minutes to focus upon action recommendations and their follow-up. Several related points about the agenda and structure of the committees were proposed in this way:

> Particular attention should be given to possible changes in the content of discussion and in the presentation of the agenda. At the moment the agenda tends to be a rather routine one, with a large number of items being lumped together under 'matters arising from the minutes' or 'any other business'. It seems preferable at departmental level to set down a list of 'topics for discussion', with any member of the department being allowed to contribute items to the list and to attend for his item if he wishes. The JCC should be encouraged to start its meeting by deciding on the priority sequence of items

on the list rather than necessarily proceeding in the order of an agenda.

We also recommend that greater attention be paid to the creation of subcommittees to deal with particular kinds of topic. (For instance a catering subcommittee for the Section Council is an obvious possibility, and a maintenance subcommittee for the Melting Shop JCC could be helpful.) Subcommittees should have a chairman with a clear interest in the topic, and might include coopted members who are not themselves councillors but who are keen and active in the subcommittee's area. Subcommittees should meet between committee meetings as required, and they should be able to make their own advisory recommendations and decisions. Each subcommittee chairman should present a brief report to the full committee, but topics in his area would normally be referred to his subcommittee for discussion, rather than requiring time in the full committee meeting. This would create more time for the committee to have less ritualised discussions about new developments, morale on the works and so on.

Another issue which had emerged from the Interlinked Phase was the need to review the patterns of industrial relations activities on the works. We made several suggestions here, including this one:

The establishment of an *Industrial Relations Seminar* on the works should be considered. This would be a kind of sounding board where present procedures can be examined by both sides in a non-partisan framework.

For example, we have observed differing ideas about who is responsible for what in the industrial relations system, about what procedures should be followed, about different people's decision-making powers and about relationships between different unions. Representatives from each element in the industrial relations system could usefully devote time to explore issues of this kind.

The Seminar would primarily be concerned with non-crisis issues, providing an opportunity to review important questions of substance or procedure. It may however also have a limited role within the industrial relations system on the works. Perhaps it should be consulted in cases of disputes affecting a wide range of employees before these disputes pass through the procedure out of the plant. This would only be appropriate if the parties to the dispute agree to this step, and on the understanding that the Seminar's role is merely an advisory one. The merits of this proposal are in terms of three principles which run as themes through this Interim Report: (a) that all kinds of problems should be tackled as near as possible to their point of origin, (b) that a multi-media approach to communication and problem solving is desirable, and (c) that the present systems do not do justice to the close interdependencies between members of the works.

As we reported earlier, such a seminar did take place and although it did not follow exactly the prescriptions in our report it did lead to several positive outcomes.

Discussion of the Report

The Interim Report was considered formally by members of the works in five separate kinds of meeting: by the Project Steering Committee, by the level one project group, by the Works Group Management Committee, by the departmental Joint Consultative Committees and by the Section Council. One or more of us was present at each of these discussions.

The Steering Committee meeting to consider the report took place a few days after its publication, and there were signs that some committee members had not had adequate time to study it. Nevertheless, discussion was lively and wide ranging. One manager objected that our account had been biased too much in favour of the shop floor: more comments should have been directed to shop-floor intransigence and unwillingness to compromise to meet the needs of the works as a whole. On reflection, we agreed that some more reference to shop-floor and trade union attitudes would have been possible and, we now accepted, desirable.

The Steering Committee was not able to take any executive action about our recommendations, although many points were accepted. Hence it fell to other groups to follow up the proposals. The works manager's project group met early in April 1975, and considered their position on the first three sets of recommendations in the Interim Report — about communciations, management styles and relations between the two plants. This meeting was interesting in that much of the report was accepted, but possible actions were left until later. This was partly because of a belief that communications, for example, were getting better anyway, so that it was best to adopt a 'wait and see' policy for the time being. But the delay was also associated with the announcement that the Works Group Management Committee would be reviewing the report in the following week and they might wish to make their views known after that.

This committee was the most senior one in the Alloy and Stainless Steel works group. It was chaired by the works group director, and its members included the general managers within the works group and those group managers with responsibility for personnel, accounting, engineering and metallurgy. The meeting to consider the Interim Report dealt mainly with very general issues, and as time was short it was decided to hold a further meeting at a later date to consider specific recommendations.

Thus, each of the first three meetings to consider the Interim Report had tended to leave detailed action planning to another group, taking few firm decisions itself. The next series of meetings were held within the departments of Tinsley Park Works, and here attention and action was focussed upon the local situation. Seven special meetings of the departmental Joint Consultative Committees were held and these worked systematically through our recommendations. To aid discussion we prepared a brief summary of the proposals and these were made available within each department. Some issues were seen as irrelevant at departmental level, but those that were relevant were seriously discussed. Not surprisingly, some of our suggestions were judged to be unacceptable, but a large number of positive decisions were taken. These included changes to the membership and functioning of the JCCs themselves, plans for visits to other departments, alterations to training programmes, improved communication networks, changes in departmental management meetings, and general wider recommendations which would be put to the Section Council.

The Section Council itself held three special meetings to discuss the Interim Report. These took place between October 1975 and February 1976, by which time a lot of the earlier suggestions had had time to mature. The third meeting took the form of the Industrial Relations Seminar described above, but the first two meetings worked through the report's proposals in much the same way as the departmental Joint Consultative Committees had done. Discussion was constructive and realistic, and many suggestions were implemented. The minutes of these two meetings were mainly presented in two columns, one headed 'Recommendations' and one headed 'Comments'. Each recommendation was summarised in the left-hand column and acceptance or otherwise was indicated in the adjacent space. Of 47 issues discussed, 31 were recorded as implemented by the date of the meeting or due to be so, and in 5 cases the recommendations were felt to be inappropriate. The records of the meetings indicate disagreement or an absence of a conclusion about the remaining 11 items. For example, the requirements of different departments were thought to make appropriate purely local decisions about frequency, location and content of JCC meetings.

One other meeting was held specifically to review the Employee Relations Project. This was in September 1975, when Steering Committee members, some senior managers and ourselves came together in the Works Sports Club to discuss the Project and its outcomes with the managing director of the Special Steels Division. We made a brief introduction, stressing how the goal had been to set up a temporary mechanism to get things moving and then gradually to replace this with more permanent changes in the regular communication and decision-making structures of the works. As with other meetings, it is difficult to summarise the varying opinions expressed during the discussion, but these quotations may serve to give an impression of what took place. They are excerpts and not continuous dialogue.

A manager: 'I was sceptical at first, but soon detected enthusiasm at all levels. Mind you, questionnaires at Stocksbridge would give the same answers ... The results have been worthwhile, the Project brought people together to discuss things. There were a lot of changes ... You won't get an end product, this sort of thing has to continue all the time.'

A shop steward: 'I never accepted that Tinsley Park was worse than Stocksbridge, the two should have been done together ... Communications are still the real problem, we need more face-to-face groups but the foremen don't want to get involved ... A lot of the items could have been done through the JCC system ... In the early days optimism was in the air, but it got too long-winded . . . Anyway, we've introduced a lot of ERP ideas as normal procedure.'

A foreman: 'There are too many meetings anyway . . . we need to deal with things less formally . . . Maintenance is still the problem.'

A shop steward: 'A lot of trivial things came up. They could have been looked at earlier . . . At the beginning there was lots of enthusiasm, people got carried away, but the problem was to keep up interest on the shop floor. There are quite a lot of people who just don't want to know about this kind of thing as long as their pay and working conditions are OK . . . Relations with management did get better, but the big issues still remain.'

A manager: 'I gained a lot from the ERP in the discipline of approaching a problem . . . It was a good idea from the outset. The main thing was that it got people into a problem-solving frame of mind . . . You may think the JCC can tackle these issues, but that was just the problem — people didn't have any faith in the JCC. We've learned now . . . I'm doing my job better.'

A shop steward: 'Items were done, but this led to other items getting raised. You're bound to have some items outstanding at any time, no matter what you do.'

A manager: 'Tinsley Park isn't much different from other works. But perhaps it's had the British disease more acutely — we like to blame other people, never ourselves . . . The good thing the ERP has done is to make managers and men talk to each other . . . It's not a question of whether the plant is ready to take over from the ERP; I'd hate to suggest that the ERP was running the plant — just the opposite . . . A lot of the improvements came from the Works Council and the Section Council getting more able to handle problems . . . Don't forget that we've been putting money into better communications, maintenance and the like — that's one reason why things are better.'

A manager: 'It was disappointing that the engineers didn't join in. They have their own problems too. But generally the ERP met its objectives, it did something for Tinsley Park . . . The best thing was that it showed how the communications system had broken down at several levels. This showed up in all the groups. People didn't feel part of a set-up . . . The JCCs were failing but they're better now . . . The job is ongoing, not just for an ERP, it's something we should do anyway . . . Now we talk. Prior to the Project people didn't talk. They only found out things after action had been taken.'

A manager: 'I saw Tinsley Park as a place where people didn't believe each other, where everyone grumbled. Maybe in a situation like that you need to do something like the ERP to start the wheel moving. Then it's up to the people on the site.'

That review meeting was the final formal activity associated with the Employee Relations Project. However, some of the ideas in the Interim Report continued to be discussed in separate meetings over the ensuing period. For example, a divisional working party on joint consultation established early in 1977 took as its starting point an examination of the Report's recommendations and their implementation throughout the Division.

7   Differences between the departments

This account of the Employee Relations Project has up to now been about the works as a whole, and very little has been said about differences between departments. It was clear from the outset that each department had its own approach to the Project, and we shall now look at the varying patterns of involvement before turning in the next chapter to a more detailed evaluation of the Project's success.

The pattern of commitment

In the Melting Shop the Project started off with much enthusiasm from the department manager. He was a keen participant in the level one project group and his own group very quickly identified a formidable list of issues for discussion. However, soon after this had been drawn up he was promoted out of the works, and the momentum which he had generated was quickly lost. The new Melting Shop manager knew nothing about the Project on his arrival and he was particularly absorbed with settling into his departmental responsibilities. These were compounded by the commissioning of very large new plant in the Melting Shop and much of his time was devoted to tackling the problems which this created.

The new Melting Shop manager expressed a wish to get to grips with what he saw as 'the real issues' when the time was ripe, and he defined these as questions of communication and the delegation of responsibility. He accepted that these were central concerns of the Employee Relations Project and for that reason he supported the formal parts of the project, but at the same he preferred his own way of tackling these problems without the aid of the ERP apparatus. This meant that his commitment to the Project was more to the letter than the spirit of it. To be fair, he was heavily loaded with ongoing changes, and this load was increased by his attendance on a three-month management course after only nine months in the job (just as the ERP entered its final stages).

Not surprisingly his outlook came to colour the views of other members of his department. Some of his section managers were themselves unhappy with increased pressure from the shop floor and with the limited response to their own project group recommendations, and they increasingly began to play a more passive role in the Project. Meetings in the Melting Shop were often difficult to arrange and sometimes poorly attended; and the department's response rate to the project questionnaire in August 1974 was the lowest in the works. This was partly due to lack of encouragement from managers and foremen, but may also reflect the fact that the shop-floor employees of the Melting Shop were a relatively satisfied, well-paid group who felt no strong need for change. In other words, the scope for change may have been limited because of the reasonably good climate of employee relations which prevailed in that department.

Nevertheless, a significant minority in the Melting Shop were enthusiastic about the Project. As time went on they became disappointed that progress was less than in other parts of the works. This was also true of the Mill, where the participation and commitment of several central figures was limited.

The Mill manager moved to a job in Divisional Headquarters at the end of December 1974, and he had been looking forward to a transfer of this kind for several months. In anticipation of his expected transfer he had not wished to become deeply involved in the Project. He had been reluctant to participate in the level one project group or to commence his level two meetings, since he hoped that the section manager who deputised for him would undertake these roles in his stead.

However, this section manager had strongly negative opinions about the Project and was unsympathetic towards some of its advocates within and outside the works. The attitudes of these two managers amounted to a somewhat reluctant participation in the Project. This was demonstrated by their infrequent instigation of action and a preference instead to respond to pressures from other sources in the works or from ourselves before they arranged meetings or followed through recommendations.

Other features of the Mill which were associated with this relatively lower commitment include the fact that the work operations and equipment in the department were, on the whole, smooth-running and effective. The Mill's mechanised process efficiently undertook its important function within the works, and communication between trade unions and management was good, since the senior steward and the department manager had built up their own open channel for discussion and debate. Furthermore, the Mill had no manager or foreman representative on the Project Steering Committee, and thus was less influenced by ideas and pressures from this group.

The situation in the Billet Finishing department was different. The department manager accepted the Project's value throughout and tried hard to make use of it. He spent considerable time at project group meetings and regularly delegated and encouraged other participants to undertake recommended tasks and actions. His section managers were mostly keen to take advantage of the Project, although there were certainly times when the increased workload and lack of shop-floor response caused them some irritation.

Some members of Billet Finishing had been troubled by the apparently low status of the department relative to the other production departments, and they saw that the Employee Relations Project might be a means of increasing departmental self-respect and influence on the works. It was also true that relationships within the department had in recent years been relatively less settled than in most other parts of the works, and the scope for improvement was rather greater.

The response rate to the project questionnaire reached ninety-seven per cent in

Billet Finishing, and this department was the first to introduce a special shop-floor safety committee and planned work-group meetings with foremen; both developments associated with ERP decisions. In general, the level of Project activity in this department was very much higher than in either the Melting Shop or Mill.

The Billet Finishing manager and the Traffic manager were the two managerial representatives at department level on the Project Steering Committee. This undoubtedly encouraged their commitment to the ERP and assisted them to take advantage of it, for the Traffic department was another part of the works where the Project was well received. The section manager in charge of Traffic was convinced that the Project was an excellent means of achieving better working relationships and a more valued status for his section. The project groups in Traffic were particularly active, and many improvements of a local kind were achieved. Moreover, out of the Traffic ERP groups grew the section's first JCC, a committee which had not been able to get off the ground in the past because of people's previous reluctance to spend time in what they thought would be fruitless meetings.

This pattern of differential commitment across the works was well illustrated in the final issue of *Focus*. As well as a complete list of problems and actions in each department, a 'joint statement on behalf of management and unions' was planned in each case. The members of the Mill did not feel inclined to draft and agree such a statement so nothing was available from them. The joint statement from the other departments included the following judgements about the Project:

Melting Shop: The general feeling in the Melting Shop was that the ERP exercise as planned and mounted was not too relevant to the Melting Shop's needs and that the generally lower level of interest has borne this out.

The Project has re-emphasised the importance of 'people' rather than systems at all shop floor and management levels and the need for tolerance of other persons' positions and points of view. It is felt that ERP did highlight the need for some informal arbitration procedure on the works for significant industrial relations problems.

It is accepted that we must have systems. However, these should be kept as simple as possible.

Billet Finishing: Since the Project began, numerous changes in working practices have been implemented in order to improve employee relations at all levels within the department.

The most obvious of these has been communications, and we have introduced regular production, safety and work-group meetings, in addition to the existing JCC, in order that people can be more involved in the running of the department.

However, it will be important to make sure that these activities and the standards we have set ourselves are maintained after the ERP is completed.

The future is almost certain to produce problems in view of the nature of the current industrial climate, but with worker and management participation continuing in the spirit of the Project, most of these can be sorted out.

However, it must be realised that solutions can never be to everyone's satisfaction, and that some decisions we take have wider implications in the works and the division.

Traffic: The Project was accepted by management and union as a useful exercise, and has been carried out with interest and enthusiasm by all concerned.

In the absence of their own JCC, the Traffic and Transport Section used the Project to bring together and channel all their problems, some of them long outstanding, that affected good employee relations.

The general opinion is that the Project has been well worthwhile, but that complete success will depend on the outcomes of the larger issues, especially those concerned with improving facilities.

It has been decided to keep the group together as a department JCC.

Need and opportunity for change

We should emphasise that the need for change varied from department to department and that there were also differing opportunities to introduce new procedures and structures. There is little doubt that at the commencement of the Project working relationships in Billet Finishing, and to a lesser extent Traffic, were poorer than elsewhere. Conversely, relations in the Melting Shop, and to a lesser extent the Mill, were relatively good. These differences were associated with variations in payment systems and union structure, although other factors undoubtedly played their part. For example, the varied manual tasks in Billet Finishing were accompanied by a fragmented wage system with opportunities for many differential or parity claims. There was also some rivalry between the two shop-floor unions in this department.

Some of the differences between departments' potential for change can be illustrated through items in the project questionnaire. Responses to these items (in the form of Yes, No or Don't Know) were obtained on three occasions, and it is instructive to examine the differences in attitudes between departments *at the outset* of the Project. The percentage of respondents in each department agreeing with six selected items from the Before questionnaire (completed in March 1974) is given in Table 7.1. The figures against 'All' are for the department as a whole, whereas 'SF, NSS' refers to shop-floor employees and non-supervisory staff and 'Fmn, Mgrs' gives the percentage agreement figures for foremen and managers.

The opinions expressed by Melting Shop members show it to be a friendly department (item 1) with relatively high openness (item 2) and relatively low mistrust (item 3); communications to the shop floor (items 4, 5 and 6) tended to be rated more highly than in other departments. On the other hand, Billet Finishing was seen by its members as a much less friendly place where you could not really say what you thought and where communication between managers, foremen and

Table 7.1
Opinions before the Project

Percentage Yes before the Project

			Melting Shop	Mill	Billet Finishing	Traffic
1	There is a friendly	All	79	69	50	33
	atmosphere in my	SF, NSS	74	63	49	33
	department	Fmn, Mgrs	90	94	54	33
2	People in my	All	44	35	29	60
	department can	SF, NSS	40	25	26	52
	say what they	Fmn, Mgrs	60	78	64	100
	think without it					
	being held against					
	them					
3	Shop floor workers	All	51	54	65	46
	in my department	SF, NSS	52	58	63	48
	don't trust their	Fmn, Mgrs	50	39	82	40
	managers					
4	Management in my	All	41	23	18	44
	department keep	SF, NSS	32	14	14	38
	shop floor workers	Fmn, Mgrs	65	56	59	67
	well informed about					
	what is happening					
5	Managers in my	All	37	66	64	55
	department only	SF, NSS	45	70	67	58
	talk to the shop	Fmn, Mgrs	15	50	37	50
	floor when things					
	have gone wrong					
6	Foremen in my	All	55	40	34	63
	department take	SF, NSS	48	30	31	62
	a lot of trouble	Fmn, Mgrs	75	80	55	67
	to listen to the					
	views of shop					
	floor workers					

shop floor workers was relatively poor. The views of the Mill and Traffic members in March 1974 emerged as somewhere in between the other two departments, with variations from item to item. Thus, the Traffic department was seen by its members as more unfriendly than was the Mill, but communication between management and shop floor was given a lower rating in the Mill than in Traffic.

It is thus apparent that the need for improvement in employee relations was fairly limited in the Melting Shop, where the situation was broadly acceptable to many people, while there was quite considerable scope for improvement in Billet Finishing. Furthermore, the opportunity to introduce changes in Billet Finishing was much greater. As was illustrated in chapter 2, work in the Melting Shop was highly capital intensive, the process being large scale, technologically sophisticated, and costly. Billet Finishing was a more labour-intensive department with small groups of self-paced employees working relatively independently with hand tools. Operational procedures and technology were more open to change in Billet Finishing than in other production departments. Similar factors enhanced the scope for change in the Traffic section, which had the additional advantage of relatively small size.

In summary, this chapter has supplemented the previous account by illustrating how the Employee Relations Project was used differently by the four participating departments. For a variety of reasons the Melting Shop and Mill showed less commitment to the Project than did Billet Finishing and Traffic. In part these variations reflected their different starting points (some places had better relations than others from the beginning of the Project) and in part they reflected different opportunities for change (through differing technologies, discontinuities in management and so on). However, this does not diminish the importance of management style and attitude. Despite a widespread acceptance of the ERP, a small number of managers felt considerable unease about its general approach. This unease did not usually turn into outright opposition but it was sufficient to reduce the impact of the Project in the areas for which they were responsible.

8   Evaluating the Project

We have almost completed our narrative account of the history of the Employee Relations Project. Previous chapters have from time to time included information about the Project's effectiveness, and we will now look more systematically at the evaluative evidence which was gathered. Evaluating a large-scale programme of this kind is far from easy, and a practical framework for evaluation studies will be presented in chapter 14. This will be in terms of the stages through which a programme passes, raising evaluative questions about each stage.

Our concern in this chapter will be with the later stages of that framework, and attention will primarily be focussed upon the outcomes of the Employee Relations Project and reactions to it. Material about these was submitted to the works in February 1976 in our Second Report, covering seven different kinds of evidence. These were:

1   Operational changes arising from the Project.
2   Changes in attitudes on the works.
3   Retrospective accounts of changes and the Project's involvement in those changes.
4   Participants' opinions about the Project.
5   Our observation of changes in behaviour and outlook.
6   Departmental dispute levels.
7   Cost of the Project and its effect on productivity.

No single one of these criteria is adequate as a measure of the Employee Relations Project's success, but in combination they permit a broad-based assessment of considerable validity.

Operational changes arising from the Project

The first evaluative criterion is the number and kinds of operational changes brought about through the Project. We have described how each project group identified problem areas and developed its own recommendations for action. These were followed through, and the issues, recommendations and actions were noted upon Problem Record Forms. The full set of these actions was summarised in the fifth issue of *Focus* and an analysis of this material is given in Table 8.1.

The left-hand column shows that 337 items were identified as problems across the works as a whole. A large number of these (135) covered equipment, safety and working conditions, and 79 concerned personnel issues: training, conditions of employment, promotion, amenities, staff appraisal, manning levels, overtime and so on. The remaining 123 issues dealt with communication problems and relationships of various kinds.

This general pattern varied somewhat from department to department. For example, a relatively high proportion of the problems raised in the Mill and Traffic were to do with relations between departments, and personnel issues were relatively more frequent in the Melting Shop and Billet Finishing and Test House. (Although the Test House is administratively separate from Billet Finishing, its members met together with Billet Finishing employees throughout the Project.)

Table 8.1

Issues raised for action during the Project, classified according to content

	Action items arising from project groups						Recommendations in the Interim Report
	Overall within departments	Melting Shop	Mill	Billet Finishing and Test House	Traffic	General issues passed to the works manager	
Equipment, safety, working conditions	135	32	17	53	33	3	7
Personnel issues	79	29	14	31	5	9	11
Relations between departments	56	7	22	11	16	5	9
Relations between management and shop floor	36	14	4	15	3	3	16
Other communication issues	31	9	6	10	6	2	9
Total	337	91	63	120	63	22	52
Percentage of departmental problems resulting in action (see notes (a) and (b))	80%	76%	56%	88%	92%	See note (c)	See note (c)

Notes
(a) Action about a problem is sometimes difficult to define. It involves some steps to remedy a situation, but this remedy may not satisfy all the people involved. Not all of the actions which were commenced were followed through to a final conclusion.
(b) Some actions were ongoing before and during the Project. In these cases the Project was only one of the contributory factors.
(c) All the issues in the last two columns were followed up in some way. Because these issues are major ones affecting many individuals or groups it is not easy to identify and count up actions of the kind referred to in the previous columns. See the discussion of this point in the text.

Based upon an analysis of the Problem Record Forms we have calculated the proportion of issues which were turned into action in the course of the Project. Of the total number of 337 problems raised, it appears that around 265 (80%) resulted in some form of action. It is very difficult to be completely accurate about this figure, since some actions were not fully completed, others satisfied only a proportion of the people involved, and others had already been discussed before the Project took place.

The action percentages at the bottom of Table 8.1 are thus likely to be over-estimates and should be reduced in some cases. All things considered, we conclude that about 200 problem items arising from project groups were successfully turned into action. The percentage figures for each department shown in Table 8.1 should be altered in line with the overall reduction suggested in this conclusion, but the rank order of follow-up remains as shown: relatively more actions were initiated in Billet Finishing and in Traffic, and relatively fewer in the Melting Shop and the Mill.

The sixth column in Table 8.1 summarises the general issues that had been passed to the works manager. As was described earlier, many of these were fundamental and difficult questions, and the works manager and his colleagues devoted considerable time to their examination. In practice clear-cut action was not considered possible, and management's replies in the fifth edition of *Focus* were more in terms of explanation and suggestion than of solution. However, the fact that the Project cast a searchlight on the issues meant that many of them were given continuing consideration. In this way the Project's influence was often extensive, with many issues still being examined after its formal ending.

The final column in Table 8.1 classifies the 52 recommendations of our Interim Report of February 1975. These have been outlined in chapter 6, along with a description of the follow-up meetings that were convened to consider them. As was noted there, many of the suggestions were turned into action, although it is extremely difficult to place a precise figure on this.

In summary, the project groups achieved some 200 changes within their departments. The more general issues passed to the works manager were less clearly affected, but the Project ensured that they remained in the forefront when decisions were subsequently being taken. A number of important actions followed the Interim Report, and the discussions arising from the report ensured that a range of difficult issues of wide significance did not get overlooked. The key question is whether this number of improvements would have been introduced in the absence of the Employee Relations Project; we believe not.

Changes in employees' attitudes during the Project

The goal of the Project was not merely to introduce operational changes. Some shifts in *attitude* were essential to its success, so that we need to know whether people's views about central issues of employee relations altered during the course of the Project.

Information about this was obtained by administering twelve questionnaire items on three separate occasions:

Before the Project, in March 1974 (52% response rate)
During the Project, in August 1974 (83% response rate)
After the Project, in June 1975 (66% response rate)

Measuring changes in attitudes across a large works is not easy, and there are a number of problems attached to this method of evaluation. One of these is the fact that the sample of people replying is rarely identical throughout; another arises from the likelihood that attitudes may have been affected by factors unconnected with, in this case, the Employee Relations Project. Particularly relevant here is the economic recession which developed during 1975. The After questionnaire was completed at a time when resources were limited and when the British Steel Corporation was attempting to reduce costs in a variety of ways. This kind of climate is one that will impose strains on relations in most organisations that are striving for change and development.

The overall pattern of results is shown in Table 8.2. The twelve statements listed there had been presented to members of the works with a request that they answer: 'Yes, that is true', 'No, that is not true', or 'I'm not sure'. Table 8.2 indicates the percentage of people replying 'Yes, that is true' to each question on each occasion. Separate figures are provided for all people answering the questionnaire ('All'), for shop-floor employees and non-supervisory staff ('SF, NSS'), and for foremen and managers ('Fmn, Mgrs').

We have also included the results of tests of statistical significance for each group of three percentage figures. As the note to the table indicates, these tests were calculated from more complete information than merely the percentage agreement figures, but only the latter are shown in the table for ease of reading. The figures in the 'statistical significance' column should be read as follows:

0.01 – highly significant differences in statistical terms between the answers on the three occasions; a probability of occurring by chance of less than 1%.

0.05 – moderately significant differences in statistical terms between the answers on the three occasions; a probability of occurring by chance of less than 5%.

n.s. – no significant differences in statistical terms.

Note that the reference is to some change between the three sets of figures (Before, During and After) for each item. The difference between any two sets of figures (e.g. During and After) is not necessarily statistically significant in cases where the overall pattern includes a significant change. The location of the major differences can of course be checked from the percentage figures in the table. For example, the 'All' figures for item 1 show a big difference between Before and During and between Before and After, but not between During and After.

Table 8.2

Questionnaire replies before, during and after the Project

Total works samples

(Sample size: Before 460,394,66; During 713,625,88; After 578,513,65)

		Percentage agreement			Statistical significance
		Before	During	After	
1	There is a friendly atmosphere in my department				
	All	58	73	70	0.01
	SF, NSS	55	75	71	0.01
	Fmn, Mgrs	77	70	66	n.s.
2	People in my department Can say what they think without it being held against them				
	All	38	47	39	n.s.
	SF, NSS	31	44	38	0.05
	Fmn, Mgrs	73	62	47	0.01
3	Shop floor workers in my department don't trust their managers				
	All	58	52	44	0.05
	SF, NSS	58	51	45	0.05
	Fmn, Mgrs	56	57	38	n.s.

		Percentage agreement			Statistical significance
		Before	During	After	
7	Most people in my department are keen to work hard to get the job done				
	All	68	82	72	0.05
	SF, NSS	67	85	74	0.05
	Fmn, Mgrs	75	60	51	0.05
8	Most workers in my department could be given a lot more responsibility than they have at present				
	All	45	56	53	0.01
	SF, NSS	44	58	55	0.01
	Fmn, Mgrs	48	43	43	n.s.
9	The traditional ways of working in my department hardly ever get questioned				
	All	50	62	58	0.05
	SF, NSS	53	64	62	n.s.
	Fmn, Mgrs	36	48	35	n.s.

No.	Statement	Group				Sig.
4	Management in my department keep shop floor workers well informed about what is happening	All	24	23	26	n.s.
		SF, NSS	16	21	23	n.s.
		Fmn, Mgrs	60	39	47	0.05
5	Managers in my department only talk to the shop floor when things have gone wrong	All	57	62	54	n.s.
		SF, NSS	61	66	57	n.s.
		Fmn, Mgrs	34	37	31	n.s.
6	Foremen in my department take a lot of trouble to listen to the views of shop floor workers	All	41	48	43	n.s.
		SF, NSS	36	46	42	n.s.
		Fmn, Mgrs	70	67	57	n.s.
10	My job is dull and monotonous	All	33	35	29	n.s.
		SF, NSS	36	38	32	n.s.
		Fmn, Mgrs	3	14	7	n.s.
11	The major decisions about Tinsley Park get taken outside the works	All	77	76	68	n.s.
		SF, NSS	76	74	67	n.s.
		Fmn, Mgrs	79	88	77	n.s.
12	Shop stewards in my department usually put their own personal views across to management rather than those of the shop floor	All	48	53	47	n.s.
		SF, NSS	46	53	49	n.s.
		Fmn, Mgrs	58	53	39	n.s.

Note: Levels of statistical significance have been calculated from means and variances (by two-way analyses of variance) rather than from the percentage agreement figures shown in this table.

Table 8.2 contains a large amount of information. Three points are worth special comment here:

1   There are clear indications in items 1 to 3 that the shop floor and non-supervisory staff had come to report more friendliness, less potential victimisation and less distrust. Within the overall objective of improving employee relations these were major goals of the Project.

2   There is some evidence of raised aspiration levels. Items 7, 8 and 9 suggest a greater willingness to work, to accept responsibility and to look out for better ways of doing things. These were also important objectives of the Project. (The items tapping these questions are clearly affected at the After questionnaire stage by the shortage of available work.)

3   The Before questionnaire data reveal some considerable disparities between the views of managers and foremen and those of their subordinates. As the Project proceeded these disparities were reduced, and both groups came to have more similar views of the situation. This suggests greater mutual understanding and consequently, it may be argued, a more accurate assessment of reality. Item 2 illustrates this feature well, but items 1, 4 and 6 are also of interest.

In summary, the opinions recorded in Table 8.2 reveal several overall trends consistent with a successful Project. Some of the items show an improvement at the During stage and then a decline at the After stage. This is understandable in view of the enthusiasm which existed in many sections at the During time, and the economic problems facing the works at the After time.

Separate analyses of this material were carried out for each department. No significant shifts are visible over the twelve questionnaire items in the Melting Shop. This stability is associated with a lower level of departmental interest in the Project and with the fact that there was only limited room for improvement to start with (see chapter 7). There were several improvements in the Mill, indicated by statistically significant changes in the responses of shop-floor employees and non-supervisory staff to items 3, 4, 5, 6 and 8; for example the initial figure of 58% of shop-floor employees and non-supervisory staff reporting mistrust of management (item 3) had dropped to 37% after the Project. Billet Finishing showed substantial improvements on items 1, 3, 4, 6, 7 and 8, so that for example 70% of shop-floor employees and non-supervisory staff reported that their department was a friendly one after the Project against only 49% before. The small number of people in Traffic department makes it less probable that changes over time there will be reflected in the measures of statistical significance, since the number of people answering each question is one important element in the statistical formula. The most marked change in responses from Traffic was to item 1, where the percentage of shop-floor employees and non-supervisory staff reporting a friendly atmosphere increased from 33% before to 59% after the Project.

To summarise this second form of evaluation, there were significant changes in outlook on the works during the period of the Employee Relations Project. These were most marked in Billet Finishing and least marked in the Melting Shop, a pattern similar to that described in the previous chapter.

Retrospective accounts of changes

The Before—During—After questionnaire procedure has the disadvantage that other factors might be responsible for the observed changes in attitudes rather than the Project alone being influential in these. The likely impact of a changing economic climate has already been noted, and changes in the management team were probably also relevant in some cases. A second part of the After questionnaire was therefore specially designed to obtain more direct information about the Project's role in changes on the works.

This second part of the questionnaire completed in June 1975 contained eleven questions of the following form:

HAVE ANY OF THE FOLLOWING THINGS CHANGED IN YOUR DEPART-MENT DURING THE LAST 18 MONTHS?

Place a tick in the appropriate box

	got better	no change	got worse
1. SAFETY			

	yes	don't know	no
1a. If safety has *got better* or *got worse* has the Project played any part in it?			

	got better	no change	got worse
2. RELATIONS BETWEEN MANAGEMENT AND SHOP FLOOR			

	yes	don't know	no
2a. If these relations have *got better* or *got worse*, has the Project played any part in it?			

Analysis of this material hinges upon two main questions: Did more people report changes for the better than for the worse? And did those reporting that things had got better think that the Project played a part? The results for the total works sample are shown in Table 8.3.

Table 8.3

Changes in departments during the last eighteen months
Total works sample (Sample size: 578)

	Issue	Changes	%		Issue	Changes	%
1	Safety	Better	39**	7	Being kept in	Better	30**
		Worse	10		the picture	Worse	12
		Stat. sig.	0.01		about what's	Stat. sig.	0.01
					going on in		
					your depart-		
					ment		
2	Relations	Better	22**	8	The way prob-	Better	20**
	between	Worse	9		lems are	Worse	11
	management and	Stat. sig.	0.01		tackled	Stat. sig.	0.01
	shop floor						
3	Relations	Better	18**	9	Your amenities	Better	19**
	between unions	Worse	9			Worse	25
	and manage-	Stat. sig.	0.01			Stat. sig.	n.s.
	ment						
4	Relations	Better	23**	10	Standard of	Better	9**
	between fore-	Worse	5		maintenance	Worse	48
	men and shop	Stat. sig.	0.01			Stat. sig.	0.01
	floor						
5	Relations	Better	22**	11	Relations	Better	6**
	between	Worse	9		between	Worse	18
	management	Stat. sig.	0.01		Stocksbridge	Stat. sig.	0.01
	and foremen				and Tinsley		
					Park		
6	Relations with	Better	13**				
	other depart-	Worse	8				
	ments	Stat. sig.	0.05				

Notes:
1 0.01 indicates a significantly higher proportion of Better than Worse responses, at the $p < 0.01$ level. 0.05 indicates that this difference is significant at the $p < 0.05$ level.
2 ** indicates that significantly more ($p < 0.01$) of those reporting that things were Better thought that the Project played a part in this improvement than thought that the Project played no part in it.

As an illustration of the meaning of this table consider the first item, safety: thirty-nine per cent of the people completing the questionnaire thought that safety had got better in the last eighteen months, and 10% thought it had got worse. (Therefore the remainder 51% reported no change.) In comparing the 39% 'Better' with the 10% 'Worse' we find that the difference in favour of an improvement is statistically significant at the 0.01 level. This is indicated in the column below the two percentage figures. We now have to ask about the 39% of people who reported an improvement. How many of them thought that the Project had played a part in this improvement and how many thought that it had played no part? The answer in this case is that 58% of those reporting an improvement thought that the Project was involved, against only 12% who thought it was not. (Therefore the remainder, 30%, said that they did not know.) For the sake of clarity these figures, i.e. 58% and 12%, are not included in the table, but the result is summarised by the double asterisk after the figure of 39% reporting that safety had got better. As note 2 below the table indicates, the asterisk means that significantly more of those who said there had been an improvement attributed credit for it to the Employee Relations Project than did not.

This pattern of results, encouraging to the Project, recurs on all of the first eight items in the table. Significant improvements were reported in all cases, and a significant majority of those people reporting an improvement thought it was due to the Project. In passing we should note that only a tiny proportion (usually less than 1%) reported that the Project had been influential in making things worse!

It should be stressed that over such a short period of time it is to be expected that most people will report 'no change' in the kind of issues on which we have focussed in Table 8.3. A proportion as high as 39% reporting that safety has improved and the other percentages of around 20 indicating that relations between groups of people had got better are quite substantial. The results for issue 7 (being kept in the picture) are particularly noteworthy: 30% reporting an improvement that was largely due to the Project.

On the other hand, on issues 9, 10 and 11 things were seen as having become worse. The latter two of these changes may be attributed to the economic situation at the time of the After questionnaire. The cut-back of expenditure and general limitations on resources are likely to have affected opinions about Stocksbridge and definitely reduced the availability of replacement parts. However, the minority who thought that things had got better on these issues generally saw the Project as the reason (see the double asterisk in each case).

Further analyses revealed very similar results for the two groups, shop floor and non-supervisory staff, and managers and foremen; but several large differences were found when comparisons were made between departments. The results for Billet Finishing were especially clear in endorsing the Project's influence. All the first eight items showed a significant reported improvement with credit to the Project. Numbers 9 and 10 showed that those employees who reported improvements attributed them to the Employee Relations Project, and item 11 revealed the lowest reported decline in relations between Stocksbridge and Tinsley Park. The Traffic department figures also showed significant reported improvements on items 4 and 5 (relations between foremen and shop floor and between management and foremen) and a significant impact of the Project on item 1 (safety) and item 7 (being kept in the picture). The small number of statistically significant results in the Traffic figures may again be largely attributed to the small numbers in the department.

As with other indicators, the Melting Shop employees reported least favourably on the Project's impact. There was only one item (7, being kept in the picture) where members of this department reported an improvement arising from the Project. Members of the Mill reported improvements due to the Project on two items, safety (item 1) and in relations between management and shop floor (item 2).

To summarise this third criterion of the Employee Relations Project's success, people generally reported significant improvements in the areas of central interest to the Project and the Project was given much of the credit for these improvements. This was particularly marked in Billet Finishing and least evident in the Melting Shop, with the Mill and Traffic falling in between.

Participants' opinions about the Project

What did the employees of Tinsley Park Works say about the Project and its value? Many quotations have been included in previous chapters, and these help to convey the flavour of the varying opinions. Discussions at the end of the Project confirmed that the works manager (who took up his job mid-way through) had a generally positive attitude towards it and felt sure that it did a lot of good in Billet Finishing and Traffic. This view was shared by the managers of those two departments and by the group personnel manager as well as by several managers and foremen across the works.

More comprehensive evidence comes from answers to the After questionnaire item: 'It would be a good idea for BSC to try some more projects of this kind in other works.' An overall figure of 51% agreed with this (with 30% uncertain and 19% disagreeing). A larger proportion of shop-floor employees and non-supervisory staff were in favour of more projects elsewhere (55% compared to 25% of managers and foremen; with 16% of the shop floor disagreeing compared with 37% of the management group). As with other material in this chapter, responses in Billet Finishing were the most positive and those in the Melting Shop the least favourable.

Chapter 14 will consider some of the problems associated with this kind of retrospective assessment of opinion. There are major problems of selective perception and remembering as a programme recedes into the past, and it may be that the most meaningful index is in terms of how few people are opposed to it. A fairly large proportion of 'not sures' among shop-floor respondents is often likely, for example, in the present case because only 20% were involved in the project groups.

Negative reactions to the ERP were of two types. On the one hand some people felt that programmes of this kind were generally inappropriate or too costly in terms of time and money. On the other hand there were people who felt that the initial progress was valuable but that it had not been sufficiently maintained.

Observed changes in behaviour and outlook

This fifth criterion is of course limited by the impossibility of observing more than a small fraction of the relevant occurrences in a large plant. Yet we are confident that the procedures employed and the questions raised led to a number of important learning experiences for many people. There developed a greater awareness of the ways in which successful meetings could be run, and some managers and shop stewards became more effective in industrial relations by adopting more systematic and comprehensive approaches to their domestic negotiations. A number of managers spoke positively of the 'discipline' which the Project taught them – a style of tackling problems and implementing decisions that was quite new to them.

The editorial staff of the works group publications were explicit in extolling the Project, saying that it had led them to adopt a more dynamic approach to communication, in which written journalism was viewed as just one component in a multi-media system. More generally, the Project's focus upon actions, delegated responsibility and follow-up led to the phrase 'action item' or 'action point' becoming established on the works. In view of our early experience that many discussions did not crystallise into decisions about actions and follow-up, this change was a most encouraging sign for the future.

The Employee Relations Project was in part a procedure whereby people could try out different ways of working; and where new ways were retained as worthwhile we can say that people learned something useful. Without being able to put a figure on it, we are sure that a number of key individuals on the works learned some useful new styles of thinking and behaviour as a result of the Project.

Departmental dispute levels

The general concern of the Project with employee relations did of course encompass the narrower field of industrial relations, and the numbers of recorded disputes on the works are important as one criterion of evaluation. But disputes arise from many factors (union attitudes, management attitudes, government legislation, pace of inflation, market conditions and so on), so that changes from year to year cannot with certainty be attributed to any one cause. Nevertheless, the trend between 1972 and 1976 was an interesting one. The number of recorded disputes (i.e. those resulting in some imposition of trade union sanctions) in the production departments of the works were as shown in Table 8.4.

One of the 1974 disputes in the Melting Shop (the bricklayers' strike) was particularly costly to the Corporation, but the wages issue involved was an isolated one which developed outside the scope of the Project. We believe that the Employee Relations Project was one contributory cause in the reduction of disputes and also in a change in the climate of industrial relations more generally. This was also the view of the senior industrial relations officer who told us that

Table 8.4
Dispute levels between 1972 and 1976

	Overall	Melting Shop	Mill	Billet Finishing	Traffic
1972	12	2	3	3	4
1973	9	2	2	4	1
1974	3	2	0	1	0
1975	1	0	0	0	1
1976	2	1	0	0	1

the kind of dispute which had been common in 1972 and 1973 would after the Project be handled with much less difficulty. The group personnel manager made a similar point: he believed that industrial relations on the works had improved since 1972 and that part of the improvement was due to the Employee Relations Project.

We have also undertaken some comparisons between Tinsley Park Works and other British Steel Corporation plants in the area. Many different factors become relevant here, and the direct comparison of dispute levels should be approached with caution. However it is fair to record that up to and including 1974 the trend locally (and indeed nationally) was one of increasing conflict, quite dissimilar to the decline in disputes which was observed at Tinsley Park.

Other kinds of personnel statistics which are often thought to reflect the climate of a works are labour turnover and absenteeism. These are very indirect measures affected by many external factors, and it was not expected that the Employee Relations Project would have a direct impact upon them. However, analyses of data from Tinsley Park as well as other local BSC works were carried out, and the findings were, as expected, neutral with respect to the Project.

Cost of the Project and its effect on productivity

The cost of the Employee Relations Project may be viewed in terms of three components: the external cost, the direct internal cost, and the indirect internal cost.

External cost

Our own activities contributed to this cost. However, we were engaged on many other research activities elsewhere during the period and each of us worked overall for less than twenty-five per cent of his time on the Project. With four members in the team this implies that less than one full-time equivalent person was employed on the Project. This cost was borne by the Medical Research Council and not by the British Steel Corporation. However, the expenses of travel, duplicating and postage were reimbursed by the Corporation, and these came to £500 for the whole Project. A second item of external cost was the printer's bill for *Focus* which totalled approximately £2,000.

Direct internal costs

Under this heading we include payments made for Project-related activities within the works. For example, we received some lunches at the Corporation's expense (likely maximum cost £50) and a small number of project group members also received free lunches (likely maximum cost £200). Occasional members of the Steering Committee received payment for coming in to meetings off-shift and a small number of project group members also did this from time to time (likely maximum cost £300).

We have so far identified £2,500 external costs and a maximum of £550 direct internal costs for the whole Project.

Indirect internal costs

These are more difficult to specify. Under this heading we include time spent by Corporation employees on the Project which might otherwise have been spent on other work. It is clear that a proportion of management's and other employees' time was spent on activities which they would otherwise not have undertaken: was this a costly diversion from more profitable activities?

Consider first the time of managers and foremen. Most of their time is in any case spent on discussion and action to resolve operational problems. If they were not engaged on this task in Project-related activities, they would in any case be doing work whose ultimate goal was the same. There were undoubtedly occasions when managers were temporarily diverted from other tasks to work on the Project. Rapid transition from one activity to another is a central feature of a manager's job. Insofar as the Project was one form of organisational problem-solving and as managers and foremen are paid to solve problems, we believe that their work on the Project was, overall, no real cost to the Corporation. This conclusion hinges on the fact that many problems were solved through the Project and also on the recognition that managers and foremen who felt limited commitment to the Project adjusted their activities accordingly, devoting less attention to the Project and more to other work.

The part-time project coordinator should be specially mentioned here, since his principal job in Quality Control meant that Project work was outside his normal job specification. Despite occasional periods of intensive work on the Project, over its full duration his percentage of time devoted to the Project was very small (say five per cent).

The position of shop-floor employees is less clear. A number of these spent time on Project work, but this was much less than for management (twenty per cent of them attended an average of three meetings). It might be argued that the shop-floor workers would otherwise have been directly producing profitable goods for the Corporation. Our conclusion is that despite the occasional breaks from direct production there was enough spare capacity on the works for no overall negative effects on output to have resulted from time devoted to the Employee Relations Project.

This is especially clear in the Mill, where shop-floor project group meetings took place during down-shifts. The Melting Shop's heavy dependence on expensive technology ensured that meetings were only held in that department when the production schedule allowed. Billet Finishing and Traffic departments undertake work which is less paced by the production process, and the average of three meetings for twenty per cent of shop-floor and non-supervisory staff employees of these departments may have resulted in some temporary delays. But the order book was often less than full, and over an eighteen-month period the quantity of steel leaving the works was not reduced because of the Project.

In summary, we have identified a directly-measureable cost of the Employee Relations Project of £3,050, and have argued that the time devoted by employees to Project work had no negative impact on productivity when the overall duration of the Project is considered. It is our conclusion that when the costs are weighed against the benefits, the balance is a clearly positive endorsement of the Project's value.

A general comment about the evaluation of this kind of programme is appropriate here. No method is at present available to evaluate orthodox training programmes in financial terms, since both costs and operational benefits are impossible to measure accurately in terms of money. The Employee Relations Project is in many ways analogous to a novel form of inplant training. Insofar as the worth of orthodox training is widely accepted in the absence of concrete financial data, it is reasonable to treat the Project similarly: requests for a complete financial account are as inappropriate as they are for many other specific projects which go on within a works.

Conclusion

There is no entirely satisfactory way of evaluating organisational change, since it occurs at many levels in many different ways. Moreover, how satisfied you are with what has taken place depends very much on what you expected in the first place. Our expectations and subsequent claims for the Project were and are moderate. We did not set out with revolutionary change in mind, and this did not occur. However, we are pleased to have witnessed a great variety of improvements, which were notably successful in some areas in helping people to work more effectively and in greater cooperation.

Very few programmes of organisational change have included systematic procedures for evaluation, and the material presented in this chapter is therefore especially valuable. Nevertheless, a more comprehensive approach would have been possible, and with hindsight we are aware of a number of issues which deserve greater attention. These are described in chapter 14, where we introduce a seven-point plan for evaluation studies.

PART TWO

Introduction to Part Two

The Employee Relations Project illustrated many features and problems which are central to all attempts to increase organisational effectiveness. We turn now to a broader treatment of the general issues arising out of the events described in Part One.

Chapter 9 presents an overview of the relationship between external researchers and organisations. It describes how this relationship changes through the stages of 'getting in' to the firm, 'getting on' with the job in the middle stage, and 'getting out' when the task is completed. At successive stages issues of values, resources and relationships assume different levels of importance, and for successful outcomes the collaboration between researcher and organisation has to be managed accordingly.

Chapters 10 and 11 introduce eight different types of procedure which have been used in planned attempts to develop employee relations. The first of these chapters examines educational and training activities, process consultation, and meetings for intergroup communication and problem-solving; greatest emphasis is given to the last of these, through a discussion of the ERP project groups. Chapter 11 opens with a discussion of data feedback procedures, with particular reference to the value of opinion questionnaires and procedures to feed back information to employees. We then comment briefly on the methods that may be used to develop plans and policies and to establish more permanent structures and technological innovations. The chapter closes with a characterisation of the Employee Relations Project in terms of the relative emphasis given to the eight procedures described in chapters 10 and 11.

Chapter 12 presents a review of different organisational types. We examine four dominant structures and their corresponding ideologies, and discuss the principal processes undertaken by any organisation. These are set within a broader discussion of organisational goals and the factors influencing their priorities. Chapter 13 deals with the place of industrial relations within employee relations more broadly. We analyse the notion of industrial relations climate and move on to examine some of the factors making for successful joint consultation and decision-making. This chapter also includes a brief discussion of formality and informality in grievance procedures and a concluding section on the place of action research in industrial relations.

In chapter 14 we return to questions of evaluation: how should programmes of organisational change be assessed? A seven-stage model is introduced and the forms of evaluation accompanying each stage are discussed. The final chapter brings together themes from the rest of the book to summarise factors which are likely to affect the success of other programmes to develop employee relations. The place of such programmes within the traditions of organisation development and social psychology is also considered.

Throughout Part Two we not only draw material from our own experiences within the Employee Relations Project and elsewhere but we also make use of ideas that have proved helpful to other researchers and writers. Consequently there are citations and notes at the end of each chapter, to which the reader is referred by numbers in square brackets.

9 The researcher and the organisation: Getting in, getting on and getting out

We commence this second part of the book with an examination of the relationships between researchers and the organisation they are working with. Our aim is to describe the changing nature of these contacts during a period of research collaboration, and we will illustrate our general themes with material from the Employee Relations Project.

It is a truism to say that each story has three parts: beginning, middle and end; but in the course of research within organisations this tripartite division has particular validity. Each of the three stages contains special processes and problems for both parties. These may be introduced in terms of three principal features and their varying importance at each stage:

1 *Values:* do the researchers and the organisation have similar goals, beliefs and ethical concerns?
2 *Resources:* what sort of contribution, in terms of competence, task performance, skills and effort, does each side of the relationship expect from the other?
3 *Relationships:* to what extent do respect, trust, openness and liking characterise the parties' interactions, communications and attitudes?

Our main theme here is that each of these features is important throughout, but that each one takes on a different level of importance as a research programme moves forward through its stages. In outline the pattern is as follows:

During stage one, the important period of access, engagement and induction, *values* are of greatest importance.
During stage two the emphasis shifts to the availability of *resources* and the quality of *relationships*, as the parties develop patterns of cooperation (or conflict) and exchange.
During stage three, the period of disengagement and withdrawal, the importance of resources and relationships declines while there is a resurgence in the importance of *value* issues.

These changes are represented visually in Figure 9.1. The events in each stage will now be examined in more detail.

Getting in

The initiation of the Employee Relations Project was partly a question of the opportunistic alignment of self-interest. For our part, we had at that time spare

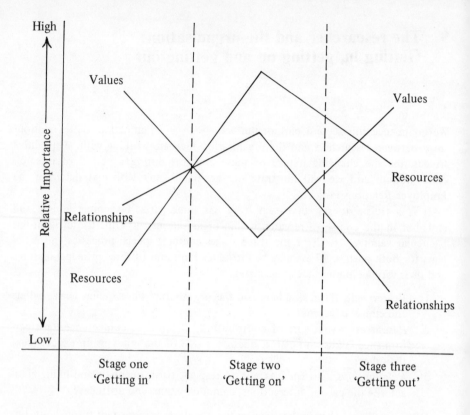

High

Values

Values

Relative Importance

Resources

Relationships

Resources

Relationships

Low

| Stage one 'Getting in' | Stage two 'Getting on' | Stage three 'Getting out' |

Figure 9.1   Resources, relationships and values at three stages in the life of a research project

research capacity and were broadly surveying local industry for research opportunities that fitted with our goals and expertise. The British Steel Corporation management we encountered during this 'surveying' activity were simultaneously thinking about several possible information-seeking programmes in different problem areas and work-sites. Our side of this interaction was very much open-minded: we did not have a fixed image of the research at that stage, although many other projects from the Unit are more closely specified from the outset (see chapter 1).

The origins of most companies' interest in research are also variable, ranging from a problem-centred focus on highly specific goals, to a mild interest in research activity and a casual acceptance of the researcher's initiatives. In the former case the organisation is looking for a specific technical service, and in the latter it is not likely to be greatly diverted by activities which are by and large seen as harmless and peripheral to more central issues. Between these extremes, the desire for an outsider's involvement may serve complex interests within the company. The researcher is usually initially unaware of these, ignorant of the organisational politics underlying his acceptance, and he may never become fully aware of them; for example, whose career is advanced by the successful 'contract', or whose interests are thwarted by its outcomes.

A valuable perspective on these issues has been described by Cherns [1], who has shown how differences in an organisation's needs and the researcher's approach can combine to produce characteristically different types of 'engagement'. He classifies engagements according to the nature of the problem, the type of solution and the methods used. Within this framework the principal roles of the researcher are these:

1 'Subordinate technician', in which the organisation determines in advance all three features: the nature of the problem, the type of solution required and the methods the researcher is to use.
2 'Engineer', in which the problem and the solution are predetermined but the researcher may select his methods.
3 'Consultant', in which the nature of the problem is specified in advance, but the type of solution and the methods to be used are left to the discretion of the researcher.
4 'Action researcher', in which all three features (problem, solution and methods) are open to discussion between the parties.

Cherns makes the point that in many industrial research engagements a tension develops between the two parties as they strain to achieve greater or lesser freedom. Typically, the organisation inclines toward a preconceived and circumscribed vision of problem, solution and methods, whilst the researcher generally wishes to keep options and definitions as open as possible during the initial dialogue.

We were looking for a potentially fruitful engagement of the action research kind, so that we observed at first hand something of this tension in our initial dealings with BSC management. Their needs had eventually coalesced into a decision for the same sort of survey feedback exercise that had been conducted elsewhere in the Corporation (the Ravenscraig Survey, described in chapter 1). Apart from having doubts about certain aspects of the design of that study, we also wished to retain the freedom to identify the nature of the plant's problems from our own enquiries, rather than accept at face value the analysis presented to us by management. Our orientation to this tension was that it was not necessarily a source of discomfort to be avoided, but that it could be desirable to the extent that it encouraged the parties to engage in a direct dialogue about each other's needs and intentions.

This dialogue is most accurately characterised by the term 'negotiation'. In its course communications ostensibly centre on ways, means and objectives, but beneath the surface there is another negotiation in progress that is in many ways more crucial to subsequent events, and this is one in which the currency of the exchange consists of values, images, goals and moral obligations [2].

Each side is 'sizing up' the other, in a way that is almost directly analogous to the early 'reconnoitring of the bargaining range' that has been described for union—

management negotiation [3]. Each side wants to know what underlying value system provides the motivation for the encounter, for from this spring the overall goals and objectives of the parties. On the surface, however, researchers and organisations may deal with one another as if they were unaware of their value systems and may take great pains to reassure the other party about what they do *not* believe or intend to do. Thus the researcher typically devotes a great deal of time and effort to establishing his credentials and trustworthiness in the eyes of the organisation [4], signalling the message that even if he ultimately does no good he will certainly do no harm. For his part, the researcher wants a reassurance that his efforts and professional integrity are not going to be impugned by the firm, and that he will not be used as a pawn in an internal game of organisational politics (as in cases where consultants may have been used as a smokescreen for redundancy programmes).

We may think of three possible types of outcome from these initial negotiations: breakdown, limited-range contract, and open-ended contract. Breakdown may take a surprisingly long time to occur. The organisation may spend much time exploring its needs and the researcher may take great pains to display his techniques, experience and qualifications, before one or other of the parties finds himself drawn to the conclusion that no mutually beneficial bargain can be struck. On the company's side, a single key decision-maker may feel there are too few tangible benefits in the programme, and that it involves risks to what is thought to be a well controlled organisation. On the researcher's side, breakdown may arise from a growing awareness that crucial research or ethical criteria would be overridden by the restrictions imposed by the organisation (for instance, restricted publication of findings within the works or outside). There are, of course, more mundane and technical reasons for breakdown (lack of resources, a sudden change in economic circumstances, etc.), though these may sometimes conceal the fact that there is a yawning gap between the objectives of the bargainers.

Yet even when it is apparent that the two sides want quite different things out of their relationship, some limited-range bargain may nonetheless be struck. Sufficient tangible benefits to either party may be apparent to promote such an agreement. In so doing, some mild self-delusion and limited collusion is often accepted by both sides to facilitate the deal. Whilst each in his heart of hearts knows the other does not entirely share his values and objectives, it may sometimes happen that comments with obliquely contrary implications are made, the researcher to the effect that he is operating within the 'unitary' framework that what is good for management is good for everyone [5], and senior managers to the effect that their ultimate altruistic goal is the enhancement of employee well-being. In these cases it can happen that each takes the other's declarations with a pinch of salt, whilst drawing up a limited agreement that secures valuable data for the researcher and information that may lead to increased efficiency for the organisation.

A more open-ended commitment to collaboration is the third type of outcome that may emerge. Whilst this is not the goal of all access negotiations it is usually the desired end for action research projects. However, even in this type of engagement the terms of reference are never entirely unspecified. The researcher neither wants nor gets complete *carte blanche* to do as he pleases. Action research is problem-centred, and the openness desired is the freedom to explore organisational problems and methods of resolving them. This may be entirely possible within some sensible boundaries of mutually acceptable controls, for example, in time-scale, resources, feedback of results and so on. The openness resides on the *inside*, in the commitment of both parties to flexible collaboration. We have described, using Chern's analysis, the tensions that can accompany this sort of deal.

Another important factor in the early negotiations is the kind of research organisation which is involved. Trist [6] identifies three types of research groups:

1   *Centres within user organisations*, offering a research service to their own institution (e.g. Government research departments).
2   *University departments*, fitting research into their activities as centres of learning and teaching, usually within one professionally-defined discipline.
3   *Research institutes*, whose primary goal is to conduct applied research and develop theory about a wide range of problems.

In the first of these the scope for action research (in the sense defined above) is severely limited. Researchers are themselves enmeshed in the organisational power structure and are dependent upon clients for definition of their functions and research goals. (Other types of research engagement from among those illustrated above may, of course, be very appropriate for a centre within a user organisation.) The second type of research group, part of a university teaching department, often has problems mapping its conceptual orientation and its limited resources onto the complex long-term requirements of action research within industrial organisations. It is the third type of research organisation which is particularly well-placed for action research, especially if the group is financially independent of the research setting.

Our ability to achieve a mutually satisfactory open-ended agreement for action research with the British Steel Corporation was largely due to the freedom we had as members of this third type of institution. Although rather more narrowly discipline-based than some other well-known examples of this kind of research organisation (e.g. the Tavistock Institute in London, and the Institute of Social Research in Michigan) our function and orientation were clearly of Trist's third type, and in our introduction to Tinsley Park Works this helped us to shape the Project's design to meet local needs and conditions.

But the access process is not merely an aligning of expectations and perceptions with senior organisational decision-makers. There inevitably follows a series of meetings with other 'interest groups', to develop and explain details of the terms of reference, to discover areas of local sensitivity, and to develop the nuts and bolts of the programme. At this point, the whole emphasis shifts dramatically. The initial high status 'gatekeepers' perceptibly fade into the background, and the researcher finds himself dealing with a whole new set of people. This is very much a voyage of discovery for the researcher as he locates first the formal key office-holders and decision-makers, and subsequently the informal social networks of the organisation. In a broad-based project significant other 'gatekeepers' emerge at all levels: middle managers, foreman, shop stewards. In these early contacts our experience at Tinsley Park was not untypical of other researchers [7] : we devoted much time to dispelling the ivory-tower or 'other-worldsman' stereotype of the academic, whilst at the same time we formulated strategies for the conduct of the Project.

The most important part of this process for the action researcher is winning commitment from all likely future participants in the research. As we have described in Part One, this is not always a smooth or easy path to tread, and one may have to be content with no better than limited acceptance of the research in some quarters, or even grudging acquiescence in others. It is unrealistic to expect a universal and wholehearted enthusiasm for an open-ended and unpredictable sequence of events. Indeed the fact that one individual or group expresses support for the proposal can sometimes be sufficient to damn it in the eyes of another group.

Two types of formal commitment to start work are desirable. On the one hand some written agreement is necessary, probably with senior management and covering the scope of the programme, financial issues and policy on publication of results. A broader commitment is also required, through a formal decision of a body which can be seen to represent the research site as a whole. In the case of the Employee Relations Project, the first of these agreements was through an exchange of letters and the second through a decision by the Section Council (see chapter 3).

By the time these formal commitments have been made, planning begins to focus on details of method and scheduling, and the researcher's problem has changed from one of how to 'get in' to one of how to 'get on'.

Getting on

Values, underlying beliefs and objectives become less often questioned at ground level during this second stage, for the in-plant participants generally have confidence that these have been checked and ratified by their representatives, the access gatekeepers of shop-floor and management interests. The researcher needs to be careful to act out the values, of course: to be honest about how the research arose and what he wants out of it. He must also show himself able to keep confidences, admit errors (if they occur) and stand up to authority figures. The chief interest of people on site at this stage is in what the researcher actually plans to do, what demands will be made on them, and what, ultimately, they will get out of it. These are also issues that are uppermost in the researcher's mind, for his prime concern in maintaining the mobility of the research is to acquire a correct understanding of what is acceptable and appropriate for the people with whom he is dealing. This process of mutual perception and image-projection may be considered a process of 'role modelling', one that is essential to the long term success of the research.

102

Thus in this second phase early contacts at site level are highly task-oriented, and cover the resources (time, skills, energy, money, staff, etc.) which each side can bring to bear on the programme. In the Employee Relations Project this was exemplified by the way the progression of activities was structured. At the start of the Project we instituted what might be termed three 'mechanisms for momentum', three devices to expedite the tasks that confronted us. These were the Project Steering Committee, the training for group leaders, and the activities of the project coordinator.

In Part One we described how each of these was set up, and what early functions they fulfilled. For example, the Steering Committee planned the number and composition of project groups, the training established a framework for the conduct of problem-solving sessions and allowed us to demonstrate our knowledge and skills of these processes, and the project coordinator scheduled events and organised materials for smooth progress. These outward functions had the immediate effect of signalling that 'something was happening', and generated a widely felt forward momentum within the programme. All the while we were attempting to streamline the chain of activity so that events followed the desired course. This 'streamlining' took several forms.

First, there were public relations activities that we instigated, whose aim was to create reasonably uniform expectations about the Project. For example, we quite consciously reinforced use of the label 'Project' in all our discussions and written communications. The words 'study', 'scheme', and 'survey' noticeably declined and disappeared from people's descriptions of the programme. A most important element of these communication activities was the publication *Focus*, which started life as a 'bulletin of the Project Steering Committee', but later became more a joint production by ourselves and the Corporation's editorial staff. Whilst it quite clearly signalled the start and end of the Project's main stages, and factually reported on opinions and actions emerging from the programme, its whole tone and presentation was exhortative and propagandising. It is not hard to discern its repeated message of: 'don't worry too much about the snags and set-backs, keep the enterprise going'. Not that negative opinions about the Project were suppressed; indeed, some people felt that *Focus* had been too generous to the opinions of the dissenting minority. Yet care was taken wherever possible to present a balance of negative and positive views about Project issues.

The project groups and the Problem Record Forms constituted the main mechanism for the temporal flow of the Project. We have described in chapter 4 how our original plan for the sequential raising, classifying, and solving of problems was overtaken by the short-term pressure for change generated within the groups. The fact that many of them were able to introduce solutions within a short period of time led to an early flurry of enthusiastic and optimistic activity.

The programme was subsequently punctuated by several events associated with the project questionnaire and the feedback of results. These were very important signposts along the research path. They proclaimed the continuing presence of the

Project to the works, documented the scale and scope of its interests, and demonstrated our ability to fulfil the terms of the contract we had agreed.

But what is of most general interest in these mechanisms is their interdependence with the working relationships we established with people on site. These relationships assumed growing importance as activities got underway. First, we established a fairly close level of contact with many of the plant's 'opinion leaders' at several levels by our membership of the Project Steering Committee. Second, the project coordinator quickly became a friend and ally. Third, and most important, each of the four of us established an easy familiarity with many people in our separate allocated area of responsibility within the plant [8]. Whilst these relationships often contained an element of conflict and tension, there were in each area people with whom we enjoyed relations of warmth, liking, respect, and trust. Clearly, the establishment of such a climate of relations is good for the conduct of research. The researcher establishes a network of social relations that gives him information, guidance, and support, which he in turn reciprocally provides for the participants. Indeed it could be said that how well this 'intelligence' network actually maps on to the power structure of the organisation is a key factor in determining the potency of the researcher to really assist in the creation of change.

However, it should not be forgotten that close and amicable working relationships between researcher and client need some deliberate managing to prevent their subverting overall objectives. One does not want so much mutual reinforcement in the relationship that it becomes impossible to apply corrective pressure without causing dismay and hostility. Furthermore, one has to guard against a tendency for groups with a good atmosphere to fall into 'groupthink'. This has been described [9] as the tendency for creative differences of opinion to be glossed over by the group's fervour for its collective task and its desire to maintain cohesion. Whilst the composition of groups was sufficiently heterogeneous to ensure that differences of opinion did exist, forceful leadership sometimes threatened to inhibit their open expression. Our role here was thus as an irritant to our principal collaborators, the group leaders. Clark [10] has expressed the ideal balance of this relationship in the following terms:

> The essential trick in the development of a fruitful client—practitioner relationship is to create enough overlap between these two systems (the 'client' and 'practitioner' systems) for communication and action to take place, without sacrificing the differences that enhance the possibility of a creative tension. The value of the complementary relationship is reduced to the extent that either system dominates or swallows the other.

Possibly, at times, we did allow ourselves to be 'swallowed' by a group leader's desire to rush matters through to completion, rather than running the risk of evoking noncompliance by making demands on him that he would be unable to meet. In allowing as much self-determination as we did, we were attempting to steer a course between what Clark has called 'false certainty' and 'undue modesty'.

Yet this process also demands that the researcher is responsive to the demands that are made on him. Our early reluctance to give the works a written report of our impressions and opinions could be described as a form of Clark's 'undue modesty'. Yet we quickly realised that we should take seriously requests to express our views formally and publicly, and that an 'Interim Report' could serve a valuable function within the overall programme. This report was, ironically in view of its title, the first act in the third and final phase of the engagement: getting out.

Getting out

The 'contract' that had been agreed at the start of the Project was based upon the shared objective of improving employee relations. This was intentionally vague in order that the central issues might surface as the Project got underway, and closer definition of the goal was left until participants could observe and experience the Project's mechanisms. However, up to the Interim Report the achievements of the Project had been localised and separate from each other. The Report crystallised our views about the nature of the employee relations problems in the works as a whole in relation to its organisational setting, and expressed our opinions about what mechanisms and procedures should sustain improvements after the Project was formally ended.

In other words, the balance was shifting away from the minutiae of individual problems, solutions, and resources to the broader value-laden issues of communications, power, and responsibility. Our recommendations were geared to the perpetuation of those aspects of the Project that were likely to be useful in the works as we had observed it. But at a deeper level the Report and its reception were the first part in a series of exchanges marking the conclusion of the contract. Both sides were tacitly agreeing that the terms of the agreement were almost fulfilled, and that it had been conducted satisfactorily. We had publicly affirmed that we cared about the works and declared our interest in its future welfare, and the works in turn reaffirmed its respect for our efforts.

As described in chapter 6, we were at that time involved in a range of activities to explore and implement the recommendations of the Interim Report. Yet we saw these as essentially short-lived activities, and we did not feel it appropriate to extend the original agreement by adding on small projects, for example, to improve interdepartmental communication. Psychologically both the company and ourselves had accepted the initial contract and we were by now both moving towards its termination.

This was partly a reflection of those features we have previously labelled as values. Our goals from the Project included the preparation of descriptions and interpretations for a wider audience, and 'closure' was thus increasingly desirable. Some of the original 'gatekeepers' among senior management had by now moved on, and their successors were busy with new problems and objectives.

This stage was characterised by a type of dialogue that was common during the 'getting in' stage. The emphasis had returned to issues of value away from those of task performance. As such, the 'cosiness' engendered at the disengagement stage can be as illusory as its counterpart during access: it is in part a ritualised 'mutual grooming' conducted while each side examines how far its objectives have been met.

The actual timing of disengagement is usually provided for in the original agreement, though when the commitment is an open-ended one the parties will seek more 'natural' criteria for conclusion. In the case of the Employee Relations Project, the project groups were resolving or shelving more problems than they were raising, and the consequent decline of interest in the groups' activities occurred fairly simultaneously across the works. This development, coupled with the decisions made at the special consultative meetings convened to consider the recommendations of the Interim Report, created a temporary vacuum in the sequence of events, as we carried out a stocktaking of what had occurred over the previous eighteen months.

The After questionnaire and the last issue of *Focus* formally set the seal on Project-related activities in the plant, though we continued to take an interest in the progress of joint consultation and other instruments for the regulation of employee relations. One final task remained: evaluation. This could be seen as the last and most significant payoff of the research engagement. Our attempts to evaluate the changes that had taken place (described in detail in chapter 8 and set in a broader context in chapter 14) were geared to the distinctive needs of both parties. Our 'Second Report' which contained these data was written up in February 1976 as a detailed account for the organisation of the costs and benefits of the Project, and was consciously aimed at assisting any future decisions about the feasibility and desirability of similar programmes elsewhere in the industry. With this in mind we devoted much of the report to a consideration of causes of success and failure in the programme and ways in which the Project might have achieved more than it did. How much practical use this was to BSC at the time or later is not easy to ascertain [11], though management were at pains to indicate to us that we had honoured our side of the contract in a useful fashion. This illustrates the mirror imaging of getting out to getting in, insofar as the importance of 'ground-level' relationships decreases and relations with key access-negotiating agents higher up the system reassert themselves. In our discussions with these people at the termination of the Project the dialogue clearly had moved away from specific in-plant issues to questions about the overall meaning and value of what had happened.

The final curtain to the Project was the 'payoff' to us, the researchers, principally in the form of this book. Our profession is one which aims to increase knowledge and practical understanding. Success in this is often measured in terms of the number, quality, and impact of scientific and other contributions and in terms of reputation inside and outside the scientific community. Part of our formal contract with the British Steel Corporation was an agreement to consult over the form of any publications that flowed out of the study. Consequently our last

Project-related dealings with people inside the Corporation were discussions about the draft of this book which we had circulated among managers and trade union representatives. This process revealed an almost coy reluctance to put any pressure on us to make changes, as if implicitly recognising that this was our main tangible benefit from the research. In practice, feedback on the draft manuscript resulted in a number of small amendments to enhance accuracy and readability.

Of course publications such as this are only a manifestation of more fundamental benefits to the researcher. Each one of us gained valuable professional experience and expertise by conducting the research; and for our research unit we opened up new areas for future exploration.

Finally, let us briefly consider what are the implications of this discussion for action research more generally. The actual events and processes of research engagements of this kind are complex and unique in each instance. However, the issues we have considered have received little systematic research in themselves, and although researchers and practitioners have written about them at length and identified many common themes [12], no comprehensive framework yet exists to aid the prediction or subsequent assessment of the course of action research. Whilst we are conscious that our treatment here has sometimes oversimplified highly complex processes, we believe the distinctive emphasis placed on resources, relationships and values at each of the three stages in the life of a programme (getting in, getting on and getting out) might provide a useful starting point for prospective researchers and others as they interpret their own experiences.

Notes

[1] A.B. Cherns, 'Behavioural science engagements: taxonomy and dynamics', *Human Relations*, vol. 29, 1976, pp. 905–10.

[2] In practice, the Unit's previous research contacts with BSC had already exhibited our probable style and resources, but there were new issues and new discussions to be brought in at the first stage of the ERP dialogue.

[3] This term was introduced by A. Douglas, in 'The peaceful settlement of industrial and intergroup disputes', *Journal of Conflict Resolution*, vol. 1, 1957, pp. 69–81.

[4] Many examples are to be found in C.A. Brown, P. Guillet de Monthoux and A. McCullough (eds.), *The Access Casebook*, THS Company, Stockholm, 1976.

[5] A powerful critique of this approach is to be found in A. Fox, 'Managerial ideology and power relations', *British Journal of Industrial Relations*, vol. 4, 1966, pp. 366–78.

[6] See E.L. Trist, 'Engaging with large-scale systems', Chapter 4 in A.W. Clark (ed.), *Experimenting with Organizational Life: The Action Research Approach*, Plenum Press, London, 1976.

[7] See, for example, *The Access Casebook*, cited in note 4 above.

[8]   As described in chapter 3, each of us was mainly responsible for the Project's
       progress in one of the principal departments of the works, with one member
       primarily engaged in the Interlinked Phase.
[9]   See I.L. Janis, *Victims of Groupthink: A Psychological Study of Foreign
       Policy Decisions and Fiascos*, Houghton Mifflin, Boston, 1968.
[10]   See page 127 of the book cited in note 6.
[11]   However, several themes from the Project and its reports were incorporated in
       discussions and documents both inside and outside the works during 1976
       and 1977.
[12]   See, for example, the book cited in note 6.

10 Group processes in organisational change

We turn now from general discussions of the relationship between action research-ers and the organisations they work with to look more specifically at the kinds of procedures which have been used in planned attempts to develop employee relations. Any attempt to classify the techniques in this field is necessarily imperfect. However, we have found it useful to think in terms of the following eight types of change activity, recognising that there is overlap between some of the types.

1 *Educational, training or counselling activities.* Situations in which the researcher adopts a role as direct provider of information, skill, theory or advice.

2 *Process consultation.* In which the researcher observes and assists during the course of group processes. The groups may be work groups meeting on a routine basis to undertake company tasks, or they might be specially formed for the purpose, as T-groups or other types of interactive skills training sessions.

3 *Intergroup communication meetings.* Activities in which groups or their representatives are brought together to examine the ways they communicate and work with each other. Other labels for this kind of procedure include 'team-building' and 'confrontation' meetings.

4 *Problem-solving meetings.* Group discussions introduced specially to identi-fy and tackle issues which are reducing the organisation's effectiveness. Such meetings may be composed entirely of managers, of managers and shop stewards, or be spread through all levels of a plant, as were the ERP project groups.

5 *Data feedback procedures.* Techniques to gather diagnostic information about the state of an organisation and its members, and to present this information for discussion and action. The information might be financial or technical material or concerned with manpower planning issues, and on other occasions it might be questionnaire data about opinions, morale or organisational climate.

6 *Assistance with the development of plans and policies.* Researchers may sometimes submit recommendations for improvement, developed by them-selves alone or through a joint examination with management and others. These recommendations may cover pay systems, technical developments, marketing possibilities or a wide range of other issues, and their vehicle is often a formal report of some kind.

7 *Establishment of longer-term structures.* Since programmes for organisa-

tional change are necessarily of limited duration, one goal is often to initiate structures which will carry forward the principles and practices of the programme after its termination. These structures may, for example, be new communication networks, decision-making procedures, reporting-back requirements, or improved mechanisms for industrial relations.

8 *Technological innovations.* A rather different form of change activity is the introduction of new equipment, new working methods, plant layout or administrative systems. Such innovations may arise through any of the previous seven procedures.

Any single programme of organisational change will have its own mix of some or all of these eight components. In this chapter and the following one we will examine the central features of each set of procedures. Our intention is to further characterise the Employee Relations Project, by identifying its particular mix, and more importantly to draw out some general principles about the applicability of each procedure elsewhere and the factors which might influence its effectiveness. This chapter will cover the first four items in the list, those that are principally concerned with different types of group process. Chapter 11 will examine the other four procedures, and chapter 15 will deal more generally with the place of these activities within what has become known as 'organisation development'.

Educational, training or counselling activities

Some programmes of planned organisational change contain regular sessions of an overtly educational kind. These may include theoretical presentations about psychology and behavioural science and have as their goal a general widening of perspective and increased understanding of the concepts on which the programme is based. For example, much of the material presented in chapter 12 could be of value in such teaching.

The directly educational activities within the Employee Relations Project were primarily intended to improve discussion leading. Training sessions were provided in order to increase the effectiveness with which meetings on the works were conducted. Attention was restricted to project group members, although we naturally expected some carry-over to other day to day work.

Individual counselling sessions were also undertaken; these were relatively infrequent but our belief was that they were quite important. As opportunities presented themselves, we undertook private discussions with individual group leaders and managers about their style and possible ways to improve effectiveness. Such discussions can be potentially threatening and are usually inappropriate unless the individual expresses an interest in them. Several group leaders did make such requests after their initial meetings, and we attempted to help in all cases.

Unless the researcher's negotiated role contains explicit provision for counselling activity, he must necessarily tread carefully in this area. Similarly, there is not always scope within the agreed contract for broader theoretical inputs. For example, attempts to introduce lecture sessions about psychological concepts may be counterproductive in situations where managers and other potential recipients are so busy that they would resent pressure to attend. Another factor influencing the suitability of this type of activity is the level of educational sophistication and of expressed interest; some managerial groups more than others are comfortable with and interested in the concepts to be covered.

Process consultation

Process consultation is a second major form of action research activity [1]. The researcher's training and experience in social psychological processes may make him especially suited to observe and provide an advisory commentary throughout discussions. His contributions may be of different kinds, and individual researchers have their own preferred styles.

One approach is to make more apparent, without evaluative or prescriptive remarks, what is happening in a group. The researcher might thus draw attention to the frequency of comments by Mr X of a certain kind, or he might record the content of particular interactions so that he can make available a 'profile' of a particular meeting for the participants to discuss. Other researchers may have a style of stronger advocacy, commenting on activities within the group and suggesting possible explanations and alternative actions. A mixture of styles is often employed, with the researcher's process-related remarks depending upon his assessment of what is appropriate in each situation.

Many techniques have been developed for process consultation, often linked with specially-formed training groups of some kind. Interested readers may wish to follow up the references to interactive training groups provided at the end of the chapter [2]. In the Employee Relations Project and in many other cases process consultation was restricted to ongoing meetings within the company. In our case we were especially concerned with the project groups, and several approaches were adopted here. One was through the Meeting Assessment Forms which were completed at the end of some of the sessions. These forms were used directly to elicit participants' judgements about aspects of interpersonal processes in the group. As described in chapter 4, they met with varying degrees of success, but they undoubtedly helped to establish the norm that observation of·and comments on interpersonal processes were legitimate and useful aspects of the Project.

Each of us acted as a process consultant in his own way as he felt appropriate. This type of activity had been envisaged in our initial discussions and our contract with the works, but the main thrust of the Project was always seen in terms of problem-solving meetings. The atmosphere on the works was one in which suspicion was often expressed that as psychologists we were mainly concerned to institute quite unrealistic 'love-ins'. However, our assessment was that the situation required a primarily action-centred programme of face-to-face meetings through project groups (item 4 on the list at the beginning of this chapter).

Intergroup communication meetings

The third set of procedures involves specially-convened meetings between people from different sections of an organisation. It is not uncommon to find that parts of a company occasionally protect their own interests to the detriment of other parts or of overall organisational effectiveness. We recorded several instances in Part One where interdepartmental meetings and working parties were helpful in the examination of conflicts of this kind, and in chapter 12 we have further comments to make on the conflicting needs for differentiation and integration within an organisation.

Similar problems arise on an individual basis between managers representing different departments or functions, and several procedures have been developed for 'team-building' exercises [3]. The general principle is similar to that employed in the project groups: managers who routinely work together are asked collectively to examine the factors inhibiting their effectiveness and to work on possible solutions. In many cases a team-building exercise among managers will bring into focus problems of interpersonal style, leadership patterns, resource allocation procedures and communication networks.

Those intergroup communication meetings which did develop during the Employee Relations Project tended to arise naturally out of individual project group discussions. They were designed as extensions of the project groups, rather than being based on more structured procedures to measure and examine the perceptions which different individuals or groups held of themselves and of each other. Such structured 'confrontation meetings' may, of course, be appropriate elsewhere.

As with all these activities, the implementation of intergroup communication meetings depends upon the level of commitment from the participants. We had envisaged that the need for team-building exercises among senior managers at Tinsley Park Works might become apparent to them as the Employee Relations Project proceeded, but this did not widely occur. A small number of managers in the level one project group wished to examine their mutual problems, and on several occasions we advocated a start in this direction (for example, as a recommendation in the Interim Report), but the suggestions were not taken up.

Problem-solving meetings

The principal activity throughout the Employee Relations Project centred upon the identification and solution of problems through project groups. These were quite unlike the other groups which normally met in the works. They were not subject to the formalisation associated with typical committee meetings, and they were temporary, being specially formed for the Project. Indeed, few of the lower-level participants came together for specific organisational purposes beyond the contact required for their actual job. Finally, and of particular significance, the Project mechanisms increased the power of the groups to obtain information or to take action on specific problem areas which concerned them. This action was to take place within the constraints of the existing channels of communication and authority in the works.

These unusual circumstances provided an exciting challenge for some of the project groups, but frequent feelings of unease for others. Coping styles varied considerably as did commitment to the Project goals. In this section we will try to disentangle some of the most significant psychological factors involved, and to draw some general conclusions concerning the likely strengths and pitfalls of such groups in other organisational change programmes.

Three kinds of factors influencing the success of project groups will first be introduced and then examined in more detail:

1   *The group composition.* Both the leader of the group and its members varied in their attitudes towards the Project, in their discussion skills and in their power to directly implement decisions of the group. There were also considerable differences in their ability to operate under the essentially participative rules of the meeting. Furthermore, our own presence was part of the group composition and our behaviour as participant observers undoubtedly affected progress.

2   *Primary outcomes.* The effects of group action can be seen in terms of three primary outcomes:
    (a)   The way problems were defined. Here we are concerned with the meaning attached to statements of 'problems', rather than merely the problem list itself.
    (b)   Expectations of success: the extent to which a group and the Project were seen as viable, and how this varied over time.
    (c)   The group atmosphere: the group's 'feeling' or 'mood' and the motivational significance of this.

3   *The group's effectiveness.* The primary outcomes ultimately come together in a way which defines the extent of a group's effectiveness. One criterion of effectiveness is, of course, the number of problems raised and solved, and this is a criterion that we have discussed in chapter 8. The present analysis is concerned with the more dynamic features of group processes, such as:
    (a)   the extent to which problems and solutions were monitored and progressed by group members;
    (b)   the desire to continue meeting and to maintain the group;
    (c)   the flexibility of a group in reformulating action strategies when initial ones had failed.

Figure 10.1 presents the above factors in diagrammatic form. We shall now consider them in more detail, starting with the group composition.

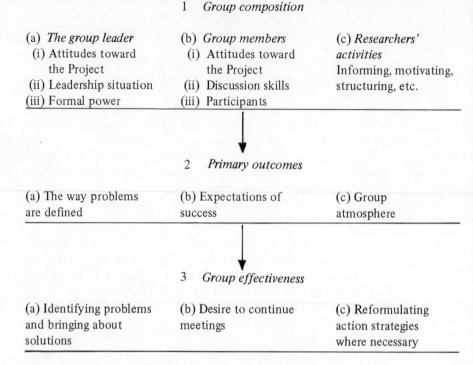

1   *Group composition*

(a) *The group leader*
  (i) Attitudes toward
      the Project
  (ii) Leadership situation
  (iii) Formal power

(b) *Group members*
  (i) Attitudes toward
      the Project
  (ii) Discussion skills
  (iii) Participants

(c) *Researchers'*
activities
Informing, motivating,
structuring, etc.

2   *Primary outcomes*

(a) The way problems
are defined

(b) Expectations of
success

(c) Group
atmosphere

3   *Group effectiveness*

(a) Identifying problems
and bringing about
solutions

(b) Desire to continue
meetings

(c) Reformulating
action strategies
where necessary

Figure 10.1   The effectiveness of problem-solving groups

Group composition

The group leader's attitudes to the Project

Our training for group leaders (see chapter 3) was based upon the assumption that it was important for the leader to have an accurate view of the Project to present to his group, and that he should be able to present this view with some enthusiasm. It was also expected that the groups would function best under a 'controlled democratic' style of leadership. The events of the training sessions left us with the firm impression that not all leaders would meet these expectations, and this was borne out in practice. For example, at the opening of the first meeting a number of leaders gave their groups extremely cursory introductions to the Project, such as: 'You all know why you're here. We want your problems, so let's have them!'

Such statements were typically followed by a stunned silence, perhaps broken by nervous laughter. One of us would then take over the introduction to the Project and then return the proceedings to the designated leader. While such occurrences were evident amongst the less experienced leaders in the lower-level groups they were by no means confined to these groups. For example, one middle management leader expressed a total disenchantment with the goals of the Project. It then took several meetings and much discussion to work through his and other people's views, but anxieties frequently re-emerged.

In contrast, some leaders readily espoused the aims of the Project and presented them clearly and concisely to their groups. Where such a stance was maintained, the group experienced fewer difficulties than when the leader was continually trying to reconcile his personal unease about the aims of the Project with the social forces urging him to continue the work of his group; forces generated by his superiors, his colleagues and ourselves. It was in these circumstances that tension was high in the group, and progress often erratic. And it was here also that we would find ourselves working particularly hard to help the group to move forward.

The leadership situation

There is an abundance of psychological evidence that the leader's situation determines whether or not a particular leadership style is effective [4]. All the group leaders' situations had the same basic components, with a clearly defined primary task (problem elicitation and follow-up of suggestions) and authority through the Project to support actions and suggestions. Yet there were major differences, notably between the situations of group leaders in different departments.

Each department had its characteristic physical setting, which was partly determined by the technological demands of steel manufacture. Hence the locations of meetings varied considerably, ranging from a prefabricated shed to relatively luxurious offices. This affected seating arrangements, comfort, and ease of communication within a group. Some group meetings were very close to the work areas; others were not.

Perhaps even more important was the psychological setting or 'climate' within a department. Some climates were characterised by less immediate production pressure and more time to think and discuss than were others. It seemed to us that the closer the department was to the actual physical production of steel, the less conducive the climate was to wideranging discussions of general problems.

Other aspects of the departmental setting were illustrated in chapter 7, where, for example, we saw variations between departments in perceived friendliness and adequacy of communication. Differences in the frequency of transfer of important management personnel were also noted in that chapter.

The group leader's formal power

The third feature of the group leader identified in Figure 10.1 is the power he holds through his formal position in the company. For example, the level one group leader was the works manager and the level two leaders were department managers or equivalent. All of these had direct organisational authority over group members as well as formal power for use in following up suggestions and taking action.

This was not always the case. At level four, for instance, a foreman may have been leading a group made up from several different sections (that is, extending beyond his own workgroup), and a shop steward group leader had only that power he could derive from his union position. However, foremen and shop stewards could sometimes take advantage of access to information which their position had given them. For example, one foreman group leader had been a member of the works job evaluation committee and he was able to clear up several misunderstandings about job evaluation in his group; similarly, shop stewards were able to report directly on decisions taken at meetings they had attended as union representatives.

The group members

Figure 10.1 summarised three influential differences between the groups: members' attitudes towards the Project, their discussion skills, and the participants themselves.

The first of these differences was particularly important, and has been illustrated on several previous occasions. We have seen how there were variations in initial attitudes and how the development of these depended greatly on the continuing success of a group, on the group leader's enthusiasm and on the climate within a department.

The discussion skills of members also varied between groups. Members of the higher-level groups were more likely to meet elsewhere in formal discussions than were the others. Yet this was a 'mixed blessing' for the Project, as there was often a tendency to undertake project group meetings in a formal style which we felt inappropriate. Groups at other levels did not meet as groups elsewhere and could move straight into a more participative style of operation. However, the lack of familiarity of some shop-floor members (and occasionally their group leaders) with the norms and requirements of effective group discussion was sometimes a problem.

In addition to these hierarchical differences, there were also variations between participants at each level. For example, some level four groups contained only production employees who all worked together, others were made up of production and service workers, and still others were composed entirely of clerical staff. The content and style of discussion was naturally different across these cases.

Ideal and actual leadership styles

Before moving on to other issues introduced through Figure 10.1, we should first take a general look at group leaders' styles. From the discussion so far and the presentation in chapter 4, we might infer an 'ideal' style for a project group leader. He would be someone who:

(a)   was participative to the extent that he encouraged all people to express their views on problem areas, suggesting issues when the conversation lagged. At the same time he would not dominate the group with his own definition of problems, nor permit others to do so;

116

(b)   could impose sufficient structure to condense the information flowing from the group into separate issues and to monitor progress on actions. In this structuring role he would need to adopt many of the skills of good chairmanship by preparing for a meeting, communicating the purpose of each meeting to the group, allocating responsibility, and summarising the conclusions of the meeting;

(c)   was clearly sensitive to differences in sympathy to the Project and its aims, not permitting his own prejudices to over-influence the course of events. This might also involve some 'selling' of the Project in order to help engender enthusiasm and commitment in the group.

(d)   was able effectively to harness his own and others' formal power, and the Project's power, to ensure attainment of his group's objectives.

This picture of the 'super group leader' was (perhaps not surprisingly) descriptive of few real leaders. There was frequently a discrepancy between what we felt the leader should be doing and what he was actually doing; and sometimes the leader himself would express unease about the effectiveness of his style. One of our functions was to try to handle this problem. This was possible in some areas, by giving further information, undertaking secretarial chores, summarising and progressing action, but it was far more difficult in the areas concerning formal power and where intimate knowledge of the job and the group members was important.

There were a number of cases of leadership which lacked some essential ingredients. Illustrations are:

1   *Too task oriented.* One manager was essentially a hard working, hard driving person who would characteristically prepare a long list of issues for discussion. This had the unfortunate effect of preventing people raising their own problems in their own words. He failed to check with group members whether consensus was being achieved, and he rarely used a direct question to bring in people who might be interested in the matter to hand. He generally tended to create dependence by offering or pushing his own solutions to problems.

   This person was not unlike others who would try to 'manage' the group in the way they would manage their production tasks. Indeed for them the relatively democratic procedures seemed odd and inappropriate in circumstances where they themselves 'knew the answer'.

2   *The over-hard sell.* In his first meeting with his group, an enthusiastic shop steward asked his 'brothers' to air their views about the Project. Before anyone had a chance to say anything he promptly quashed possible doubts: 'This is something new, things are happening already. It's worth pursuing. I think it's got tremendous possibilities . . . Yes, the proof of the pudding is in the eating, but we've got to cook it first. Well,' he continued, banging on the table, ' . . . are we all agreed it's worth going on?' A chorus of 'yes' followed. And so the strong, almost ideological, stance of the leader pervaded this, and other meetings. Ultimately it tended to be his views which

prevailed in a climate of mock democracy.

3   *Too passive.* A few leaders were so passive that little progress was achieved at all. This often resulted in an easy-going, relaxed atmosphere in which most people chatted happily but where few of the Project goals were achieved. Sometimes someone else in the group would emerge to assume the task-oriented role, but more often than not it was up to us to fill that gap.

4   *Unprepared.* Apart from the problems of the balance between task- and people-oriented styles of leadership, one feature common to several group leaders was their lack of ability and/or enthusiasm to prepare for a meeting. It was not uncommon for a leader to arrive at a meeting and turn to his group or to us and ask what should be done today. This naturally acted as a disincentive to some less keen members of the group. Basic discussion skills of these leaders often left something to be desired; comments tended to wander in all directions and decisions sometimes went unrecorded.

Researchers' activities

We have mentioned on several occasions the types of activity that we ourselves engaged in. These are identified as the third feature of group composition in Figure 10.1. In fact, the range of our behaviours expanded as the Project developed, and it would be useful at this point to summarise the main tasks we undertook:

1   *Informational activities.* Here we provided information about, for example, the progress of the Project in general, what other departments were doing, future activities, and the progress in specific action areas. We frequently presented the overall context to a group to remind them that they were part of an interlocking set of activities.

2   *Motivational activities.* We tried to engender a climate within a group whereby members would feel free to participate in the discussions, and openly comment about and/or support others. Also, we helped to set up particular goals which were legitimate within the Project for individuals to strive towards, such as acting on a particular issue in a particular way by a specific date. This often involved the encouragement of individual responsibility for the action.

3   *Structuring activities.* We helped to devise and timetable action plans, provided secretarial assistance, arranged meetings, developed systems, and made our own suggestions about desirable courses of action.

4   *Power activities.* Although we had no formal power in the works, we did have some power through the Project: power to add weight to a group suggestions; power to approach people in authority; power to facilitate group decisions; and to assist in the structuring and motivational activities.

5   *Social relationship activities.* Here we were concerned with the interpersonal and attitude issues within a group. We acted in a process-observer

role, as illustrated earlier in this chapter, feeding back our impressions of the group's actions and possible sources of misunderstanding. In this role we were also able to provide support to those people who were under pressure or threat through the demands of the Project.

6   *Professional role activities.* These concerned behaviour that we considered to be appropriate in terms of our role as professional psychologists employed by a research organisation. Illustrations occur throughout the book.

Primary outcomes

So far in this section we have considered the group composition factors identified in Figure 10.1 and we have illustrated different group leader styles. Now we turn to see how the effectiveness of project groups was influenced by the primary outcomes listed in the Figure: the way problems are defined; expectations of success; group atmosphere.

The way problems are defined

The Project placed no particular constraint upon the type of problems that could be suggested by group members, and indeed the range of issues which emerged was enormous, varying from very specific 'niggles' such as an inadequately maintained piece of machinery, to broader problems of liaison between different departments and between levels in the organisation. Yet the reasons behind a person stating a particular problem depended very much on that person's work role and the nature and dynamics of his project group. We are able to gain full understanding of the meaning of a person's 'problems' only if we view his statements against the background from which they emerged.

It was clear that some group members could not easily perceive their daily work activities in terms of 'problems': the concept of 'a problem at work' was for them an abstract notion. When these people were prompted by the group leader to suggest possible issues, it was not uncommon for them to react: 'Well, I suppose it would be nice if that machine (procedure, etc.) was improved.' And this might ultimately appear as an item on a Problem Record Form. Such a statement should be seen as of low validity, in that a group member did not clearly 'own' the problem to a sufficient extent that he would devote energy towards solving it. Consequently, many participants opted out of action, looking more to the leader or ourselves to do something.

On other occasions progress would be limited for a different reason. In certain groups, members would very readily respond to the request to identify problems limiting their work effectiveness, and poignant descriptions of, say, working relationships or communication issues would emerge. The usual mechanism for assigning responsibility for actions on the issue would be employed, and a time would be agreed to accomplish the action. Nevertheless, the action deadline would pass, and nothing would be done. The man responsible might say that he had been 'too busy' or 'couldn't contact the person he wanted' or he simply might not arrive at a meeting. It soon became apparent that there were some problems that people really did not want solved. They did want to talk about them and they were important to them, but important as problems which should continue to exist in their own right not as issues to solve. In this way their reactions seemed to indicate that some of the existing problems were important in providing a legitimate and necessary focus for surplus energies. For example, where a degree of inter-level conflict was expressed, this could reinforce a 'them and us' culture which was psychologically rewarding to the members of that culture. Hence some of the problems which had been generated were in a sense an intrinsic part of working life, not necessarily seen as completely 'bad things' to be entirely eradicated. They cemented a kind of stability in relationships and provided a focus for conversation and action; if they were really bad, 'someone else' would do something about them, someone who would more readily accept the risk or effort involved in attempting a solution.

Another theme in terms of problem definition stemmed more directly from group members' preconceptions about the Project and beliefs about the works. Certain groups were so convinced that no-one was really interested in responding to their problems that they would present them very wearily, usually adding that they had tried unsuccessfully time and time again to get the problem solved. This would start a cycle of events where a negative outcome was almost inevitable: the problem would be raised and some half-hearted action would be taken. Progress was therefore minimal, and then group members would say: 'I told you so – no one's interested in our problem!' It was very difficult to divert such self-fulfilling prophecies from their predetermined course.

Not all the groups and issues can be characterised as above. Many participants very firmly grasped the Project mechanisms and used them to their fullest extent. Hence problems were defined in ways in which action could, and would, be taken; these groups were often initially highly energised by the thought of having some direct control over their own situation, and being able to approach people or departments for specific action on their problems. These were veritable model groups for the Project as they were very much self-sustaining. Indeed, the internal group energy was often such that many problems were solved in a very short period using the group's current resources.

While these characterisations of problem definition did in fact fit particular groups quite accurately, many were a mix of the orientations such that some problems tended to go unsolved for the reasons mentioned, and others were worked upon and ultimately solved. Yet there were a number of organisational factors outside the groups which substantially influenced expectations of success within them. Let us turn to these now.

Many recommendations from project groups required reactions from senior members of the works. Sometimes the structural remoteness of, say, a department manager or the organisational constraints upon him would considerably hinder a fast response and such delays were soon discouraging for even the most enthusiastic groups. Managers' communications to groups were sometimes in written form and were vague or evasive. Face-to-face encounters usually left a group far more satisfied, even if no direct solutions to their problems had been found. This point has been examined in chapter 4.

The power to sanction particular decisions was usually in management's hands, and any new operation required higher-level support if it was to be effective. Thus the Project relied on the responsiveness of the organisational system to complement and implement group decisions and activities. In some departments there was a weight of activity building up at lower levels with only limited response, encouragement and support from the top. This applies as much to the scheduling of meetings as to actions on specific problem points. When, for example, a shop-floor worker knocked on a manager's door to ask him questions about problems arising from a project group, or to attend a meeting, this was an important step forward. However its significance could only be reinforced if management made their initial response quickly, openly and constructively. Sometimes this occurred, but sometimes it did not. In the latter case, disillusionment and cynicism were likely to set in.

The contrasting frames of reference used by people at different levels in the organisation sometimes posed particular communication difficulties. For example, it was not uncommon for a manager to be asked to explain to a project group why certain equipment was not renewed, or why the physical working conditions in a particular location could not be improved. The explanation would usually be in terms of cost factors, budgets and priorities, all apparently sensible economic reasons. But often shop-floor group members would perceive this as the 'language of managers', whilst their perception of the problems was more in terms of difficulty and inconvenience in operations and discomfort at work. This could lead to a 'credibility gap' and a still higher degree of dissatisfaction, especially when the manager's response had been in a letter rather than through his personal presence and discussion at the meeting.

While 'communication' issues are often cited as if they are themselves an explanation, they might also be seen as symptoms of other difficulties. They sometimes seem to highlight the cultural differences between different levels and interest groups in the works. Communication during the Employee Relations Project was worst when different groups were unable to see the problem from others' points of view. Managers and workers sometimes showed a marked reluctance to examine an issue in terms familiar to the other party. Conversely, some of the more effective project groups were those containing a person who could act as a 'link-man' by attempting to translate between the different parties and so facilitate understanding and negotiation. In some groups this person was the leader himself, in others it was a group member with a special interest in a particular problem. On certain occasions we would attempt this role ourselves.

While a group's enthusiasm to pursue their ERP role clearly related to the type of response they received from people they contacted, the strength of their desire to proceed was usually directly proportional to the time it took to initiate action, receive feedback and take any necessary follow-up action. Sometimes problems had to be passed through several layers of the organisation (perhaps to other project groups) before a meaningful answer was possible: this took time, occasionally several months. It could often take weeks to schedule a meeting between the group and a particular spokesman on a problem. On other occasions the person in the group who had agreed to take initial action on an issue would, for whatever reason, not do so in the designated time, so creating further delays. Finally, industrial action and holidays added their contribution to setting back the Project activities.

Some project groups seemed to suffer particularly from an accumulation of delays, and saw no early positive results from their actions. In these groups, desire to continue became noticeably lower than in others where a number of successes attributable to group action occurred early in the Project.

Time delays were just one of the various factors which contributed to the atmosphere in a group. Let us next look at this notion of group atmosphere as the third primary outcome of group activities.

Group atmosphere

The main systematic device we had for gauging the atmosphere in the discussion groups was the Meeting Assessment Form. In the early stages of the Project, this was completed by all group members at the end of a meeting, and the group's comments were discussed at the beginning of the next meeting. Such a procedure is an instance of 'process consultation' as described earlier in the chapter, and it is based upon the assumption that the process by which a group functions, and the feelings which emerge, are critical in determining the content of what the group achieves.

The data that we obtained from the Meeting Assessment Forms and from our general observations of the groups, indicated that there were fairly discernible changes in project group atmosphere over time. These can be roughly divided into four stages: uncertainty, enthusiasm, wariness, and pessimism.

Most groups felt rather uncertain and unclear about the Project in their first meetings. This is exemplified by Meeting Assessment Form statements such as:

'I have reservations about the outcome of this'.
'I came to the meeting very unsure about what it would offer.'
'What can this Project do that we haven't done before?'

But after the first one or two meetings it seemed as if most fears had been allayed, and uncertainty turned into enthusiasm. For example:

'Progress is certainly being made towards action.'
'Very formative; these meetings could work out very helpful to all.'
'A very instructive and meaningful discussion of a wide variety of problems; it took place in a friendly atmosphere.'

In these meetings groups were already tackling problems and in some departments solutions were emerging. Hopes were high and most people thought the Project had quite a lot of promise. Yet, if anything, many group members seemed to set their hopes too high, expecting big changes in a very short period. Such changes rarely occurred fast enough to maintain the climate of optimism, so that by the third and fourth meetings the atmosphere could be described as 'wary'. Characteristic Meeting Assessment Form statements were:

'The meeting was not up to standard with a distinct falling off of actions required, and too many points deferred for further reference.'
'Our actions may not be very useful after all.'
'There's a lack of enthusiasm to tackle the jobs in hand.'

There was a noticeable change in aspiration level at this point in time almost reversing the earlier stance: people began to have very low expectations of what could be achieved, and indeed they often forgot earlier successes which had previously been hailed as important steps forward.

The effects of the various delays discussed previously were now beginning to accumulate, which added to the growing feelings of pessimism:

'No one cares much any more.'
'These meetings will not achieve anything.'
'I knew right from the beginning that management had absolutely no interest in the Project.'

Various factors helped to exacerbate these feelings. Firstly, group membership could vary considerably, and rarely in the later meetings would there be full attendance. Some people reported that they would not come because they were 'fed-up' with the lack of progress in the group. Yet, ironically, staying away from the group simply slowed down its progress even more, particularly if the absentee was expected to take some action on problems. As noted in chapter 4 this difficulty was compounded by changes in leadership in some groups.

This account of the sequential changes in group atmosphere over time is, of course, a very general one. Some groups managed to maintain the aspirations characteristic of the 'enthusiastic' stage throughout their life, while others did not progress beyond the first stage of uncertainty and scepticism.

The variability of work roles represented in a particular group was important. Some groups contained people who carried out similar jobs, and they were naturally more united in terms of what they felt the Project could do for them. This contrasted with groups that were made up of people from different sections who had fewer common points of contact. Yet such groups could sometimes generate extremely lively debates on their working relationships, and some people claimed that it was a sobering experience to find out how other people saw them!

Problem-solving groups — some general conclusions

This discussion of the Employee Relations Project problem-solving groups highlights five major themes concerning their effectiveness in programmes of organisational change:

1 The group leader's attitudes and style.
2 The many roles of the researcher.
3 The context of problem generation.
4 Organisational support for the group's activities.
5 Aspirations and expectations.

The group leader's attitudes and style

The group's achievements are clearly very dependent upon the leader and his sensitivity to and understanding of the situation. Many aspects of the leadership situation which faced ERP group leaders will be present in other organisations. Thus group members' uncertainties, political interests, unfamilarity with participative techniques, together with differences in the physical setting and psychological climate of departments, should be predictable to a sufficient extent to be discussed and worked upon during briefing and training sessions. Similarly, an appreciation of the stable, formalistic aspects of the intended programme should certainly be susceptible to training.

Yet it is less reasonable to expect that the group leader will possess, or will be able to learn, all the behavioural skills necessary for effective leadership — particularly when they may be very different from those which are effective in his usual task situation. Leadership style training tends not to be particularly successful as it often attempts to change relatively permanent areas of personality [5]. A similar problem can arise in attempts to change the attitudes and preconceptions of a group leader. Our experience suggests that negative attitudes can detrimentally affect the progress of a group, perhaps irrevocably, yet at best one can hope for only limited attitude change during training by providing accurate information on which any necessary change can be based. But if a person feels threatened because his beliefs are too severely challenged by the information provided he may reject it and become still more entrenched in his negative attitudes. While it is most undesirable that such a person should lead a problem-solving group, as he may simply stifle it, it is often politically essential that he performs this function. In such a case the activities of the researcher in the group are of particular importance.

124

When we embarked on the ERP we had no clear idea about the range of activities we would need to engage in in the project groups. But in retrospect we see that we could not have functioned effectively by adopting one specific role to the exclusion of all others. Some textbooks of organisation development (see chapter 15) define the action researcher's role in a particular fashion: for example, as a 'process consultant', or being 'non-evaluative', or as a 'fly on the wall' observing, or 'not being prescriptive'. We take the view that the researcher working with problem-solving groups has to have at least half a dozen hats to wear, and requires the skill to know when to change them. He cannot possibly be truly 'neutral' about specific issues, as he has a particular professional expertise and he is often asked to show it. He cannot be entirely 'non-directive', as he has a set of personal values which influence him. Also, by attempting to 'sit outside' the group to be 'objective', he can easily lose sight of the meaning of the group and specific issues to the group members, and his understanding of the process therefore becomes limited.

We would not like to convey the impression that we were always flexible, clever and perceptive enough to change our behaviour to suit the demands of the situation. Some groups were relatively ineffective and other researchers could perhaps have encouraged greater progress. Indeed, over time it became evident that we differed amongst ourselves in the emphasis that we gave to the various roles described in this chapter. For example, some of us adopted a more positive, structuring role, making sure that the groups had agreed on action and had allocated somebody to execute this action. We sometimes wrote up notes for the group leader if he found this difficult. Others took a less directive approach, more in line with traditional thinking in organisation development. This view is based on the assumption that group members will learn more, and be less dependent on the researcher, if they grapple with their difficulties themselves.

On balance we have concluded that a more structuring approach, where we 'showed the way it should be done', was more effective in helping to maintain the formal activities of the Project. This was partly because many groups did not meet sufficiently often as a group to develop their own strategies and norms, and also because the culture of the organisation tended to create a climate where people were fairly dependent on authority figures for the direction of their activities. Yet the structuring role seemed less desirable in senior management groups which were functioning workteams in themselves and where self-help was the customary way of operating.

Clearly, the action researcher's role has to be tuned in to the culture of the organisation and its subgroups. Much of the work of the Employee Relations Project was with shop-floor people, whereas the bulk of the organisation development literature concerns managers and professional staff. It is unwise to generalise preferred researcher roles from one setting to all others. Nevertheless, there is force in the customary argument that a structuring style can encourage dependence on the researcher so that organisational members do not bother to create their own procedures for coping with future problems. For this reason we paid much attention to the institution of longer-term structures in the form of improved consultative and other mechanisms.

The context of problem generation

A similar issue arises for the mechanisms of the ERP itself. One valuable feature was the initiation of a very clear method to elicit, record, and progress problems and solutions. Yet dependence upon any such method may lead to information being squeezed into meanings which were not intended by the persons raising an issue. In other words, the researcher may exclude the true psychological meaning of a problem by imposing his method upon it. In this way we sometimes lost sight of the context of a person's problems and made unwarranted assumptions that he was likely to devote considerable energy to their eradication.

Organisational support for the group's activities

This is a key theme which emerges in most parts of the book. If members of a group perceive that their efforts are not reciprocated by other significant people in the organisation they can soon lose the will to participate. This illustrates why it is necessary very firmly to set down the foundations of the programme from an organisationally wide base, right from the start. Of course, that is easier said than done, and it was a dilemma that we wrestled with throughout the Project. Our evidence from progress in different departments suggests that the more initial overall commitment that existed, the more successful were the groups (see chapter 15).

One feature that is worth re-emphasising is that the group needs to perceive support. Sometimes groups would actually get support, but not perceive it as such because of the way it was communicated. Thus, it is most desirable for some work to be undertaken before meetings on the likely difficulties in communicating with the problem-solving groups, alerting likely participants to the difficulties that might be encountered and how they could be overcome. At the heart of such an effort should be an examination of the differences in language and concepts used by different professional and non-professional groups in the organisation.

Aspirations and expectations

The extent to which people in a project such as the ERP believe that worthwhile changes have come about depends upon the shifts in their expectations and aspirations. We felt that expectations in some groups were set unrealistically: whether unrealistically high or unrealistically low. One role for the researcher in the group is to encourage discussion on what the group is likely to be able to achieve through its actions, emphasising the place of the group within the organisation as a whole. This requires some understanding of the issues involved in overcoming structural barriers to change, and in particular the likely time-scales involved. Such action should help to throw into perspective the power of particular groups to effect changes, and where expectations of success are likely to be greatest. Thus we might avoid the occasions where a group becomes frustrated because a change which it desires does not come about overnight, despite the organisation's attempts to speed up what is inevitably a long sequence of decisions.

Notes

[1] A helpful general introduction is provided by E.H. Schein in *Process Consultation*, Addison Wesley, New York, 1969. See also the chapter by M. Beer on 'The technology of organization development' in M.D. Dunnette (ed.), *Handbook of Organizational Psychology*, Rand McNally, Chicago, 1976.

[2] See, for example, C.L. Cooper, *Theories of Group Process*, Wiley, London, 1975; N. Rackham, P. Honey and M. Colbert, *Developing Interactive Skills*, Wellens Publishing, Northampton 1971; N. Rackham and T. Morgan, *Behaviour Analysis in Training*, McGraw-Hill, London, 1977.

[3] Illustrations are provided in S. Gellerman, *Behavioural Science in Management*, Penguin, Harmondsworth, 1974.

[4] This point is examined by F.E. Fiedler and M.M. Chemers, *Leadership and Effective Management*, Scott Foresman, Illinois, 1974; and by S. Fineman and I. Mangham in P. Warr (ed.), *Psychology at Work*, Penguin, Harmondsworth, 1978 (2nd edition).

[5] See, for example, S. Fineman, 'Changing managers or changing situations', *Industrial and Commercial Training*, vol. 7, 1975, pp. 410–13. A comprehensive account of research on the issue of changing leaders and/or situations is provided by J.G. Hunt and L.L. Larson, *Contingency Approaches to Leadership*, Southern Illinois University Press, Carbondale, Illinois, 1974.

11   Data feedback and other procedures

The last chapter identified eight procedures for planned organisational change and discussed aspects of the first four:

1   Educational, training or counselling activities.
2   Process consultation.
3   Intergroup communication meetings.
4   Problem-solving meetings.
5   Data feedback procedures.
6   Assistance with the development of plans and policies.
7   Establishment of longer-term structures.
8   Technological innovations.

The present chapter carries forward this discussion to examine the remaining procedures, with particular emphasis on data feedback since this figured prominently in the Employee Relations Project.

Data feedback procedures

A traditional function of consultants of all kinds (financial, technical, engineering as well as psychological) is to gather data about the state of an organisation and feed it back for discussion and action. The type of material which is collected is naturally dependent upon the consultant and his purpose; in our case it is material about people, their relationships and their attitudes which is of central concern.

Data feedback activities by psychologists in organisations may be viewed in terms of the length of the feedback cycle. Short-cycle feedback occurs, for example, in process consultation of the kind illustrated in the previous chapter, whereas longer feedback loops are present in the activity which has become known as 'survey feedback'. Two forms of this were featured in the Employee Relations Project. During the Interlinked Phase (see chapter 6) a substantial amount of information was gathered about industrial relations mechanisms and styles on the works. This information was fed back to shop stewards and managers through summary reports, and major themes were subsequently developed in our Interim Report.

However, the principal use of survey feedback was through the project questionnaire, described in chapter 5. We will now consider the general applicability of such opinion questionnaires and examine some of the factors influencing the likely success of survey feedback in general.

The process has three stages: the systematic collection of opinion data by questionnaire, the preparation of summaries of the material so gained, and the presentation of these summaries to the original respondents for them to examine and make recommendations about possible action. Both managers and non-managers can thus be involved at several points, although it is usual for outside researchers or consultants to assist with questionnaire design, statistical analysis and preparation of summary information.

Some differences between our application of survey feedback and the more usual ones should be noted. In many cases the survey feedback exercise stands on its own, so that the first stage is the design and completion of a questionnaire with the feedback group discussions following later. We had preferred to see survey feedback as only one element in an integrated programme built around project groups. Furthermore, we chose to initiate meetings of these groups before moving into the questionnaire stage, in order to increase initial commitment and to ensure that the survey questions would be particularly appropriate for the workforce. Another difference was that the project groups also served as the groups through which results were fed back; in other studies workgroups covering all members of a department have sometimes been brought together specifically to discuss the results of a survey.

The value of survey feedback has already been documented [1], and we expected that our amendments would create an overall programme which was more effective than survey feedback alone. This expectation appears to have been borne out, but the structure of the Employee Relations Project was such that the survey feedback component did not operate in quite the conventional way. We turn now to examine eight features of the process which the Employee Relations Project and the wider research literature indicate to be important. These concern: the involvement of shop-floor participants; management's commitment; the questionnaire items and layout; the feedback process; a mechanism for decision-making; organisational willingness to use the results; the outside researchers or consultants; and the location of the survey feedback component in the overall programme.

The involvement of shop-floor participants

It is by now generally accepted that survey feedback will have limited value unless the questionnaire respondents have a substantial involvement in the process. There are, of course, difficulties in specifying the minimum level and breadth of involvement which are required, but there has to be evidence that many employees want the programme to be undertaken. Management's wishes are important here, and we will consider these shortly, but it is shop-floor and non-supervisory staff employees who usually make up the bulk of participants.

How does one encourage and gauge involvement? Written publicity is obviously important (in our case through several issues of *Focus*), as is discussion with a representative group (in our case the Project Steering Committee). But it is extremely hard to assess the interest of a workforce numbering several hundred and scattered across a wide area. Planning discussions will often be held with shop stewards, and their role as opinion-leaders means that their views can be particularly significant.

We have described in Part One the initial reactions of Tinsley Park shop stewards, and have traced their changing opinions across the months of the Project. Although they had, on the whole, initially welcomed the Project, there had from the outset been some doubts in their minds about the project questionnaire: 'the lads don't like filling in bits of paper' and 'you can only really learn what people think by talking with them'. We had responded that the project group meetings and other discussions on the works would provide a more detailed picture, and that the questionnaire was mainly included in order to confirm the generality of opinions expressed in meetings.

In practice, then, the project questionnaire was expected to be a less influential mechanism for change than the project groups. The overall response rate through voluntary completion sessions in works time was eighty-three per cent, and despite an indifference in some sections the level of shop-floor involvement was probably not untypical of large-scale surveys. However, there were substantial variations between workgroups, influenced primarily by management's commitment to the exercise.

Management's commitment

We have already stressed in chapter 7 how the progress of the Project as a whole was greatly influenced by the strength of management interest. This was especially well illustrated through differing attitudes to questionnaire completion.

In one department, management gave strong support to planning and scheduling, rooms were available as required and workpeople arrived punctually with an accurate idea of what was expected of them. Additionally, they were interested enough to make frequent comments and recommendations in the section of the questionnaire provided for these, and they often left the sessions discussing the kinds of changes they would like to see. In another case, the manager who had been designated to organise questionnaire completion had omitted to take any action or to tell his subordinates about the arrangements. The turnout in a third department was initially rather low, and when we pointed out to the relevant manager that he was expected to encourage his employees to take part, he replied: 'Oh, we've slipped up then. I said to them that they shouldn't attend if they didn't fancy it.' In both these cases, steps were taken to retrieve the situation and the final response rate was reasonably good.

Enough has been said to indicate that the commitment of managers and shop-floor people is likely to work together to influence the success of survey feedback. It is hardly surprising that if a foreman or higher manager gives the impression that filling in a questionnaire is unimportant or of low priority, then his subordinates will see it in these terms. And indeed it was not uncommon for a latecomer to say as much when he eventually arrived to attend the completion session.

The reasons for differing levels of managerial commitment to survey feedback are similar to those underlying differing views about projects like the ERP in general. We have seen in chapter 7 how a number of managers felt that the Employee Relations Project was of limited interest to them. This was sometimes because of pressing requirements elsewhere, sometimes because they did not recognise any major problems requiring solution, or because the style of the Project was inconsistent with their personal outlook. These kinds of reaction are particularly likely to be aroused by a questionnaire survey [2]. Such exercises may yield results which are critical of management and give the criticisms a spurious appearance of precision: 'Eighty-nine per cent of shop-floor workers in department A think in this certain way, against only twenty-seven per cent in department B.'

Most people resist suggestions that their work is open to criticism, and the visibility of critical survey results is such that defensive reactions by managers are to be expected. These reactions can take several forms, perhaps denying the worth of the items ('These are all leading questions', or 'These questions are ambiguous'), or objecting to the whole idea ('People will always grumble if you give them such an easy opportunity'). Other reactions might accept the value of the approach, but deny its suitability for the present circumstances: 'The survey was carried out at a bad time', or 'It's management's rejection of the pay claim which has caused all these results.'

Quite clearly, comments of this kind may have some validity, and survey feedback exercises should be carried out at times and with methods which minimise the difficulties. In practice, however, it is still possible to accept the existence of a number of constant biases but to find interest in the rank-ordering of results: 'Granting that the questionnaire and the time were not ideal, why does workgroup X score consistently more positively than workgroup Y on this set of items?'

More generally, the most appropriate interpretation of survey results is one which attributes responsibility to several causes. Some of these might be in the nature of the items or associated with the time of questionnaire completion, but other causes are likely to lie in genuine organisational or managerial problems. A managerial reaction which shifts responsibility for the results of a questionnaire survey to people, events and circumstances but excludes management as a partial cause is usually open to question.

Questionnaire items and layout

The third feature identified as influencing the success of survey feedback is the questionnaire itself. A number of practical issues are relevant here. For example, the items should be appropriate for the departments concerned, so that preliminary interviews and discussions about current issues will usually be required. This argues against the use of standard questionnaires which might be applied in a variety of companies, although a standard approach is often claimed to have the virtue of allowing comparisons with previously obtained data. Our belief is that the benefits attained through local relevance as a springboard to action outweigh the possible advantages of external comparisons, especially since the meaning of questions tends to alter from company to company so that the validity of comparisons is in any case uncertain.

The project questionnaire at Tinsley Park Works undoubtedly gained strength through drawing issues and phrases from project group discussions. Care was also taken to create an attractive layout, with two-colour printing and varied typefaces. However, one possible disadvantage of too 'professional' a questionnaire design is that it may arouse the reaction that the survey must have been expensive, using up financial resources which could be better spent elsewhere. Attractive presentation is thus not to be overdone!

Another aspect of the questionnaire which can influence the success of a survey feedback programme is the kind of written response which is required. Our experience is that three-point or five-point response scales running from agreement to disagreement are the most acceptable. (The project questionnaire used three points.) Nevertheless, some respondents will wish for more alternatives and others for less, and some minor dissatisfaction has always to be expected.

A related issue concerns the appropriateness of a 'not applicable' box as an additional response alternative. This is most likely to be useful if the questions are of very general scope or if many different types of respondents are to use the same questionnaire. The 'not applicable' option at Tinsley Park was rarely used, but it was noticeable that it was most likely to be ticked by clerical and other staff employees in response to matters more directly relevant to the shop-floor than to themselves.

One general issue which will face anyone attempting to obtain questionnaire responses from a shop-floor population concerns the level of literacy in that population. A small percentage of most workgroups of unskilled people will be unable to read the questionnaire or to grasp anything but the simplest of terms. To put these people into a situation where they have to tick responses uncomprehendingly is clearly undesirable, and one should be alert to the person who has 'forgotten his glasses' or presents other excuses for non-attendance.

The feedback process

A fourth factor influencing the success of survey feedback is to do with the feedback channel itself. Several aspects of this need to be considered.

Some projects have relied entirely upon feedback of results through notice boards or written reports; this is much less effective than a system of discussion meetings [3]. The level at which the feedback occurs is also important, in that results need to be clearly relevant to individual departments or groups. The chosen level of feedback will depend upon local circumstances, but mere presentation of responses for a large works as a whole lacks the immediacy and precision required to engage interest. At Tinsley Park the material was grouped in terms of each department's results, split into 'shop floor and non-supervisory staff' and 'managers and foremen', with the overall works figures in these two categories given for comparison.

The main examination of results was through the project groups themselves. This allowed us to use the established mechanisms of the Project, but it had the disadvantage that specialised small groups were asked to comment upon the overall views of the department as a whole. Other programmes have fed back data for each individual workgroup to discuss its own responses. This has the advantage of very direct relevance to the discussions, but it requires more complex statistical and administrative work.

Another aspect of feedback concerns the person who conducts the meetings. In general, it appears that interested line managers are more effective than personnel specialists or outside consultants, although the manager's own commitment to the exercise will clearly also be influential here. Managers who have previously studied the material and are familiar with its main characteristics are also known to be more effective than those not previously briefed [3].

For the bulk of the workforce at Tinsley Park our principal channel of feedback was *Focus*. Meetings were held with the Steering Committee and with senior managers, but no formal presentations were made to shop-floor groups via their foremen or managers. This approach to the feedback process differed from other studies, and may well have reduced the effectiveness of the survey feedback exercise in relation to its usually-defined goals. However, within the ERP as a whole, the feedback procedures employed were in general successful in maintaining the Project's momentum and in confirming the importance of issues already under discussion through the project groups. It is likely that an additional network of group meetings would have been seen as an unnecessary burden on an already very busy works.

A mechanism for decision-making

The main objective of survey feedback is to provide a company with information about itself which it can use to improve its effectiveness. A crucial stage is thus the point where the information is turned into action. Is there a formal procedure for using the feedback material to identify major issues, for examining possible solutions, choosing from amongst these, nominating the people responsible for action, and following up their progress?

Those feedback discussions which did take place at Tinsley Park were not structured in this way, and their success was accordingly reduced. In retrospect, albeit slightly caricatured, it seems that we tended to assume that the mere presentation of information would spontaneously lead to decisions about change. This was not so, and a more closely structured procedure and briefing for feedback leaders would have been desirable.

On the other hand, there was ample opportunity for managers to study the survey results and to base subsequent decisions upon them. We have informal evidence that this occurred quite widely, and it was not uncommon to hear managers cite particular questionnaire responses in the course of their routine meetings. Survey feedback can lead to action in the absence of a formal mechanism for decision-making, but the existence of such a mechanism is assuredly a help.

Organisational willingness to use the results

It is convenient to separate out willingness to use the results as a sixth factor influencing the success of survey feedback, although it is clearly associated with other features mentioned here.

Shop-floor and management concern for the programme becomes especially important at the action stage. Workpeople and their trade union representatives have a major role here, since the distinguishing feature of survey feedback is the part-ownership of the results by employees below management level. Conventional attitude surveys yield data and interpretation for management alone, but survey feedback is for all employees. It follows that if non-managers fail to use the process, then one goal has not been attained. In a sense, the material is for shop stewards and their members to apply, and this fact needs to be made explicit and welcomed from the outset.

By the same token the material is also for the use of managers, and we have already commented on the understandable reluctance of some to respond positively at Tinsley Park. A key to understanding this is to be found in the role of higher management in shaping the behaviour of their subordinates. Studies have repeatedly indicated that unless senior management show interest, manipulate incentives, and attempt to mould expectations, then survey feedback is unlikely to yield extensive action by their subordinates. Few managers can do everything that they would like to do, and priorities have to be set; the ordering of these priorities is in part determined by senior management and their indication of what kinds of behaviour are to be rewarded. A survey feedback exercise is thus likely to be less than fully effective if encouragement and pressure from senior management are lacking.

The outside researchers or consultants

The seventh factor influencing success is the part played by outsider researchers or consultants. It is apparent that these must earn trust and respect within the company, but the bases of their acceptability are difficult to specify.

Most companies initiating survey feedback will be doing so for the first time, so that detailed knowledge of procedures and problems will be lacking. Here is one major advantage of the outside researcher or consultant. A second advantage is his range of skills in questionnaire design, statistical analysis and interpretation, planning of meetings, training participants, guiding discussions and helping with disagreements. Within-company resources might instead be devoted to these tasks, and effective survey feedback exercises may well be mounted on that basis, but two problems concerning the internal researcher should be noted. First, is he part of a continuing personnel or other function or does he have to be drawn from other tasks for the period of the exercise? In either case there may be difficulties of personal career development and of relationships with colleagues after the exercise.

Second, the in-company researcher needs to be known as a relatively non-partisan person; selecting a manager with, for example, strong anti-union views for the role would clearly be unwise. Since the situations where the project is likely to be especially useful are often those where attitudes have hardened over the years, there may be problems here.

The location of the survey feedback component in the overall programme

A final issue requiring comment is the place of a survey feedback exercise in a larger programme. In some cases it may stand on its own, and the themes examined in this section will naturally be applicable. Especially important, however, will be the process of gaining interest and commitment prior to the questionnaire itself. We noted in chapter 1 how the impact of previous surveys has sometimes been limited by inadequate preparation and 'unfreezing'.

When the survey feedback exercise is part of a larger programme, as with the Employee Relations Project, its goals and possible impact may be somewhat different. We have noted how the Tinsley Park questionnaire did not lead to major changes directly through feedback groups, but that it had several other important functions. It gave everyone the opportunity to express their opinions on issues of personal importance and for some groups it maintained the Project's momentum. The fed-back results were available for use by anyone who chose, and this widespread availability provided public evidence that the promises made at the outset of the Project were being upheld. For reasons of this kind, the feedback exercise was undoubtedly worthwhile.

Conclusions

Our aim in this section has been to explore some of the factors making for success in data feedback exercises. We have concentrated upon the longer-cycle process of survey feedback. The involvement of shop-floor participants and management has been identified as of principal importance, together with a general organisational willingness to use the results of an investigation. Practical aspects of the questionnaire items and layout, the feedback process, and mechanisms for decision-making have also been noted, together with the role of outside researchers or consultants. In addition, we should mention the extent to which change is required in the first place; without a strong perceived need for change within the company, the use of survey feedback is in any case inadvisable. Finally, the location of the feedback component in a larger programme has been seen to have an important influence on goals, procedures and evaluation criteria.

Assistance with the development of plans and policies

The sixth type of action research activity identified earlier is one involving assistance with the development of new plans and policies. In practice this may be achieved through participation in planning groups and an ongoing contribution through discussions, or it might occur through the presentation of formal reports to management or to the company as a whole.

There is a tendency for some psychologists and other behavioural scientists to prefer not to make formal recommendations themselves. They note that commitment arises more readily from internally generated suggestions, and they may sometimes be nervous about the obvious limits to their knowledge of detailed technical operations on the plant. Yet the diverse character of the eight procedures for change which this chapter and the previous one have examined indicates clearly that there is a need for flexibility in the researcher's role. There are undoubtedly circumstances where his knowledge, his status within the organisation, and the wishes of management make it helpful for him to spell out his own views about possible changes in structure and policy.

This occurred in some project groups of the ERP, and in the later stages through our Interim Report. In this we reviewed a variety of issues and made our suggestions available to all levels of the works. A formal report has considerable merit in that it focusses attention on topics which may otherwise not attain a priority which ensures their formal examination. In the case of the Employee Relations Project we have described in chapter 6 how the Interim Report recommendations supplied the agenda for some ten special meetings of managers or of managers and workpeople.

In general this element of the Project had more immediate impact than the survey feedback component. This was partly because the Interim Report constituted a visible decision point, being introduced towards the end of the Project. In part also it was because care was taken to create a formal structure of meetings to examine and evaluate the recommendations, although this was less explicit at senior management levels.

The factors governing the effectiveness of recommendations are similar to those described in the previous section, although in this case the value of the suggestions themselves and their political practicality are additionally important. One problem is that changes of major significance are likely to have implications outside the single works in question, so that recommendations soon come up against the boundaries of the programme as initially conceived and agreed. Because of the scale of operations and the interdependence of issues, senior management's willingness to examine the broader aspects of their organisation is undoubtedly the principal influence upon developments at this level. However, within most large organisations the constraints upon even quite senior managers are severe, and a range of top managers need to be convinced before large innovations are possible. This point is further considered in chapter 15.

Establishment of longer-term structures

A major aim of any programme like the ERP is to provide structures which will create the means to continue improvements attempted by the programme itself. This can, of course, be achieved by a variety of the procedures already described.

The central goals of the Employee Relations Project were in terms of better problem identification and joint solution in the area of employee relations, and several components were built into the Project to help towards those goals. But it was important to look beyond the end of the Project, so that new procedures for negotiating, new communication channels and new decision-making networks became continuing parts of the works' operation. This is partly a question of the changed definition and execution or roles, and we have illustrated throughout Part One the ways in which such changes evolved.

Technological innovations

The final type of change activity which we have identified is in terms of technological innovation. One obvious way to improve a company's effectiveness is to improve its technological efficiency, through new equipment, processes or raw materials. Such change programmes are more the province of the engineer, the metallurgist, the chemist, the purchasing expert or the computer scientist than the psychologist, so that a programme to develop employee relations does not often become heavily involved in technological change.

Yet there are circumstances in which the more psychological change processes can be fruitfully linked with technical innovation. For example, the human factors implications of new production systems need to be studied at a very early stage if useful suggestions are to be made. In programmes like ERP, problem-solving discussions necessarily lead into questions of possible technical improvements, and dozens of minor changes to equipment and working practices resulted from the project groups. Other change programmes in the area of job design and work structuring have a stronger component of technical innovation.

Concluding remarks

It was noted at the beginning of chapter 10 that each programme of organisational change has its own mix of the eight sets of change activities. It is helpful to conclude this discussion with a summary statement of the emphasis given to the eight components in the Employee Relations Project. This will allow comparisons with future programmes of similar purpose.

We have attempted a rough scaling on each component below. It is essential to recognise that the profile is in terms of the Project as it actually took place; in some cases the original intention might have been for greater or lesser emphasis.

1	Educational, training or counselling activities	Little emphasis
2	Process consultation	Some emphasis

3	Intergroup communication meetings	Some emphasis
4	Problem-solving meetings	Considerable emphasis
5	Data feedback procedures	Moderate emphasis
6	Assistance with the development of plans and policies	Some emphasis
7	Establishment of longer-term structures	Some emphasis
8	Technological innovations	Little emphasis

Finally, we should once again stress that the eight approaches are, of course, to some extent interdependent. For example, data feedback procedures can flow into problem-solving meetings, and assistance with the development of plans often requires the establishment of longer-term structures. Such overlap is to be expected in any complex programme of change.

Notes

[1] Useful examinations of survey feedback may be found in D.G. Bowers, 'OD techniques and their results in 23 organizations', *Journal of Applied Behavioural Science*, vol. 9, pp. 21–43; F. Friedlander and L.D. Brown, 'Organization development', *Annual Review of Psychology*, vol. 25, 1974, pp. 313–341; W. French and C.H. Bell, *Organizational Development*, Prentice-Hall, Englewood Cliffs, 1973; F. Heller, Chapter 15 in A.W. Clark (ed.), *Experimenting with Organizational Life*, Plenum Press, London, 1976; and the chapter by M.G. Miles and co-authors in W.G. Bennis, K.D. Benne and R. Chin (eds.), *The Planning of Change*, Holt, New York, 1969.

[2] See the chapter by D. Sirota ('Why managers don't use attitude survey results') in S.W. Gellerman (ed.), *Behavioural Science in Management*, Penguin, Harmondsworth, 1974.

[3] See S.M. Klein, A.I. Kraut and A. Wolfson, 'Employee reactions to attitude survey feedback', *Administrative Science Quarterly*, vol. 16, 1971, pp. 497–514.

12 Organisational types: ideals and realities

The previous three chapters have examined the character of relationships between action researchers and organisations and the main procedures which have been used to assist the development of employee relations. We turn now to look at organisations in terms of their context, processes and structure. The ideas are first summarised in a general schema and will then be applied to Tinsley Park at the time of the Employee Relations Project.

A schema of organisational types

The word 'organisation' has two main meanings, associated first with giving 'orderly structure to' and second with achieving 'wholeness' or 'working interdependence among parts'. We will examine the structures commonly found in industry and elsewhere and consider how these contribute to the achievement of working interdependence. Figure 12.1 presents the main topics of this chapter in the form of an illustrative schema. This is in terms of three sets of concepts: those to do with the contextual factors relevant to decisions about how to organise; those processes which occur in organising; and finally, a typology of structures which define the dominant and regularly occurring processes. In practice the three sets of concepts are intertwined both in content and in time.

The left-hand section of the schema summarises principal organisational goals and indicates how their priority is determined by various conditioning factors. The central section indicates that an organisational system needs to manage three principal sets of activities (maintenance, breakdown and development) and that these processes are undertaken by varying combinations of social differentiation and social integration. By 'differentiation' we mean that different people with different skills and statuses do different things to manage the processes, and by 'integration' we mean mechanisms which are designed to bring together the efforts of people in different parts of the system. In a sense differentiation attempts to create order, and integration attempts to create unity. The last part of the schema implies that this complex set of processes results in each organisation having a dominant type of structure which has developed partly under the influence of senior decision-makers' beliefs about what 'managing' involves. We stress 'dominant' type of structure here because in different parts of the organisation there may be different types.

Organisational goals

The first six goals in Figure 12.1 are taken from Perrow [1], and seem relatively

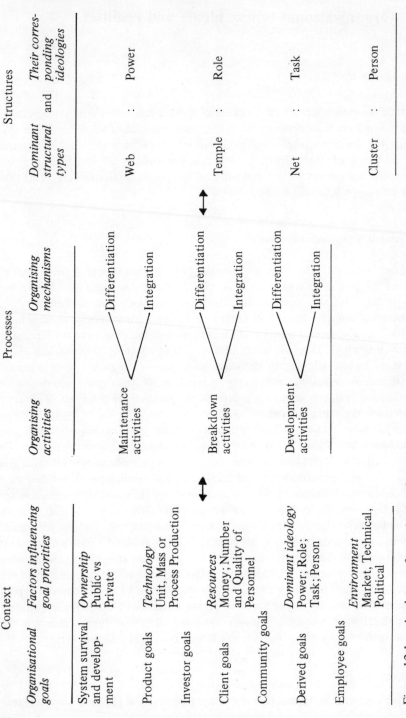

Figure 12.1   A schema of organisational types

140

self-explanatory although one or two require some clarification. In service organisations such as hospitals it may sometimes be difficult to distinguish between client goals and product goals since the product is a service to the client and will, one assumes, meet the client's needs. Community goals refer to the efforts of the organisation to legitimise its activities in the broader society. Such goals are often high on the list of priorities for fringe organisations like new political parties, and for organisations under some threat from society, cigarette manufacturers for example. Derived goals are those which are not directly connected with the organisation's main function but have developed out of some related activities. For instance, the staffs of some welfare organisations often get involved in radical politics.

We have added employee goals to the list in the Figure because organisations cannot function without satisfying the needs of their employees. Furthermore, the development of large trade unions illustrates how employees can no longer be classified as part of the organisation in such a way as to include them within goals relating to the maintenance and development of the system.

Factors influencing goal priorities

Organisations may give each of these goals a different priority, and the Figure lists some of the factors which can influence those priorities. Ownership refers to whether the organisation is family owned, publicly owned or is owned by shareholders. This last form of ownership is likely to lead to a higher concern for the goals of its investors. The family owners of the firm might see themselves as the investor, and thus give their own satisfactions high priority. Or they may choose to give higher priority to the product, or to the employees if they have a paternalistic tradition.

Obviously the type of production technology (the second influencing factor) affects goals. However, although each particular technology is designed in the first place specifically to achieve product and client goals, production systems can last many years and their influence over goals may change with time. The simplest classification of production methods is 'service' versus 'manufacturing', with 'manufacturing' divided into three types: unit production systems, where the output is made in single units (computers, ships, hand-made pottery); mass production, where the output is weighed or counted (cars, television sets); and process production, where there is continuous throughput of much the same materials, as in petrochemicals or continuous-casting steelmaking [2]. Production in unit production technologies is uniquely designed to meet client needs, so that these have priority, whilst in mass production systems product goals may have high priority: once the product is made it must be good enough to sell in large numbers. Where the technology is complex and capital intensive the organisation may need to borrow money to sustain it, so that investor goals may become more important. The changing fortunes of a company are likely to affect goal priorities in all types of organisations.

The third influencing factor under the 'Context' heading of Figure 12.1 is resources. If money or people are in short supply, then investor and employee goals are likely to become priority issues. The effects of the dominant ideology (the fourth factor) permeate the whole organisation, having their influence on goals and the means to achieve goals since they affect strategies of control and coordination. This influence is further emphasised in the right-hand section of the schema by directly linking the four types of dominant ideology to four types of organisation structure.

The power ideology characterises people who are motivated by their ability to influence the fate of people and events through their own forcefulness and ability. Entrepreneurs often have this characteristic. Things happen because they decide they will happen. Their powerful, charismatic personality often carries others along with them, so that they may generate great loyalty. The corresponding organisational form takes a web as its metaphor, with specialist strands moving out into the organisation but held together by the strong central component. Such structures are political organisations with few rules and procedures but much concern for doing what the 'centre' wants, often based on experience and/or intuition rather than logic. 'They judge by results and are tolerant of means [3].'

Many successful family businesses have this web form. They run into difficulties when the business grows too large for the centre to retain its charismatic influence and control. Web organisations also run into problems when the leader leaves or retires or is involved in a struggle for power with another person (perhaps a member of the family) who also has strong power needs [4].

The structural analogy for the role ideology (the second one listed in Figure 12.1) is the Greek temple with strong supporting pillars (professionally trained specialists) coordinated by the pediment on top, the managerial team. Its less complimentary title in Western countries is bureaucracy, and it is characterised by clearly defined roles, set standards of behaviour and performance for role occupants, documentation of records and achievements, with limits of authority and responsibility clearly defined, and the requirements for entry to valued positions closely specified to guard against nepotism. The temple structure is founded on a commitment to rationality and legalistic responsibility, and if the environment remains stable for long periods then it can be a very effective organisational form. But bureaucracies are difficult to change quickly, since they encourage individuals to identify with a particular specialism or profession, and lengthy educational investment is hard to put aside. The segmentation created by the division of labour also makes effective communication a difficult and time-consuming task. Whilst the armies of clerks predicted by Parkinson do not usually take control, their presence indicates the reliance on written and numerical communication [5]. Another much maligned characteristic of bureaucracies is convoluted decision-making, or 'buck-passing'. Organisations designed for economies of scale almost always have a temple structure and a role ideology, and many claim that this is the dominant organisational form of the twentieth century [6].

The task ideology (the third one in the Figure) has goal attainment as its god.

Getting the job done takes priority over people and systems: 'the task culture utilizes the power of the group to improve efficiency and to identify the individual with the objective of the organisation' [3]. The metaphor of the net can be used to describe the dominant organisational form of the task ideology, in that a net is similar to a 'matrix structure'. This has become the jargon term for describing systems which organise their work partly or wholly into tasks done by temporary groups. The task groups draw people from specialist sub-units which have their own functional heads, and any one person from a sub-unit may work on one or more projects at a time. The projects are managed by project leaders so that a team member has two bosses, one for his sub-unit and one for each project. The dominant ideology is to complete each current task, and the project managers and the functional managers work hard to negotiate the attainment of this goal. It is a flexible system in organisations where task priorities change quickly and influence is based on the capacity to solve particular problems at particular times, contrasting greatly with a role-based system where task responsibilities are determined by formal status and prescribed authority.

The modern aerospace industry in North America is characterised by the matrix form though other types of institutions have adopted it [7]. Whilst it is an ideology which has great psychological appeal to some highly trained managers, organisations contain many routine tasks which do not supply the challenge and change that feeds the task-oriented appetite. It is difficult to obtain close control and coordination in the matrix (net) structure and the main method is resource control determined by top managers. When tasks become more predictable and volume and costs become important, the net structure is often found to have too many holes to ensure survival and the organisation may be forced to change towards a role ideology and a temple structure. The net system demands high personal qualities of flexibility, creativity and commitment and is therefore vulner-able to the poaching of high quality personnel. It may also lose people through the strain imposed by a constant task emphasis. As in so many other cases, the seeds of its downfall lie side by side with the seeds of its success.

When the person is at the centre of the dominant organisational ideology (the final possibility listed to the right of Figure 12.1) there is an immediate tension between the needs of the individual and the demands of the organisation. It is not surprising that these tensions can become too great to control when the diversity of individuals becomes large. Person cultures therefore tend to occur in small organisations where superordinate goals do not intrude on the basic goals of optimising the person's needs. Communes, families, small consultancies and professional partnerships might nurture this kind of social system. The cluster is suggested as an appropriate structural analogue of such a system since no one element of the cluster is dominant, and there is no constant pattern to the spatial or power arrangements within the cluster. Whilst this is rarely the dominant form in work organisations, there are many individuals who embrace its ideology and try to use the organisation to create a sub-cultural niche of this kind. Research specialists, organisation development groups and university professors sometimes succeed in operating in this way.

The difficulties of living out this ideology even amongst people committed to it are well documented in the many failures of communes [8], but for those that work well no other way of organising seems as adequate. Indeed, recent legislation in Scandinavia is pushing even large bureaucratic organisations towards the person ideology. This legislation is aimed at making all entries to the organisation, and departures from it, the subject of participative decision-making between managers and employee representatives.

These four conditioning variables of ownership, technology, resources and ideology are all potentially affected by the fifth one shown to the left of Figure 12.1, the organisation's environment. Political, economic and knowledge factors individually and together act to create a stable or unstable environment which may affect the other conditioning variables and ultimately the goals of the organisation. Thus organisations differ in the priorities they give to different goals, and in unstable environments the priorities within an organisation are also likely to change quite rapidly.

System processes

As we stated at the beginning of this chapter, organisations need to develop distinctive processes to achieve internal order and effectiveness. These processes have been classified in many different ways, some of which are complex [9]. We have adopted what seems to be the simplest and most general classification, one which applies equally well to a marriage as to a large organisation. It identifies three main activities: maintenance, breakdown and development.

1 *Maintenance processes.* These are all those activities carried out to keep the system in a steady state. In large organisations maintenance activities are to be found in specialised forms in the production system, the financial system, the administrative functions, and personnel and sales departments. These undertake the day-to-day running of the organisation. Note that this is the sense in which we are using the term 'maintenance'; the familiar use in terms of engineering maintenance falls within the next heading.

2 *Breakdown processes.* These may need to be carried out in any section of the organisation which experiences a crisis or functional breakdown. Such 'breakdowns' are not confined to equipment or machines, so that any part of the organisation may be required to contribute to the breakdown process. However, this work tends to be specialised in top management, marketing departments and parts of engineering and production, with specialists in industrial relations increasingly evident on the crisis management scene.

3 *Development processes.* These are activities concerned with finding new markets, products or operating procedures which will increase the capacity of the organisation and in the long run improve its chances of surviving and competing successfully. Marketing, research and development, organisation and methods, organisation development and corporate planning are the

specialist departments which bear the brunt of these activities, but the development of maintenance and breakdown processes may also be included under this heading.

Organising mechanisms

Lawrence and Lorsch [10] have proposed that social systems have two main ways in which they ensure that organising activities are carried out. One is by a strategy of differentiation: breaking down tasks into well-defined parts and allocating them to particular individuals who are trained to do them efficiently. This takes place in two directions. First, it occurs vertically, so that more and more difficult jobs are given to people with higher qualifications and greater experience. Usually, greater authority is also granted with this increase in task difficulty or responsibility, and higher status, pay and other marks of distinction may be attached to such roles. This naturally leads to the classical Greek temple structure based on role ideology. Second, differentiation occurs horizontally, so that, for example, at the top of a large organisation the managers who report to the chief executive may all have the same status and authority but each be a specialist in his own area (production, marketing, etc.). At the lowest levels in large mass production technologies the differentiation may be so fine as to distinguish by title persons who open cardboard cartons and persons who place the central dividing sections inside them: openers and inserters!

Such extreme task differentiation obviously demands some complementary mechanisms to coordinate the activities of these different roles. This may be called integration. In the Greek temple model horizontal integration is achieved by having a little pediment at each vertical level which coordinates the various pillars beneath it. Integration is also achieved by rules and procedures which attempt to legislate the direction and frequency of communication. Face-to-face contact between managers at adjacent levels is also used to facilitate coordination. As organisations have become more complex and the environment more turbulent and less predictable, some organisations have developed specialist integrative roles either on a permanent or temporary basis. Indeed, some of these are large enough to be established as separate departments, so we have the paradox of specialisation being used to achieve integration.

The schema in Figure 12.1 attempts to convey that each of the three organising activities of maintenance, breakdown and development can be achieved by differing degrees of differentiation and integration. We can look at different organisations to see how the three activities are principally handled. For example, in one organisation there may be very little differentiation in breakdown processes so that each manager and supervisor is expected to tackle problems as they arise. In another there may be high differentiation with different specialists handling production breakdowns, industrial relations problems, customer complaints, shareholders' complaints and so on. Integration in the first organisation may be unsystematic but based on face-to-face contact or a network of informal grapevines. In the latter it will occur mainly at the top levels and then be passed down on a 'need to know basis'. The first organisation is likely to develop a web or a net structure whilst the second is likely to resemble the temple structure.

Within the same organisation the different system processes of maintenance, breakdown and development may have different degrees of differentiation and integration and thus give rise to different sub-structural types. In a medium-size manufacturing organisation both breakdown and maintenance processes may follow the temple model with a specialist maintenance department for production breakdowns and a personnel department for the 'human' problems. However, development processes might be much less formalised so that marketing, product development, training and systems development may be carried out by a diffuse group of interested managers with a web or, less likely, a cluster structure. As organisations get larger the tendency is for all these processes to become specialised [11], resulting in a temple structure or a series of temple structures, each with some degree of autonomy according to how the organisation is decentralised — by product or by region.

Our schema takes a 'contingency' approach to organisations. Each organisation weights its methods of managing the processes of maintenance, breakdown and development in idiosyncratic ways to suit the particular circumstances, or contingencies, in which it finds itself. There is no one best way of organising. Any of the four main structural types may be approximated as a result of quite different combinations of environmental and ideological factors: the structural types we have defined are notional 'pure' types which are rarely identifiable in real life. One emphasis of this framework which is absent from many organisational theories is on the values or ideologies of the controlling 'élites', which are seen to have a major influence on the choices made. Environmental, technological and resource factors do exert considerable constraints, but ideology plays a major part [12]. The schema provides a way of thinking about why particular structures occur, but it does not, and cannot, predict which structures will occur. However, it can be used to suggest a way of examining the structure and processes in particular organisations such as Tinsley Park Works.

The schema applied to Tinsley Park Works

It is appropriate here to treat Tinsley Park Works as an organisation itself, so that Stocksbridge will be regarded as part of the plant's environment even though within the context of British Steel Corporation as a whole the two sites were regarded as one functional unit. Research has confirmed that one of the effects of belonging to a larger corporation is to centralise decision-making at the top of the organisation [13]. Indeed, some control is often taken out of the organisation altogether so that key decisions are made by other parts of the corporation. In our case, we have seen how some deicisions were made by managers at Stocksbridge and some beyond there. Stocksbridge Works was, of course, itself subject to superordinate control of this kind.

In terms of the schema, centralisation is here acting as an integrative device to coordinate and control the highly differentiated structure that exists in a large industry like steelmaking. Although Tinsley Park Works had no specialists to deal with marketing and sales, it was specialised into production departments and by service functions such as engineering, quality control, personnel and industrial relations. Its dominant structural type was the temple with a strong powerful roof holding the pillars together; and the roof was located above the level of the plant, so that the Works Manager at Tinsley Park had only limited authority over some areas of activity. This differentiated structure, with centralisation, rules and procedures as the main integrating mechanisms, is the one that dominates two of the three system processes of maintenance (mainly through production) and breakdown. Plant breakdown on the site was handled by engineering and other support services or was contracted out. Social system breakdowns were handled by the formal management system or by the industrial relations functions largely controlled from outside the works.

The structure of development processes at Tinsley Park was much less clear. Technical development was principally carried out beyond the works itself though managers on the site were involved in managing and planning new plant installations such as those in progress in the Melting Shop. For this task they used a task group system similar to the net or matrix structure. There were trainers for each of the production departments but they concentrated on operator training, and supervisory and management training was guided from Stocksbridge and even further afield in BSC.

The development of the managerial and administrative system was the responsibility of the Works Manager, although all department managers were, of course, responsible for their own departments. In this way the development processes were not entirely specialised but were horizontally differentiated across the plant. They were on the whole given lower priority than system maintenance work. However, the Employee Relations Project itself might be regarded as an attempt to increase awareness about development processes, and for this we were used as a temporary specialist group approximating to a net structure. Limited attention to development processes is not unusual in plants which are solely production units and are subject to continuing contextual pressures.

A return to the schema in Figure 12.1 allows us to consider the goal priorities and some of the factors which may have influenced them. Tinsley Park Works was built to produce steel on a more or less continuous basis. The selling function was located physically and organisationally outside the works, and production is its *raison d'être*. The technology was a mixture of process and batch production and one consequence of the high capital investment involved was that profitability depended greatly on a high rate of production. In many industries with this kind of production technology some stockpiling occurs during turndowns in the market in order to ensure continuity of future production. This has not usually occurred in British steelmaking, where the convention has been to produce to order. Thus the industry has been more vulnerable than some similar types of production systems to market forces.

Survival goals probably come next, from those in Figure 12.1, and survival was largely guaranteed by continuing to meet production goals in an efficient and profitable way. The goals which we would guess to be the next priority were employee goals and the priority they had was partly derived from the British Steel Corporation itself. The Corporation's policy was to get human relations and communications in better shape, and the Employee Relations Project was a sign of this concern. The high differentiation within BSC as a whole made integrating these social policies very difficult indeed, and the variety of payment systems, administrative procedures, different customs and practices that had been brought together through nationalisation lay at the root of some of the industrial relations problems of Tinsley Park Works and BSC as a whole. The other goals in the schema had very low priority on the works compared to these three, mainly because they were issues handled by other parts of the Corporation. This provides an example of how the wider environment of the organisation (BSC) influences the goal priorities of a subordinate system (Tinsley Park Works).

Given the concern with product and survival goals and the close links between them, then the choice of a role ideology and a temple structure follows logically, since it is the most appropriate one for handling continuing production in a relatively stable environment. All choices involve compromises however and we now consider some of the consequences of the organisational structure which had developed at Tinsley Park.

Some possible consequences of organisational structure

In recent years there has been a tendency to concentrate on the negative consequences of organisational structures. But structures are designed to achieve control and certain sorts of coordination and we should be seeking to find out how well they are able to achieve these.

One of the major advantages of structures founded on role ideology is that people are likely to know how to do their own particular jobs well. Thus, given adequate resources and the will to work, specialisation and the standard procedures associated with it tend to ensure a reasonable capacity for the necessary system maintenance activities. That is, they ought to be able to produce a satisfactory quality and quantity of output and to maintain the organisation in a viable condition. This was true of Tinsley Park Works. It was cost-effective and the Melting Shop in particular was regularly achieving new output levels during the Employee Relations Project. The Mill was working below capacity, but that was largely because the Melting Shop could not produce enough steel to keep it busy; for this reason the Melting Shop furnaces were being updated and extended.

In terms of system breakdown activities, we have seen in Part One that there were difficulties with engineering support for several reasons. One was that the engineering services were short of resources, machines, materials, men and time, but another reason points to the Achilles heel of specialisation in jobs and functions. This is the problem of integration which accompanies high specialisation. Role structures are designed to create adequate role performance and coordination up and down the hierarchy, but they create problems of integration between the differentiated functions. The dilemma is that the different specialists have different goals and tend to work primarily to the goals of their profession or function even where it is at some cost to the organisation as a whole. Examples of this at Tinsley Park included the move for engineering maintenance to reduce its costs, which produced long-run problems for the production departments (see 'Catch 22' in the shop floor project group described in chapter 4). This lack of integration is also shown in the relations between the Rail Traffic men and the Melting Shop. The Melting Shop would strive to achieve a record output, but could do so only at the cost of increased work for the Rail Traffic personnel who had to haul more trains and take away more slag. Because of the increased pace this often led to the Melting Shop 'slagging on to the floor', which made Rail Traffic's job more difficult and more dangerous. As Traffic personnel received smaller financial gains for increased output than did the Melting Shop, relationships between these two groups of specialists were thus strained.

However, many breakdowns on the site were in the social rather than the administrative or production systems. The initially high level of strikes and stoppages at Tinsley Park compared to Stocksbridge was one of the reasons why the Employee Relations Project was introduced. Whilst the causes of such stoppages do not primarily lie in aspects of the structure or technology, it is possible to argue that the structure and technology encourage a pattern of acting and reacting which lowers the threshold for social breakdowns (see chapter 13). We have already indicated that high specialisation and longish chains of command tend to produce psychological reactions which lead the worker to identify more with his own activities than with those of the broader organisation. Since the worker is the 'expert', he is in the end concerned to protect himself by making sure his own task is properly done. He is less prepared to compromise his standards and run the risk of retribution in order to help people in other roles. In the temple structure the high centralisation of authority encourages this because mistakes tend to shoot up high in the organisation as lower level people do not have the authority to handle them. Foremen at Tinsley Park were sometimes unclear about their own authority and responsibility, particularly for discipline. Furthermore, they were sometimes unwilling to take disciplinary action since they felt that they may not get the support of higher management for their action.

Other problems caused by breakdown activities came from the numerous interface issues which existed for long periods between some of the departments: engineering and all the production departments, and traffic and most of the production departments, to say nothing of the relationships between Tinsley Park and Stocksbridge. Some of the major successes of the Project involved setting up discussions between departments to work on these problems, but continued attention will be required to maintain any improvements at their new level. These are, of course, only specific examples of the general problem of interdepartmental breakdown, and indeed all the features we have identified here are common in other bureaucracies.

To summarise the argument: high specialisation produces differentiation which makes integration difficult. High centralisation of authority creates a tendency to pass the buck upwards rather than take a risk to help another job or department. These structural factors do not create the most fertile of soils in which consultation and collaboration can take root. Thus, even though joint consultation systems may exist, they often act rather like another bureaucratic mechanism, for they are frequently built on the same structural differences of hierarchical level and centralised decision-making which make the day-to-day management of system breakdown a difficult process in the first place.

There is perhaps a clue here to one of the major difficulties of all bureaucratic structures. In any system based largely on regulations and rules it is in a sense paradoxical that people are unclear what their roles are. Yet some foremen at Tinsley Park Works were unsure of the limits of their authority, and we may view this as follows. The bureaucratic approach has virtues when applied to the definition of job duties, performance standards, routine communication channels, etc., which are more or less publicly identifiable phenomena. However, when the same bureaucratic thinking is applied to the control of social behaviour (discipline about attendance, timekeeping, insubordination, low quality of work, etc.) it works less well because the standards of behaviour, definition of insubordination and so on are much more difficult to specify. Whatever standards are formally legislated, actual behaviour ends up being negotiated so that some foremen trade-off better production for laxity over timekeeping or apparent insubordination. Since they can then pass responsibility for these breakdown behaviours upwards, a situation is created where no-one is sure what really should happen.

It must be made clear, however, that such outcomes are not inevitable in temple structures. Organisational behaviour is not determined by structural, technological or attitudinal variables alone. Each plays a part and its importance differs in each organisation. One could almost say that any structure will work if the people want it to. Some structures may make the working more difficult, but if the will is there the difficulties can be overcome. The problem is that a temple structure and a role ideology can restrict freedom of movement and curtail interest in new ways to manage the processes of system breakdown, both social and technical.

This brings us to the development activities on the site. The technological innovations in the Melting Shop and the fact that the whole plant was relatively new, indicate that there were many managers experienced in handling large complex technical developments. However, the mechanisms for the development of human systems were much less sophisticated. For example, 'team-building' as a procedure of the kind illustrated in chapter 10 was poorly appreciated. The involvement of lower level personnel in organisational decision making was limited, although it was beginning to increase even before the Employee Relations Project.

In the Melting Shop level four project groups the men ruefully pointed out that, if the management had built the rail extensions at both ends of the track rather than at one, then it would have been possible to empty (teem) both ladles at once. 'But we were never asked', they said.

Apart from isolated initiatives from individual senior managers little was done to stimulate site-wide mechanisms which could have provided increased integration. A thriving Sports and Social Club did constitute one means of developing cohesion and group identity, but social activities of that kind are not task-based and the identification does not necessarily transfer to task activities. Additional mechanisms to promote development are therefore needed.

The schema points us towards considering the degree to which these activities should be specialised or differentiated, and how integration could be achieved. In a highly differentiated organisation the procedure is often to create a specialist role or roles to carry out development activities. These might be trainers or organisation development specialists, or people 'assistant to' the main functional heads such as production, finance and administration. Examples of specialist 'integration' roles are known and their purpose is to promote the general development of the system [13]. The problem is how to integrate them; how to get them accepted. Indeed the not uncommon line versus staff conflicts present these issues in a slightly different guise.

An alternative strategy is to go for low differentiation by adding development activities to the responsibilities of the line managers. The effectiveness of this depends on their skills and capacity for change as well as their present level of work. The problem here is how to integrate the different developments that might occur. There is a need to examine how the development activities in different departments work to ensure they are not in conflict with each other or other systems of working. This is probably a more complicated approach to the problem, but it might well have greater eventual benefits since it raises the capacities of people across a wider spectrum of the organisation.

The Employee Relations Project moved matters in this direction by arranging for managers and others to attend meetings in other departments. For example, the Traffic Section Manager started to attend meetings in the Melting Shop and would occasionally take his foremen with him if their presence was appropriate to the matters under discussion.

One may conclude that the mechanisms and values behind temple structures have an inhibiting effect on organisational concern for development activities. They are largely designed to satisfy the requirements of system maintenance, and special additions to the structure need to be created if development activities are to be adequately undertaken. At Tinsley Park Works the acceptance of the Employee Relations Project, initiated as it was by staff responsible for development but based outside the works, may itself be an example of the recognition by at least some people that these processes had been under-emphasised.

If formal mechanisms do not exist to manage system development activities then the rise of informal mechanisms requires some stability of personnel; and the turnover of senior and middle management personnel at both Tinsley Park and Stocksbridge was relatively high. This was particularly galling to some Tinsley Park employees, since many of the 'new' managers were from Stocksbridge and were seen as benefitting from the experience to be gained at Tinsley Park before moving on to greener pastures. They were also sometimes regarded as people who had been promoted unfairly over local men. These anxieties made successful development activities difficult, as they do in most large multi-site organisations.

Criticism is, of course, relatively easy. Solutions to the development problems are more difficult. The question is where to break into the circle of structural, technological and attitudinal constraints. Without a major change in overall corporate policies the structure of many plants is certain to remain highly dependent and relatively centralised. Due to high capital costs, production technologies will only change in minor ways. Similarly, the attitudes and values of a workforce will not change overnight. One choice seems therefore to be some form of structural intervention. The first step may be to try to ensure that the present structure works as effectively as possible. Apart from developing the motivation to make it work, this may involve ensuring that present definitions of roles are clear, non-overlapping, non-underlapping and well understood by all whom they affect. A second improvement is similar in nature and focusses on the breakdown activities; the kinds of changes recommended for the joint consultative and industrial relations systems at Tinsley Park are examples in this area. As to development activities, these either need to be made a key element in each manager's job description and included in his annual appraisal, or a special development role needs to be created. It would seem important that wherever possible this type of role is located on the actual site and not at some superordinate part of the organisation. For example, some members of Tinsley Park Works retained the view that the Employee Relations Project had been imposed by Stocksbridge and was not really 'owned' by Tinsley Park, even though we tried hard to create awareness of a genuine local ownership. It may also be that a specialist organisation development role could be set up to develop skills in on-the-job coaching, team-building and other integrative activities until such time as they are a self-sustaining part of the local managerial style. This strategy has the dual advantage of maintaining the existing levels of both differentiation and integration. We finish where we began, in a search for order and unity.

Notes

[1] These ideas are presented in detail in C. Perrow, 'The analysis of goals in complex organizations', *American Sociological Review*, vol. 26, 1961, pp. 859–66. A more general treatment may be found in C. Perrow, *Organizational Analysis*, Tavistock, London, 1970.

[2] A particularly influential writer in this area is J. Woodward. Her account of the relationship between production technology and organisational structure

can be found in *Management and Technology*, Her Majesty's Stationery Office, London, 1958; but a more comprehensive and analytical presentation appears in her book *Industrial Organisation*, Oxford University Press, London, 1965.

[3] The four ideologies are taken from R. Harrison, 'How to describe your organization', *Harvard Business Review*, September 1972, but they are elaborated and related to structural types in C. Handy, *Understanding Organisations*, Penguin, Harmondsworth, 1976, pp. 176–85.

[4] The problems of transition from an authority system based on charismatic power to one rooted in traditions and conventions are vividly depicted by Max Weber in *The Theory of Social and Economic Organization*, The Free Press, Glencoe, Illinois, 1947.

[5] *Parkinson's Law, or the Pursuit of Progress*, Murray, London, 1958 hardly seems to need a mention. One of the better empirical tests and theoretical elaborations of those ideas is to be found in J. Child, 'Parkinson's progress: accounting for the number of specialists in organizations', *Administrative Science Quarterly*, vol. 18, 1973, pp. 328–48.

[6] See P. Blau, *Bureaucracy in Modern Society*, Random House, New York, 1958.

[7] Matrix systems and the qualities demanded by them are described in L. Sayles and M.K. Chandler, *Managing Large Organisations: Systems for the Future*, Harper and Row, London, 1971.

[8] Accounts of the successes and failures of communes can be found in A. Rigby, *Communes in Britain*, Routledge and Kegan Paul, London, 1974.

[9] For a more complex description of social system components see E. Wight Bakke, *Bonds of Organization*, Wiley, New York, 1952, and the chapter by the same author in M. Haire (ed.), *Modern Organization Theory*, Wiley, New York, 1959.

[10] See P.R. Lawrence and J.W. Lorsch, *Organization and Environment*, Harvard University Press, Cambridge, Massachusetts, 1967.

[11] The relationship between number of employees and organisational structure has been discussed by J. Child, 'Organizational structure and strategies of control: a replication of the Aston study', *Administrative Science Quarterly*, vol. 17, 1972, pp. 163–76.

[12] See J. Child, 'Organisational structure, environment and performance – the role of strategic choice', *Sociology*, vol. 6, 1972, pp. 1–22.

[13] See for example the book referenced in note 10.

13 Employee relations and industrial relations

In this chapter we turn to issues of union–management relations and the way these are part of 'employee relations' more generally. The component of the Employee Relations Project most directly concerned with these issues was the Interlinked Phase, so named because it was additional to but linked into the main sequential phases of the Project (see chapter 6).

We commence with an examination of how 'industrial' and 'employee' relations are interdependent, and then move on to a discussion of plant-level 'industrial relations climate'. The third and fourth sections of the chapter cover two principal mechanisms for industrial relations problem-solving: joint consultation and grievance procedures. In examining factors bearing upon the effectiveness of these we will focus on the advantages and disadvantages of formality. Finally, we will take a broader look at the prospects for research in this important area.

Industrial relations in employee relations

There were five main reasons for our early concern with industrial relations within the Employee Relations Project:

1   The pattern of industrial relations problems in the works had been the principal motivation for senior management's interest in some form of investigation, and changes in this area were central goals of the Project.
2   The programme of action research we envisaged would require the initial formal agreement and longer-term commitment of the major interest groups on site, namely the representatives of management, supervision and shop floor.
3   We intended that the Project as a whole would be mainly directed at relations between the shop floor and management, so that as a matter of course we would be working within the framework of the formal industrial relations system.
4   No matter what changes emerged through the Project, at the end of the day the major strain of events would continue to fall where it had always fallen, on the formal and informal processes of union–management relations.
5   Industrial relations is a research area of particular importance, yet one which has been neglected by our professional discipline, psychology. This theme is taken up again at the end of the chapter.

Given this conviction that industrial relations should be given particular attention within the Project, there remained a definitional problem: how should 'industrial' be distinguished from 'employee' relations; and a practical problem: how should this distinction be translated into the design of the Interlinked Phase? Without allowing semantics to take up too much of our discussion, our orientation may be summarised as follows. We viewed employee relations as the broad climate of interpersonal relationships throughout the works, whilst we saw industrial relations as the more focused relations between the principal protagonists in the joint decision-making system: shop stewards, branch officials, line managers, and personnel specialists. Parallel with the industrial–employee relations distinction may be drawn a line between 'formal' and 'informal' systems of relations, such that industrial relations are primarily located in formal systems. This line of distinction is a fluctuating and uncertain one, since formality often has more to do with physical and bureaucratic settings than people's behaviour. Nevertheless, within the 'formal' system we would include all those dealings among union and management representatives which follow custom and practice 'rules' or which are conducted in officially recognised meetings (e.g. joint consultation and negotiation). These formal joint regulatory activities are conducted against a background of informal and less structured dealings at the workplace and elsewhere. Just as there is a 'grapevine' in every firm underlying the formal channels of information exchange, so in industrial relations there are complex networks of interpersonal relationships, with accompanying expectations and beliefs, that underlie formal interactions and decision-making. The formal system creates the framework within which many informal processes operate, and yet which at the same time reflects, often in a concentrated form, the character of these informal dealings.

For the researcher this poses a dilemma. To which end of this dimension should he first attend: to the informal system of employee relations or the more formal industrial relations system? We favoured an emphasis on the former, on the grounds that by directing our efforts as broadly as possible we would necessarily become involved in improvements in formal systems as well as in the less formal aspects of employee relations. Rather than attempting a more restricted but detailed *'Industrial* Relations Project', our solution was to try to 'have it both ways', by incorporating the more focused Interlinked Phase into the wideranging plans for the Project. As described in chapter 6, the Interlinked Phase consisted of an inquiry into joint consultation, union–management relations in grievance-handling at various levels of the organisation, and a statistical analysis of disputes data and other personnel records.

Industrial relations climate

It is helpful to characterise a works in terms of its broad 'climate' of industrial relations. By this we mean the pattern of problems regularly faced by managers and union representatives, the outcomes of these problems, and the attitudes and beliefs that pervade dealings between unions and management. As in the case of geographical climate, the notion is a complex one made up of a variety of components, extending beyond a simple 'good–bad' dimension [1].

According to this conception, climate applies primarily to the industrial unit of the plant, though the notion may also be useful to discuss large organisational sub-units (e.g. largely autonomous departments). It is more than the 'sum of the parts' where the 'parts' are individual actions, attitudes, and issues, since it is shaped by interconnected events at department or plant level (e.g. disciplinary procedures, consultative machinery). In the discussion that follows we will look at climate-influencing factors at plant level or above, and drawing on the findings of the Interlinked Phase we will illustrate how they interact with the characteristics of person-to-person dealings at shop floor level. The more wideranging influences on climate may be viewed under four headings: socio-cultural context, corporate structure and policy, economic and political environment, and technology and organisational structure.

Socio-cultural context

We start our analysis with the most difficult factor to define, yet the one that is perhaps most universally acknowledged as a crucial influence on plant-level climate. Its apparent intangibility is because socio-cultural context is largely historical; in some ways it only 'exists' as a collective memory, glimpsed by the outsider through the traditions and folklores of the community, and reflected in the complex network of beliefs, customs, socialisation practices and relationships of its 'occupants'.

In industrial relations, the burden of the past is of weighty significance. For example, to properly understand the current climate of industrial relations in the South Wales mining or the Midlands car industry, it is important to know something about the historical antecedents of the people and their work. Similarly, to gain a correct appraisal of the industrial relations climate at Tinsley Park some appreciation is needed of the industrial relations tradition of the Sheffield area. The region has long been a prosperous centre of manufacturing industry, and of the metals and allied industries in particular. Not only was the area a 'crucible' for the industrial revolution and a fertile region for subsequent industrial developments but it also was a principal site for the birth of the modern trade union movement. Unions and management in the city thus have a long history of mutual dealings and this has bred a kind of 'militancy without extremism'. Both sides of industry appear to be relatively unafraid of the risks of conflict inherent in adopting tough bargaining strategies, suggestive of an ultimate faith in the manageability of conflict. A reflection of this is the relative infrequency of full-blown strikes in the area, illustrated by the initial pattern at Tinsley Park Works of fairly frequent disputes but relatively infrequent lost production because of them. The more peaceful contrast of Stocksbridge at the beginning of the Employee Relations Project is also better understood when the integrative features of the rural community context of this sister plant are taken into account. Further-more, the growth of white-collar trade unionism, well advanced in Sheffield, might be seen as an additional factor fostering common consciousness within these work settings [2].

On the other hand, the urban environment is one that accelerates change and mobility; within the catchment areas of city-based industries there are invariably people who are relatively unfamiliar with the community's traditions and customs. In urban settings, instability often arises from the disruptive turnover of key personnel, and this can rebound on the industrial relations climate by unsettling bargaining relationships and undermining confidence in future cooperation.

Corporate structure and policy

The predominant 'temple' structure described in chapter 12 demands flexibility of movement up, down, and across its main 'pillars' and 'arches'; movement which may increase the feelings of remoteness, powerlessness, and dependence of those at or near the bottom of the long hierarchy. Frequent transfers of key personnel may, of course, encourage these feelings. In terms of industrial relations policy, the temple structure at Tinsley Park meant that the local autonomy that management tried to foster through the 'ship' system was sometimes felt to be illusory. When there were major decisions to be taken, precedents to be set, or important conflicts to be resolved, then the Stocksbridge-based industrial relations specialists were usually decisively involved.

From a corporate point of view, this type of power structure might be thought ideal, with policies covering all major eventualities located at the centre of the organisation, and the nuts and bolts being worked out at plant level, but the actual practice often falls short of the ideal. This was apparent in the interview data of the ERP Interlinked Phase. A series of questions asked management and union representatives their relative frequency of interaction with opposite numbers, and their satisfaction with way these people handled problems and grievances [3]. Whilst this revealed that 'crew' relations in the department 'ship system' were generally good, there was dissatisfaction with the amount of influence wielded by people not 'on board the ship'. Principally this took the form of resentment that decisions taken at departmental level, or jointly with the site's senior industrial relations officer, had to be ratified or modified centrally, coupled with a feeling that when outsiders did have a say in decision-making their judgement was sometimes based on insufficient local knowledge and sympathy. This type of criticism is often expressed with exaggerated force in large organisations, but however far removed from the truth it is, it can be detrimental to the local climate by undermining the basis for trust and cooperation.

Economic and political environment

Some observers would point to this third area of external influence as of paramount importance, particularly industrial relations practitioners themselves who tend to suffer the impact of changes in government policy and planning more acutely than most. Enough has been written elsewhere on the subject of the effect of state controls on plant level industrial relations for it not to concern us at length here. However, brief mention may be made of an interesting fresh view of the topic that has been provided by recent research at Edinburgh [4]. The focus of this work has been 'the psychology of inflation', and research has shown how economic trends govern people's expectations and their bargaining behaviour. These researchers have extended their argument to show how pay policies might aim to break the ensuing spiral. There were certainly signs at Tinsley Park Works that the accelerating rate of inflation during the Employee Relations Project was directly reflected in employees' material aspirations, and thus constituted an important source of potential conflicts. Yet while the economic, legal, and political climate of the times does have a direct bearing on the industrial relations climate with firms, it does this in a fairly undiscriminating fashion. The impact at plant level differs from establishment to establishment by virtue of other factors: principally traditions and technology. The influence of the former we have already considered, and it is to the latter that we now turn.

Technology and organisational structure

We have already considered the influence of corporate structure and policy, and illustrated in chapter 12 and in this chapter how the size and hierarchical complexity of organisations like the British Steel Corporation can create decision-making problems for people at plant level. More local structural features are of equal importance as determinants of plant level industrial relations climate (such as the nature of the process, organisation and concentration of labour, and sub-unit differentiation and integration) as well as impinging differently on the climates of individual departments. The Interlinked Phase of the Project revealed that sharp differences existed between the main areas of the works covered by the Project, and, moreover, that these were more situation-based than person-based. The data showed that it was not the quality of one-to-one relations between union and management representatives that chiefly determined feelings about the departmental climate of industrial relations but the type and frequency of problems that people had to deal with. More precisely, equipment maintenance was a major problem in all departments, but the amount of difficulty this created was distinctly uneven. Traffic, whose maintenance needs were strongest, suffered most, whilst the Mill's relatively trouble-free self-sufficiency made the problem of overstretched maintenance facilities only a relatively minor source of discomfort. In Billet Finishing the fragmented work organisation created problems of management control, commonly expressed through management anxiety about stop, start, and break times. In the Melting Shop, the high pressure on production and the carefully tiered hierarchy of job grades combined to make problems over bonus rates and job regrading a prime focus of attention.

In short, the industrial relations climates of clearly identifiable sub-units are often directly related to those features that make them identifiable in the first place. Cohesive high intensity production departments generate quite different issues from differentiated ancillary areas, and the type and flow of problems that union and management representatives have to tackle together determine their dissatisfactions with past and present situations, their expectations about the future, and their confidence in their own competence and powers. What is particularly interesting from the data of the Interlinked Phase is that this pervasive issue-centred climate did not appear to damage interpersonal dealings and relations, although it did cause problems at the interface between departments. Within departments managers and stewards were able to maintain good relations even when problems were flying at their thickest and fastest. This is encouraging in its implication that clearcut benefits to the industrial relations climate on site might be brought about through improved mechanisms and operating procedures.

Before turning in the next section to an examination of some of these possible improvements, let us take stock. How far can the various strands we have discussed be pulled together as the basis for a coherent theory of industrial relations climate? Other writers' attempts at this do not give grounds for optimism, mainly because of a not unnatural tendency to overemphasise the dominant thinking of their own professional discipline or their personal experiences.

Considerable attention has been devoted in North America to the organisation of work groups [5] and union leadership characteristics [6], whilst in the the UK community characteristics and social class [7] have been highlighted. None of these approaches is itself adequate to account for the climate of industrial relations at Tinsley Park Works. This is not because the plant was in any way extraordinary, but because of the range limitations of the models. Each one may help in some way, but when taken together, rather than giving us an integrated framework, they suggest that 'climate' exists differently in a number of different spheres: in the area of interpersonal dealings on the shop floor, at the level of interdepartmental problem-management, in terms of workers' and managers' value-systems, and through the formal mechanisms for containment and expression of conflict.

It is this diffuseness and intangibility which makes the measurement of industrial relations climate so difficult. The concept itself appears to be a fruitful one, but users of the concept (including ourselves) have not yet specified it in sufficient detail and breadth to be successful in explaining industrial relations activities within a single, albeit multidimensional, framework. That is a task we must defer until some future occasion.

Joint consultation and decision-making

Joint consultation in industry has had an uneven history, and today its status is controversial. It is seen by some as an ideal form of employee participation, in which the great fund of shop floor wisdom and opinion have the chance to contribute positively to the quality of decision-making. In other quarters it is derided as a poor substitute for negotiation which ultimately reinforces managerial prerogatives and power. There are plausible arguments on both sides of this debate,

159

and it is not our purpose to attempt to add decisively to one side or the other. Our aim is to use the data from the Interlinked Phase to illustrate some of the limitations inherent in consultative systems as well as the factors that help them to operate with optimal effectiveness. We will take up the wider issue of the relative merits of different types of joint decision-making later in this discussion.

As was described in chapter 6, we were introduced at an early stage to the low repute in which people on all sides at Tinsley Park held joint consultation. The questionnaire and interview data of the Interlinked Phase examined the details of this by asking consultative committee members to identify which issues they felt were handled effectively and poorly by joint consultation. This, of course, begs the central question in the debate described above, namely what constitutes effectiveness, but for now it will suffice to define 'effectiveness' simply as 'to the general satisfaction of parties directly or indirectly affected by it'. By this criterion the consultative system was initially ineffective – generally failing to fulfil people's needs for action and involvement in decision-making, and instead largely functioning as a bureaucratic framework for processing very minor problems or as a forum for the expression of frustration and aggression. These are important functions in one sense, but clearly are not those for which the consultative system was principally designed. To gain a comprehensive appreciation of the conduct of consultation we elicited committee members' opinions about seven facets of the system: outcomes, quality of discussion, formal powers, agenda and minuting, chairmanship, physical arrangements, and temporal arrangements (timing and length of meetings).

There was least overall satisfaction with the outcomes of consultation; neither management nor unions felt they were getting what they wanted from it. Both sides were also equally unhappy about the quality of discussion: interviewees felt that the group atmosphere in meetings and people's conduct left much to be desired. There were more mixed feelings about the formal powers vested in the committees, with a majority expressing the opinion (most often on the union side) that the constitutional powers were insufficient [8]. There was also widespread dissatisfaction with the contents of agenda. Although opinions were again mixed, people were generally more favourably disposed to the composition of committees, though there was some criticism of attendance rates. Both the temporal and physical arrangements were generally thought to be suitable, though there were occasional complaints about the rooms used and the excessive duration of meetings. People were generally complimentary about the chairmanship, though this may be due in part to an understandable reluctance to express criticism of the individual shop stewards and managers performing this role. However, there were enough dissenting voices to forestall any complacency about the chairman's role and his responsibilities for the conduct of meetings.

To gain further insights into the main causes of the perceived ineffectivness of consultative mechanisms we subjected the quantified response data to correlational analysis [9] to try to find out which specific dissatisfactions with features of the system were related to general feelings about the system as a whole. The results of this analysis showed that of greatest importance was people's satisfaction or dissatisfaction with the outcomes of consultation, and that this in turn hinged partly on the design of agenda and feelings about the powers of committees. Quality of discussion was also a key influence on overall satisfaction, and here the standard of chairmanship was thought to be an important underlying influence.

These findings have wider implications than just for Tinsley Park, and the recommendations of the Interim Report that grew out of them might be applied to consultative systems elsewhere. The most important of these recommendations was that joint consultative committees should lead to and be seen to lead to concrete and valued outcomes. This is easier said than done, but one way of helping to promote the change and to provide pressure for meaningful outcomes is through the mechanisms for reportage and feedback. Most committee minuting is unsuited to action and change, usually being concerned to convey the content of speeches and acknowledge their authorship rather than committing people to action in the immediate future. Moreover, the delay in producing minutes (usually they are issued just before the next meeting, attached to agenda), does not allow them to be a vehicle for feedback on short-term decision-making or for progress-chasing in the longer term. We recommended that instead of, or at least in addition to, this kind of minuting there should be a listing of action points, naming the people committed to carrying out or chasing actions rather than, or at least as well as, the people who first suggested them. In other words we recommended that the system used in project .groups be adopted in joint consultation; and, indeed, the subsequent implementation of this proposal did go some way to achieving the desired ends.

Similarly, agenda should be drawn up at sufficiently short notice to ensure their topicality, and provision should be made for sufficient participation by possible contributors to create a representative list of important issues for discussion. We felt this was especially important for Tinsley Park's lowest level committees (the departmental joint consultative committees) where reports by chairmen (i.e. department managers) sometimes served as the only agenda item. This practice had the unwitting effects of making JCC's unnecessarily remote from outsiders, making outsiders unaware of the possible scope of discussion, and forestalling any possible intention to suggest additional topics. On the subject of formal reports to committees, it was apparent that too much time was often taken up with their presentation, and that their consideration and discussion could be aided by prior circulation to members.

This leads us to the lynchpin of successful consultation: management's approach to it. Since consultation is a system of participation that does not fundamentally disturb management's decision-making prerogatives then the onus is on management to make it work. This can only be done by genuinely allowing the system to be used for feedback on key decisions in important areas and for a first canvas of factory opinion on burning issues. In this, management must take initiatives and make sure that views expressed in joint consultation have a real impact on subsequent events. Management frequently point to trade union aggressiveness and pettiness as a cause of JCC failure, but this is often partly a reaction by shop floor representatives to the feeling that management only consult because they are told to and have no serious desire to open themselves up to influence from below. This perception may be false; management may have merely relegated participation down their list of pressing priorities and be genuinely unaware that they appear to lack trust in their subordinates. Either way, the effect is the same; consultation degenerates into a sterile cycle of attack and defence.

A key figure in breaking out of this cycle is the chairman. Bad chairmanship often goes unnoticed, or at least unremarked, in committees, and people are often unaware of the chairman's potential power to speed up discussion, ensure a flow of opinion and response from all parties and generally promote clear decision-making. In the minds of many people the chief problem is one of committees' restricted powers, and this is true insofar as they cannot compel decisions on people. But it is often overlooked that key decision-makers usually sit on JCC's and have the power to initiate and enact outcomes that are collectively desired by the consultative committee members. Thus it is entirely possible for action-oriented joint consultative committees themselves to reach verdicts on certain issues and to recommend actions with some force. Clearly this is insufficient for those who wish to replace consultation with negotiation, but the re-assertion of an action emphasis will go some way to satisfying those people whose disgruntlement is based mainly on a dissatisfaction with outcomes.

The last important factor underlying the success or failure of the joint consultative committees is their composition. Without an appropriate membership a committee is unlikely to be respected by its own participants or by the people outside whom it claims to represent. This is often mistakenly reduced to the question of whether only shop stewards should sit as employee representatives. Hopefully, shop stewards will want to be JCC members and management will want them to be; anything else in a strongly unionised industry would render consultation vulnerable to the charge that it is undermining existing systems of employee representation and would eventually ensure its ultimate irrelevance. Similarly, it is vital that the members on the management side are people who have the power to deliver the goods: membership is not a job a senior manager should delegate to his juniors. Conversely, it is equally to be urged that no person whose opinions are relevant to the outcomes of a JCC is automatically excluded on technical grounds, such as their lack of formal status within the union. In other words we are advocating that stewards are encouraged to sit on consultative committees ex officio, but that committees are also open to ordinary union members and other grades (subject to some necessary size limitation).

This flexibility is particularly important where committees operate at the lowest level of the organisation, partly to avoid the suspicion and misunderstanding that can be aroused by remote and uncommunicative committees, but mainly to ensure that all shades of shop-floor opinion have an opportunity for direct expression. A flexible system of this sort then becomes a basic form of employee participation, and encourages the shop floor to seek direct involvement and management to accept it. One way of operating such a system would be by having a fixed proportion of 'regular' seats with others being filled on a voluntary, perhaps rotational basis.

Often more relevant than who may attend meetings is who actually does attend: 'apologies for absence' can be the most telling item on the agenda! Indeed, one of our recommendations in the Interim Report was that people who were regularly unable to attend should forfeit their membership and an alternative person be nominated.

A final thought may be extended to an ostensibly less important issue, though one that can have damaging effects if not given proper attention: the temporal and physical setting for consultation. Careless or thoughtless planning of this prompts the reaction, however unjust, that management have little commitment to the system and are prepared to spare it little consideration. In other words the significance of this aspect is not only practical, it is symbolic and symptomatic and as such worthy of a vigilant regard.

At this point let us return to a consideration of some of the wider implications of consultation within the industrial relations system of the plant. Perhaps the most fundamental issue here is that of power and power-sharing. Recent debate on the subject of industrial democracy has tended to concentrate on decision-making at the top of organisations, and it is at this level that legislated power-sharing has most often been advocated [10].

Joint consultation can never achieve the goals intended through this type of power-sharing, but it can nevertheless be of considerable practical importance. Effective consultation requires strong additional joint regulatory rights elsewhere in the system, such as may be provided by collective bargaining or high level power-sharing. In other words, well-meaning consultation alone is unlikely to provide sufficient opportunity for upward influence on decision-making, and may consequently be swept away by union demands for 'more negotiation'. Ideally, one might envisage the flexibility of shop-floor level consultation enabling it to be a source of inspiration, ideas, opinions and facts that complement and fortify higher level joint decision-making. To achieve this goal in most industries would require both management and unions to adopt a fresh approach to 'industrial democracy', and for this the assistance of legislation might be needed.

Formality and informality in grievance procedures

A high degree of formality in joint decision-making, whether in the shape of consultation or negotiation, is often blamed for the degeneration of union—management dealings into ritual debate between polarised opinions. Under such circumstances it is not unusual to observe people in the formal setting behaving in ways that are out of character with their usual informal style. Yet most would agree that formality is necessary for the maintenance of orderly industrial relations, for without it fairness cannot be seen to be done, trust may be weakened and representation become haphazard. It was with these considerations in mind, and in response to disquiet over the confused conduct of plant-level industrial relations in much of British industry, that in 1968 the report of the Donovan Royal Commission [11] urged both sides of industry to recognise that conflict was being inadequately 'managed' at lower levels of the industrial relations system. The Royal Commission urged rationalisation through the institution of plant-level grievance procedures to fill in the missing lower links in the chains of industry-wide disputes procedures. A recent review of trends since the Donovan Report has concluded that its proposals have had a surprisingly slow and as yet insubstantial impact on the growth of grievance procedure in British industry [12], though it has produced some change in attitudes toward workplace bargaining.

In this context Tinsley Park Works, as we observed it, was not atypical: confident in the existence of a well-established industry-wide procedure that was triggered when plant-level discussions had failed, but with no written or formal procedure for the day-to-day lower-level processing of grievances. A consequence of this, indicated by the Interlinked Phase interview programme, was that many people were bypassed in the grievance-handling process, principally the less experienced union representatives (shop stewards or branch committee members) and a number of junior and middle managers (foremen, shift managers, and occasionally section managers). In effect, this meant that problems were often dealt with in direct informal liaisons between senior shop stewards and department or section heads.

There are two contrasting ways of evaluating this high level of informality. In its favour, it may be said that this type of system has the merit of effecting a speedy and generally well-judged response to issues; it is 'logical' to take problems as quickly as possible to the place where they can be solved. This accords with the view that 'the major part of the grievance process as it actually operates is essentially an information processing system which gets information on grievances to the person(s) with authority to make decisions on them' [13]. Furthermore, formal systems can channel issues toward the 'wrong' decision-makers, whilst informal grievance handling often fits well into a close working relationship between steward and manager, and is integral to a wide range of their ongoing shared concerns. On the other hand, formal procedures may be useful as a 'crutch' for the inexperienced and reticent operator of the system [12]. It may be added that a formal procedure helps ensure that people at the bottom of the management and union hierarchy have first-hand experience of industrial relations problem-solving, and that people at the top of the hierarchy are not needlessly overburdened with minor issues that could be handled lower down. Moreover, there is an additional danger in the speed and short-circuiting of high-level informal dealings: failure to resolve a problem at a high level leaves it nowhere to go but up, into the full formal disputes machinery. Arguably it is better to have tried and failed lower down before getting to this point.

In relation to Tinsley Park Works, it was our observation that informality was successfully maintaining a good climate of industrial relations where there was already an effective working relationship between the principal parties, but we had three main doubts:

1 Over-reliance on a small number of individuals left industrial relations vulnerable to the exigencies of personnel change.
2 Too many small issues reached too high a level in the system before being
resolved.
3 Certain individuals and groups were being excluded from the decision-
making process.

We felt that the remedy for these ills was not the imposition of a 'mechanistic'
formal procedure upon an essentially 'organic' system of relationships, but the
development of a new set of norms about acceptable behaviours. We considered it
desirable that there should be a common understanding or 'custom and practice'
that wherever possible issues would be handled at their source and thereafter at the
lowest appropriate level. In other words, workmen, shop stewards, foremen and
shift managers should be more involved in day-to-day grievance handling. This
would have the effect of strengthening the industrial relations system by providing
'on the job' training for junior union and management representatives.

The feasibility and utility of this kind of grievance handling had already been
demonstrated within the Employee Relations Project, for in some ways project
groups were a type of a 'grievance procedure', albeit a temporary and limited one.
Our Interim Report recommendations were based on the need for more permanent
and self-sustaining mechanisms and practices. Our recommendations for changes in
the operation of joint consultation and the suggestion for 'work group meetings'
to be set up to improve communications and planning at shop-floor level were
designed to this end, and in the belief that these were changes that would complement and not subvert existing informal industrial relations networks and procedures. A key to the success of this kind of innovation is to make sure that trade
unions and their representatives are able to undertake significant roles (for instance,
through their functioning as group leaders in level four project groups) and that
management do not try to use the new communication channels and participative
machinery as a way of avoiding the official union system. By the latest account to
reach us from Tinsley Park before this book went to press, it would seem that
these strategies were proving helpful.

Research in industrial relations

Finally in this chapter we will consider the prospects for social psychological
research in the industrial relations field. There are now increasing numbers of
studies of psychological aspects of negotiating and the activities of industrial
relations practitioners [14], but investigations of an 'action research' kind, as
defined in chapter 9, are still relatively infrequent.

A central theme in this chapter has been the need for industrial relations to
be studied in programmes directed at changes in employee relations more broadly

[15]. This inevitably brings the researcher in close contact with shop-floor issues and questions of trade union organisation and attitudes. Such a conclusion may seem unremarkable, yet reports of work in 'organisation development' often give the impression that the action researcher has considerable freedom and legitimacy to work with management groups without concerning himself with industrial relations issues [16]. This seems to us a very mistaken impression.

Union—management relations are not merely background factors but are central to the effectiveness of all large organisations. North American researchers might point to the lower levels of unionisation and the greater emphasis on bargaining above plant level in their country, but in the UK the in-plant industrial relations network is of major significance.

What role may be foreseen for action research in this field? It is helpful to think of the roles of a third party in industrial relations in terms of a dimension of dependence: the degree to which the protagonists are dependent upon the opinions and decisions of the third party. At one extreme of this dimension are judicial roles and those of an arbitrator, where dependence is at its greatest. The other end of the dimension is where the protagonists are themselves free to operate without constraint from the third party; his role may be as an observer or perhaps as a listener who gives informal advice when asked. In between these two extremes are third-party roles as mediator, provider of 'good offices', consultant and source of administrative and emotional support.

These roles are listed in Table 13.1, together with an indication that the first four require a nonpartisan stance whereas the other four may be undertaken either by partisan or by nonpartisan outsiders.

Table 13.1
Third-party roles in industrial relations

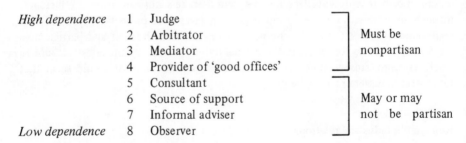

The partisan occupants of roles 5 to 8 may come from 'a centre within a user organisation', as defined in chapter 9. For example, they might be trade union or employers' association research officers. But such persons cannot move into roles 1 to 4, where impartiality is clearly required.

Our own roles as impartial third parties in the industrial relations network of Tinsley Park were largely confined to the lower half of the list. We did briefly move towards roles 3 and 4 (during the bricklayers' strike; see chapters 4 and 6), but we felt that the two sets of roles (1—4 and 5—8) did not easily mix within our agreed contract with the Corporation. This separation of roles is also reflected in the fact that third parties from universities and research centres who adopt roles 1 to 4 in conflict situations tend to remain within these, rather than also moving into consultancy activities which might assist the protagonists to work out a solution themselves.

However, such a division of roles may not always be necessary, and there is scope for broader agreements about third party activities to be negotiated at the access stage (see chapter 9). For example, a researcher may usefully work in conflict situations by attempting to marry the skills of the organisation development consultant (see, for example, chapters 10 and 11) with those of the mediator [17]. An alternative approach is to focus more specifically on industrial relations issues themselves. As noted at the beginning of this chapter, we attempted at Tinsley Park Works to 'have it both ways' by incorporating an inquiry into industrial relations within a broader project on employee relations. Our ERP experiences confirmed to us that this was a valuable perspective, but other action researchers might choose to reverse the emphasis, casting the main spotlight on industrial relations and viewing employee relations as the 'background'. It is only when one topic is pursued in isolation, without any regard for the other, that serious criticism is warranted.

Notes

[1] The notion of 'organisational climate' has received considerable research attention, principally through studies seeking to record a 'baseline' of shared employee perceptions about the characteristics of their work situation, supervision, opportunities for advancement, organisational structure, etc. The focus of the word 'climate' in this discussion of 'industrial relations climate' is more narrow, encompassing the atmosphere surrounding union—management dealings and the factors that impinge upon this.

[2] The growth of white-collar unionism in recent years has been a topic of considerable interest to industrial relations researchers, and particular attention has focused on the spread of trade unionism into the traditionally supra-union ranks of middle management. The steel industry is a case in point, and at Tinsley Park Works membership of the middle managers' union (the Steel Industry Management Association) was close to one hundred per cent above foreman level up to and including department managers.

[3] These data were analysed in two ways: (a) the measurement of intergroup differences in ratings and responses, e.g. between shop stewards and managers, or differences between departments; (b) correlational analysis (see note 9) measuring the degree of association between people's specific responses to issues (and the people that handle them) and other variables, e.g. departmental industrial relations climate, seniority, experience of consultation, etc.

[4]   See, for example, H. Behrend, 'The impact of inflation on pay increases, expectations and ideas of fair pay', *Industrial Relations Journal*, vol. 5, 1974, pp. 5–10; and 'Research into inflation and conceptions of earnings', *Journal of Occupational Psychology*, vol. 50, 1977, pp. 169–76.

[5]   An early and influential work on this topic is that of L.R. Sayles, *Behavior of Industrial Work Groups: Prediction and Control*, Wiley, New York, 1958.

[6]   A number of North American writers have described leadership of union 'locals' (branches) as a factor of surpassing importance in industrial relations, an emphasis that may be more appropriate in the USA than in the UK, though open to criticism for failing to take due account to structural influences.

[7]   One example of this approach is D. Lockwood, 'Sources of variation in working class images of society', *Sociological Review*, vol. 14, 1966, pp. 249–67; in which occupational and community factors are described as leading to four different types of 'consciousness': 'middle class', 'deferential', 'proletarian', and 'privatised'.

[8]   The written constitution for the consultative committees defined their functions as 'advisory and consultative' only, though stated that they may vote on issues and 'have power to make recommendations to management'.

[9]   This statistical technique provides a measure of how closely any two variables are associated, whether positively (e.g. a high score on one occurs when there is a high score on the other) or negatively (high score on one occurs when there is a low score on the other).

[10] *Report of the Committee of Inquiry on Industrial Democracy*, HMSO, London, 1977.

[11] *Report of the Royal Commission on Trade Unions and Employers' Associations 1965–68*, HMSO, London, 1968.

[12] A.W.J. Thomson and V.V. Murray, *Grievance Procedures*, Saxon House, London, 1976.

[13] See page 29 of the book referred to in note 12.

[14] See, for example: I.E. Morley and G.M. Stephenson, *The Social Psychology of Bargaining*, Allen and Unwin, London, 1977; N. Nicholson, 'The role of the shop steward: an empirical case study', *Industrial Relations Journal*, vol. 7, 1976, pp. 15–26; R.E. Walton and R.B. McKersie, *A Behavioral Theory of Labor Negotiations*, McGraw-Hill, New York, 1965; and P.B. Warr, *Psychology and Collective Bargaining*, Hutchinson, London, 1973.

[15] This theme has been developed by T.A. Kochan and L. Dyer, 'A model of organizational change in the context of union–management relations', *Journal of Applied Behavioral Science*, vol. 12, 1976, pp. 59–78.

[16] A recent example of this kind of writing may be found in M.S. Myers, *Managing Without Unions*, Addison-Wesley, New York, 1976. The field of organisation development is examined in chapter 15.

[17] See, for example, C. Margerison and M. Leary, *Managing Industrial Conflicts*, MCB Books, Bradford, 1975.

14 Evaluating organisational change

How should programmes like the Employee Relations Project be evaluated? Participants in the programme, other members of their organisation, and outside observers all have an interest in deciding whether a programme was worthwhile and in learning from its successes and failures. However, the wide scope and long duration of many change programmes raise considerable difficulties for the attainment of balanced and reliable evaluations of what has taken place.

In this chapter we present a framework for evaluation which aims to bring together many important features in a comprehensive and practical model. Seven stages of change are outlined, and our suggestion is that the evaluator should look systematically at the effectiveness with which each one has been carried out. The stages may be introduced as follows:

1   *Identification of problems.*   For example: How are current problems and needs assessed?   How are they seen by different individuals and groups? How wide a perspective is taken?   How much agreement is achieved about objectives?

2   *Assessment of resources.*   For example: What types of external assistance are investigated?   Is the experience of other organisations examined?   How realistic are the assessments made of internal resources: money, equipment, time, enthusiasm, knowledge, skills?

3   *Choice of strategy.*   For example: How well are possible options considered? Against what criteria is the chosen strategy judged?   Who makes the choice? Is it appropriate?

4   *Execution of the chosen strategy.*   For example: How are the methods applied?   How skilfully and efficiently do the principal agents undertake their tasks?

5   *Interim reviews and adjustments.*   For example: What adjustments to the previous four stages are considered as they unfold?   How are any revisions to earlier decisions introduced?

6   *Establishment of longer-term structures.*   For example: What changes are introduced into day-to-day operation to sustain improvements identified in the previous stages?

7   *Assessment of effectiveness.*   For example: What outcomes have been achieved at what cost?   How do participants feel about the programme? Are there significant differences between parts of the organisation?   Has the experience generalised for future application?

A seven-point plan for evaluation

In practice these seven stages are interlocking and more interdependent than such an introductory presentation suggests, and the sequencing of events can also vary from situation to situation. In broad terms however we can suggest that to evaluate a programme of change is to consider the effectiveness with which each of the seven stages has been carried out. This broad statement requires modification to suit individual circumstances, for there could be features of surpassing importance within one of the stages which make detailed assessment of others less relevant. And the overall pattern of changes also requires some assessment; for example, it may be felt that individual stages were carried out in a suboptimal fashion, yet that the overall benefit of the programme was considerable.

Our seven-point plan for evaluation is thus an idealised one, and we envisage adaptations to fit local needs. The evaluative material about the Employee Relations Project presented in chapter 8 fell mainly within stage seven of the model, in that we were dealing with specific questions of outcomes, reactions and costs, issues that were thought to be of principal importance at the time. In the present chapter we will examine in more general terms the evaluative questions which arise in each of the seven stages, drawing illustrations where appropriate from our experiences in the Employee Relations Project.

Identification of problems

It is clear that change programmes have their origin in a decision taken somewhere in the organisation that some form of action is required, but the processes leading up to that decision and commitment to it vary widely between situations.

We described in chapter 9 how there is often tension between organisation members and action researchers during early discussions about a project, as the former look for relatively tight definitions of the problem and the latter prefer to retain a broad perspective and to delay final decisions. Yet there usually has to be some shared appreciation of a problem within a company before widespread action will be taken, and the belief that something needs to be done has to be held with moderate intensity as well as by sufficient numbers of people. In practice there will usually be divergent views about the nature of principal problems, and discussion within a company is essential over a period of time to allow ideas to develop and become clear.

These initial discussions will usually combine and even confuse questions of objectives and means to achieve those objectives. As a possible course of action begins to emerge from the exchange of ideas, additional and initially separate objectives and procedures may be attached to the programme. These may be formal and explicit: the company might decide to take the opportunity to analyse its absenteeism or labour turnover figures. But the subsequently identified objectives may also be more personal and implicit: a manager might decide that active enthusiasm for whatever is initiated will aid his promotion prospects, or a group of employees might see an opportunity to press forward a longstanding grievance.

In other words there are circumstances where agreement about the kind of action to be taken may be achieved although the desired outcomes from that action are viewed differently by different people. In evaluating this first stage, one might wish particularly to consider the extent to which problems are identified and agreed rather than the degree to which a plan of action was seen to be acceptable for divergent reasons.

More broadly it is tempting to evaluate the processes of stage one by asking whether the organisation succeeded in finding and agreeing upon the 'right' problem. However, it is possible, indeed likely, that what appears to be the major problem at the time will change as people take steps to resolve it. For example, poor supervision may turn out to involve poor production planning, and poor planning may become a question of poor communication. The most appropriate evaluation for stage one centres upon the effectiveness of the search for problems and upon the processes whereby members of the organisation are brought into that search. In this way any consensus that emerges will be valid for those involved because it is based upon informed choice. These conditions can then lead to internal commitment, so that initial action is determined and directed, even if the main problem eventually turns out to be different from that initially identified [1].

Another question to be asked about stage one in the sequence concerns the boundary of the problem as defined. Any organisational problem has ramifications which can extend into other parts of the system, and a decision has to be taken about the limits of these ramifications: how wide is the programme of action to extend? For example, if poor communication within a department is identified as a serious problem, are attempts at improvement to be restricted within that department? Or are the boundaries of the problem to be set more widely, embracing features of the works as a whole?

There are advantages in setting narrow boundaries (within the department, for example), in that positive action may be relatively more feasible; but the disadvantages are equally clear, in that problems associated with the broader organisational structure may be excluded from consideration.

In the case of the Employee Relations Project, the boundary of the problem was initially set in terms of the works itself. Even within this definition the engineering workers were excluded by their own choice (see chapter 3), and this was undoubtedly a significant limitation. As was illustrated in Part One, the Project was nevertheless able successfully to tackle a wide range of issues within the works, and to identify broader issues for senior management consideration. The tension between small, localised programmes and larger, more diffuse activities is difficult to resolve, and we return to it in the next chapter.

Assessment of resources

The second step in our idealised model of change involves an examination of what resources are available for possible action. These resources may be knowledge provided by other companies who have identified similar problems and themselves attempted solutions, or they may be in the form of external consultants or researchers who claim some expertise in the areas defined.

Particularly important, however, is an examination of internal resources. Has the organisation enough money to undertake possible programmes of action? The expense of these will exceed the definable costs described in chapter 8 to include finance for new procedures or equipment. As the Employee Relations Project moved forward, it was suggested by several managers that provision at the outset of a fund to implement desirable Project recommendations for which money was not available would have been useful to maintain momentum and enthusiasm. In this respect, perhaps the initial assessment of resources for the ERP was less than perfect. On the other hand, it was after the initial decisions had been taken that the general economic climate deteriorated, and the impact of this was not foreseeable at the outset.

Other internal resources include equipment and time. In terms of programmes like the ERP these may be linked through a consideration of whether technical developments are also envisaged during the period. It was clear in sections of Tinsley Park Works that important managers were extremely busy with the installation of costly new equipment, so that the time they had available for the Project was consequently diminished. In assessing the resources for possible projects, we should ask how far other major developments are likely to compete for substantial investment of energy and time and what priority is likely to be assigned to each.

Furthermore, we need to make a realistic assessment of the interest, knowledge and skills of likely participants. This is extremely difficult, and the process will inevitably overlap with other stages, for example, the identification of problems and the establishment of their boundaries (step one) and the execution of the chosen strategy (step four). The skills of the participants are of particular significance here. In cases of job redesign, have the job-holders the necessary ability to undertake more challenging work; and in programmes of downward delegation can the foremen accept the greater responsibility which is to be granted them? This assessment is not merely of the skills thought to be available at the time, but also of the resources for training and further development. The latter question extends beyond the quantity and quality of training staff to cover questions of possible release from productive work and the time available for broad-ranging training schemes. A general problem is that one often does not know if resources are capable of meeting new demands without putting them to the test; some form of experimentation is thus often necessary.

Choice of strategy

The third stage in the sequence we have proposed is the choice of a strategy to deal with the identified problems in the light of the resources available. In some circumstances, of course, this third stage will not be reached, since a decision may have been taken that the problem is not sufficiently serious or widely accepted, or the resources may have been deemed to be inadequate.

In evaluating the third stage we are interested in the extent to which possible options are considered, who makes the choice, and the criteria adopted during decision-making. Of central importance also is the type of programme which is chosen. The decision here will partly depend upon the assessment of internal resources, in that, for example, some organisations will be more suited than others to an examination of their interpersonal and intergroup relationships. In the case of the Employee Relations Project, the decision was for a flexible system of problem-solving groups which could themselves select the kinds of issues to be tackled. In other cases an initial choice of different procedures (see chapters 10, 11 and 15) might be appropriate [2].

These themes provide a convenient background for two general points about evaluation. The first of these is its essential subjectivity. There are no clear quantitative markers that allow us to say that a programme of change was or was not 'good'. The conclusion depends on the observer's expectations and aspirations, and also on the frame of reference he brings with him. For example, our frame of reference suggests the desirability of widespread discussion before a programme like the ERP is undertaken. Such discussion serves to explore possible options, but goes beyond that to present new ideas, to explore possible areas of agreement, to communicate intentions, to accept the existence of disagreement, and to permit the beginnings of changed opinions and behaviours. However, a busy manager might point to the practical problems involved, the need to make rapid progress, and the fact that the likely outcome is already clear; he might be more concerned that agreement was in fact reached, placing less emphasis on the breadth of discussion and non-managerial consideration of options. Judgements about a programme are thus unlikely always to coincide.

The question of the subjectivity of evaluation will be considered again later. The second point to be introduced here is the parallel between the evaluation of change programmes like the ERP and the more limited evaluation of training. Several techniques for training evaluation have been developed in recent years [3], and there are many useful applications of these. But it should be noted that most training is not evaluated at all, usually because of the high cost and difficulty. In the light of the very restricted knowledge about the evaluation of training, we should not be too discouraged that the evaluation of much more complex and diffuse programmes of organisational change is far from easy [4].

Execution of the chosen strategy

The fourth step in evaluation is particularly problematic: how well are the plans applied and how effectively are the methods undertaken? Principal attention here naturally falls upon any consultants or action researchers, and it is to be expected that their performance will be closely watched. In the case of the Employee Relations Project, consideration has to be given to our own effectiveness. Each of us can identify times when he might have behaved more appropriately, and we have all acquired some new behaviours and outlooks as a result of the Project. But who can assess our performance in detail, as we moved from person to person and from activity to activity?

This problem applies in all programmes like the Employee Relations Project, and it is reasonable that some systematic evaluative checks should be made as plans begin to develop. But the effectiveness of other people and activities is also of interest to the evaluator. For example, he needs to examine how well group leaders prepared for their meetings, how they handled their groups, how they followed up the decisions, to what extent managerial commitments to action were subsequently maintained, how effective were individual counselling or training schemes, how convenient were the administrative procedures, how far did staff changes hamper progress, and many other similar issues. The questions which can be asked in evaluating the processes through which a strategy is applied are clearly diverse and difficult.

Interim reviews and adjustment

Whether or not a programme of organisational change involves an external action researcher it will inevitably be 'organic' in the sense that it develops and moves in unpredictable directions with some unanticipated consequences. This gives rise to the need for interim adjustments, and programmes require some mechanism for monitoring progress and responding flexibly to events as they occur.

The Employee Relations Project was guided by the Project Steering Committee (see chapter 3), and this group regularly assessed progress and made decisions about procedure. The project coordinator was also active in attempts to encourage development and to make up lost ground in particular areas, and we were ourselves continuously working to maintain activities within the overall plan.

Although the Project was thus subject to formal and informal review, the changes which were made tended to be small ones. Three exceptions to this come to mind. Our original plan for several discrete stages (see chapter 3) was revised to allow the stages to merge into each other as necessary. Second, we came to view the project questionnaire in a changed light (see chapter 11), and third we came to see the need for an Interim Report in which we presented our own conclusions and recommendations (see chapter 6).

In retrospect we are sure that this flexibility was desirable, although it is difficult to say whether or not other adjustments should have been made. The momentum of the Project itself could have created difficulties if we had wished to introduce any major new components. The feeling on the works was that the Project should go ahead in the form which had been agreed; large additions would have to be negotiated through a re-run of the preliminary stages. To do this would clearly hamper current progress and also require a fresh investment of time and energy whose supply could not be guaranteed.

174

Establishment of longer-term structures

The sixth stage in our idealised model of organisational change extends beyond the formal ending of a specific project. It is possible for a change programme to be successful, in that the previous five stages are undertaken effectively, but for the basic situation to remain unchanged after its completion. There is therefore a need for any programme to create longer-term structures which develop and sustain the procedures and attitudes which it has introduced.

The 'structures' we have in mind include new networks of management meetings, new channels of communication, successful consultative mechanisms, adequate procedures for handling grievances and industrial relations problems, new equipment or workshop layout, changed payment systems, and so on. Also relevant are altered personal outlooks, increased motivation and enhanced skill levels. These are often very diffuse and difficult to assess, but they may sometimes be evidenced by specific behavioural changes.

The Employee Relations Project set much store upon members of the works establishing routine procedures to monitor their own effectiveness. For example, an annual review of formal management meetings and of the joint consultative committee network was advocated. Another specific change in behaviour was the growing emphasis on 'action points' and changes in the conduct of meetings to stress the outcome of a discussion and procedures to follow up the chosen action. Examination of specific innovations of this kind may be included within this sixth stage.

In evaluating the stage as a whole we are faced with a problem of deciding how long a period is appropriate for assessing the longer-term structures which have been developed. Should one examine the situation immediately after the programme, or is it better to delay assessment for, say, six months? There is no easy answer to this, but factors which might influence a decision include the purpose of evaluation and the expectations held by the observers. We return to these general issues later.

Assessment of effectiveness

The final stage of our model deals with procedures to assess the effectiveness of the programme: what steps were taken to monitor the outcomes, costs and reactions? And how far has the experience generalised for future application?

Measurement of outcomes might be in terms of significant types of behaviour, for example, dispute levels, number of meetings between different sections, number of problems solved, amount of overtime worked, level of labour turnover, or whatever indices are appropriate for the problems identified in earlier stages. An account of some of the outcomes of the Employee Relations Project has been presented in chapter 8, and some factors influencing the impact of projects of this kind are examined in chapter 15. We note there that different parts of a works are likely to have different initial needs for change, so that a consistently large impact is not to be expected.

In addition to behavioural measures there is usually a case for some form of questionnaire survey of opinions about salient issues and the nature and extent of changes achieved. At Tinsley Park Works we used two major kinds of opinion questionnaire. First, we took Before, During and After measures of people's assessments of the employee relations climate on the works. Details of items and results are given in chapter 8, where we documented, for example, an increase in judged friendliness and a significant decline in distrust between shop floor and management. A set of measurements like this spanning the period of a change programme is extremely useful, but there are difficulties. For instance, the sample of respondents may vary slightly across the three occasions of testing; and it may later become apparent that items selected for the first questionnaire do not cover all the issues subsequently seen to be important.

A second form of questionnaire is purely retrospective. We included questions in the After questionnaire to tap people's beliefs that changes (for better or for worse) had taken place in, for example, relations between unions and management over the period of the Project. We then asked whether or not the Project had played a part in any reported changes. This procedure has two advantages: information needs to be gathered on only one occasion (after the programme), and evidence is generated about the relevance of the programme to any changes that have occurred.

Some combination of the two procedures seems to be desirable, but the retrospective assessment may be particularly useful in cases where a programme has been introduced without prior plans for systematic evaluation. In these cases the lack of a Before questionnaire is often thought to prohibit detailed assessment, but this is only true for the before-and-after design, and the problem can be circumvented through the procedures described more fully in chapter 8.

However, information gathered through either questionnaire method still requires interpretation, and the problem is once again: how positive a result is required before we judge the programme to have been a success? At the very least we should require that changes reach conventional levels of statistical significance, but even then absolute differences between Before and After scores may be relatively small. Once more it is a matter of personal judgement, although of course the more extensive and relevant the changes the more convincing they will be.

A related difficulty is that changes within a social network may not always take the form of moves along a preselected dimension, such as the level of friendliness within a department or the amount of communication between management and shop floor. Another form of change, much more difficult to measure, is in terms of the judged salience or importance of an aspect of organisational life. To take an extreme example, the amount of communication within a department could remain unchanged over a period, but there could be a growing recognition that good communication is important enough to warrant increased attention when time is available. In such a case, changes in amount and kind of communication might take place at a later date, mediated by the covert and unobserved shift in priorities which has taken place during the programme itself. It is therefore helpful to attempt to assess changes in judged priorities as well as merely moves along pre-determined scales.

A quite different type of opinion should also be examined in the seventh stage of a change programme. The discussion above concerned participants' opinions about each other and about important issues identified through stage one, in the present case about issues of employee relations. But we should also examine people's reactions to the programme itself: do they think that it was helpful and worthwhile, and in what ways do they believe it could have been improved?

Some form of questionnaire study is often practicable to acquire this information and to avoid selective sampling of the reactions of particularly vociferous participants. Yet there are a number of problems. For example, should one give equal weight to all questionnaire respondents? It may be that the views of those most directly involved in a programme are more significant than others. Further problems concern timing. At what point should opinions about a programme be measured? We have reported how enthusiasm for the Employee Relations Project was high in many parts of Tinsley Park Works during the early stages, but that it declined to varying extents in different departments as time went on. Quite obviously, opinions are likely to change in many ways over a period of months, and there is no one single reaction to a programme.

It seems reasonable to place greatest weight on opinions later in a programme or after it has ended, but there is a substantial problem of adaptation to be faced here. People rapidly adapt to successful new procedures, but they tend to forget the origins of these procedures. A programme like the ERP is necessarily a temporary and minor extension to the normal activity of a works, so that as problems get solved its influential role may become forgotten. Furthermore, as time goes by new problems are likely to capture people's attention. These may be quite different from those which the programme was designed to tackle, but the fact that they are still outstanding (as in the nature of things there always are fresh problems to solve) may lead people to express doubts about the value of the programme.

As we described in chapter 3, several managers and shop stewards at Tinsley Park Works felt that in an ideal world they should be able to solve their own problems among themselves. (We agree with this, and see no place for continuing outside assistance.) But both managers and shop stewards accepted that the Employee Relations Project could be helpful in their situation as a temporary expedient. As the Project developed, we noted many occasions when satisfaction was expressed at an improvement which we believed had arisen from a project group but which was instead attributed in discussions on the works to the normal process of decision-making.

Of course, the Employee Relations Project and the normal processes of decision-maing were in practice very closely interconnected, since the same people were active in both systems. But the interdependence of Project and day-to-day decision-making, combined with people's tendency to adapt to new situations, prompts a generalisation of some importance. The successes of a programme like the ERP are often likely to be minimised in retrospective judgements whereas its deficiencies are likely to be emphasised. This means that reaction evaluation studies may yield potentially misleading results. However, this generalisation should itself be qualified by the observation that for some people the benefits of a programme will become more visible as it recedes into the past and a balanced view becomes possible.

A related problem of retrospective opinions obtained through a questionnaire survey of a whole works is that many people will have no clear view. This may be for several reasons. At one extreme an employee might only recently have commenced work in the company, so that he might know nothing of the programme in question. Or a longer-serving person might himself not have been actively involved (for example, only twenty per cent of shop-floor employees took part in the ERP project groups), so that he has no well-formed opinion. Additionally, the process of forgetting is such that his recall may be hazy or dominated by a single salient event (positive or negative). Another factor is the influence of social group values in determining individual opinions. A person with no direct knowledge about a change programme (perhaps for one of the reasons noted above) is likely to respond in terms of what he has heard his mates say, irrespective of the evidence for their conclusion.

The inference to be drawn from these facts is that a strongly positive reaction to a large-scale programme of organisational change is not to be expected. It may be that the most meaningful index is in terms of the prevalence of negative reactions: how few people are opposed to the programme? Furthermore, the reasons for opposition can provide very valuable information. We have explored the forms these took in relation to the Employee Relations Project at various points throughout the book.

Finally, in our discussion of stage seven of a change programme, we should consider the question of generalisation to other people and places. This is partly a question of the establishment of longer-term structures (stage six) to extend the application of new ideas and procedures. However, we might also ask whether an organisation has attempted to study the experience gained through a programme in one site to assess its potential relevance to other works or divisions. There are sometimes problems of organisational politics here, as the managers involved in a local change programme may be anxious to conceal its less positive features. For example, we have seen how later opinions about a programme are likely to be relatively cool, and local managers may sometimes take this to reflect adversely on their initial decision or on their execution of the programme.

In general terms, however, it is reasonable to argue that some systematic attempt by an organisation to generalise from one local project to other situations is desirable. Indeed, this book aims to extend that process, by describing specific organisational experiences and setting them in a broad interpretative framework.

Further questions of evaluation

The previous section has sketched a seven-point plan for evaluation. To comprehensively evaluate a programme of organisational change one should examine the effectiveness with which each of the seven stages has been undertaken. We have illustrated some of the problems associated with each stage, and we now move on to look at the process of evaluation as a whole.

The first problem to be considered is that of reaching an overall assessment. Within each of the steps there might be varied and conflicting evidence, and it may be difficult to reach a definite evaluative conclusion. This problem is, of course, compounded when we try to put the evidence from all seven steps together to reach an overall conclusion: has the programme as a whole been worthwhile? It may happen that assessments are inconsistent between the stages, some favourable, some unfavourable and others equivocal.

One solution to the difficulty is to ask for seven different evaluative statements as well as an overall conclusion. In this way we might aim for an evaluative profile, indicating success levels at each stage. Such a procedure is the principal recommendation of this chapter.

However, severe difficulties still remain. A major problem arises from the absence of quantitative markers in this field: how good is 'good'? It is often very difficult to form a clear opinion whether a particular stage was carried out 'successfully', as in an ideal world there will usually be scope for better performance. The practical need to reconcile conflicting pressures, to allocate time to different tasks, and to work within a specified budget all prevent the perfect execution of a programme, but it is usually less than clear whether an organisation's trade-off between its many practical requirements has created a programme of change which should be described as 'very good', 'good', 'satisfactory' or 'poor'.

Here is the essential subjectivity of evaluation, to which we have already referred. There is a need to systematise the process wherever possible, through the development of profiles as just mentioned for example, but different observers may still reach different conclusions. This may be because of their divergent expectations and aspirations or because they are adopting different time-spans for perception. Furthermore, a programme of change can lead some participants afterwards to view their plant and its problems in a manner rather different from before, and their estimate of the programme's success may be coloured by this revised perspective.

The discussion so far has assumed that an evaluator wishes to attempt a comprehensive assessment of all aspects of the programme as a whole. In such a case the seven-point plan provides a framework. However, detailed and wideranging evaluation of this kind is time-consuming and expensive, and there may be occasions when a more restricted assessment is appropriate. Such an assessment might study in depth one or two of the stages, or it might take a less detailed view of several of them.

This leads into the final issue of this chapter: can the participants in a change programme properly evaluate it themselves, or should an independent evaluator undertake this role? Involved participants (for example, ourselves in the present case) may be biased towards seeing more success than other people see. On the other hand they are much closer to the plant and its idiosyncracies than is an external and independent evaluator, so that they are better placed to bring together the facts and interpretations which are necessary for detailed assessment of all the stages.

Furthermore, experience elsewhere has suggested that an independent evaluator almost inevitably becomes drawn into the activities of change, thus losing his independence. For example, having gathered material early in the course of a programme his independent role requires him to avoid comment on what he has learnt and what he sees. This tight-lipped silence may well reduce people's willingness to divulge to him the small items of information which he must accumulate if he is to form a sound opinion. Such an independent, uninformative stance is extremely difficult to maintain. Furthermore, it might happen that he gathers information at an early stage which could in principle be used to improve the effectiveness of later stages. This presents a moral problem: should he merely observe activities which he knows to be open to improvement or should he contribute to that improvement?

The central question is again that of the purpose of evaluation. A detached 'wise after the event' style may be less effective in generating learning and change than one which encourages a dynamic interplay between a programme and its evaluation. The effective operation of any organisation requires it to gather and use information about its own progress. This applies to day-to-day management as well as to programmes like the Employee Relations Project. However, there are many possible approaches to data gathering and use, and the most suitable strategy appears to be one which operates at several levels. For example, 'short-cycle feedback' through continual monitoring of information is desirable (it figures as stage five in our model), but 'long-cycle feedback' taking a broader view from a greater distance also has its place. The former evaluation may be undertaken by participants in the programme itself, whereas long-cycle feedback may sometimes be better provided by an independent observer.

Notes

[1] This theme is powerfully developed by C. Argyris and D. Schon, *Theory in Practice: Increasing Professional Effectiveness*, Jossey Bass, San Francisco, 1974.

[2] R. Harrison suggests 'two criteria for choosing the appropriate depth of intervention: first, to intervene at a level no deeper than that required to produce enduring solutions to the problems at hand; and second, to intervene at a level no deeper than that at which the energy and resources of the client can be committed to problem solving and change' (p. 201). See 'Choosing

the depth of organizational intervention', *Journal of Applied Behavioral Science*, vol. 6, 1970, pp. 181–202.

[3]   See, for example, A.C. Hamblin, *Evaluation and Control of Training*, McGraw-Hill, London, 1974; and P. Warr, M. Bird and N. Rackham, *Evaluation of Management Training*, Gower Press, Epping, 1970.

[4]   A useful review of evaluation studies and their problems is provided by D. Gowler and K. Legge, 'The evaluation of planned organisational change: the necessary art of the possible?', *Journal of Enterprise Management*, 1978, in press.

15 Change programmes, organisation development and social psychology

This final chapter will review the aims, activities and attainments of the Employee Relations Project, and examine some ways in which it might have been still more effective. We will consider the range of factors that can influence the impact of programmes of this kind, and will examine the place of action research programmes within the traditions of organisation development and social psychology; both these disciplines have strongly influenced our approach to the topics covered in this book.

Looking back on the Employee Relations Project

The overall objective of the Project was to improve relationships between people and between groups of people employed at Tinsley Park Works and between this works and Stocksbridge. Our action research strategy was one of providing time for people to meet, improving the quality of communication between them when they did meet, identifying the problems which were causing ineffective performance, and then committing people to spend time, money and other resources to solve the problems.

From the outset the Project was explicitly seen as one of dual sponsorship, and this was exemplified through the setting up of the Project Steering Committee of union and management members. The Steering Committee helped to design the Project, monitored its progress and coordinated the production of *Focus*, the special bulletin about the Project.

The Employee Relations Project had five main components, as follows:

1   A network of project groups was established. These involved people at all levels of the works, meeting on up to nine occasions. The group leaders were managers, foremen and shop stewards, who had previously received training in discussion skills. The groups met to identify problems, to recommend solutions, and to attempt to implement proposals. Their progress and problems in these tasks have been described in chapters 4 and 10.

2   A project questionnaire was completed by eighty-three per cent of the workforce and the pattern of attitudes thus revealed was fed back to the works for discussion in a number of different meetings. This 'survey feedback' activity has been examined in chapters 5 and 11.

3   An Interlinked Phase investigated the process of union—management relations on the works and initiated some changes in structures and procedures

(see chapters 6 and 13).

4　We prepared an Interim Report containing our own analysis of the wide-ranging issues facing the works and presenting some recommendations to tackle these issues. This has been summarised in chapter 6.

5　The effectiveness of the Project was monitored in several ways. Important successes have been reviewed in chapter 8 and a broad framework for evaluation was presented in chapter 14.

These activities extended over two and a half years and the character of our involvement as action researchers has been described throughout the book and analysed more formally in chapter 9. We undertook a number of different roles: as facilitators in problem-solving discussions, trainers, communicators, counsellors, designers and analysts in survey feedback exercises, progress chasers, prescriptive consultants and so on. Some of these roles were undoubtedly discharged more effectively than others, but for a very small cost the Employee Relations Project was able to identify and clarify many of the problems existing at Tinsley Park, to demonstrate where agreement existed or where there was room for movement, and to initiate a large number of improvements which otherwise would not have occurred.

However, important problems remained unsolved. These included the quality of relationships between certain sections and departments, interunion rivalries and some works-wide communication difficulties. So whereas we have concluded that the Employee Relations Project had an undoubtedly beneficial impact, it is also appropriate to ask how it could have been still more successful.

In retrospect, one possibility would have been in terms of additional money to spend on equipment or personnel issues where all parties agreed on a solution; perhaps special expenditure could have been authorised to generate and sustain commitment and to help create a situation where success breeds on itself. This is, of course, easier said than done in times of financial stringency. Other possible improvements include more preparation and training for group leaders; facilities for spending time away from the works to examine some issues in a more concentrated way; fewer transfers of key managers so that involvement and enthusiasm were better sustained over the lengthy period of the Project; for the same reason a larger contingent of managers on the Project Steering Committee might have been helpful.

All these themes should be considered in future designs. The broad question of relations between two geographically separate but functionally interdependent works requires particular attention. There may be a case for suggesting an ancillary programme specifically to deal with problems associated with relationships between the two works. The Employee Relations Project was based within a single plant, and there were many occasions when its effectiveness was limited by this fact. An additional 'interworks project' might have been valuable, involving a selection of employees from both sites. Project groups in this latter network could have brought together members from each site who dealt with each other in the course of their work. As with the ERP project groups, all levels of employees would have participated in the interworks project, the difference being that the problems to be addressed would be those to do with linkages between the works [1].

A separate issue is the scale of changes which might be aimed for or achieved. Even with the improvements and extensions which can with hindsight be suggested, the Employee Relations Project would not have introduced really fundamental changes to organisational structure and functioning. It was not aimed at change in the sense of 'revolution' or 'metamorphosis', but at adjustment, improvement and 'tuning up'.

The pressures for fundamental change are rarely widespread, and organisational constraints are usually powerful and pervasive. The constraints upon changes in employee relations include the major objectives and procedures of management and industrial relations systems, interdependencies, regulations and precedents that are not easily shaken. Without doubt these wider constraints should be examined and sometimes challenged through projects like the ERP (and we have indicated that more could have been achieved there), but it is inappropriate to aim for their complete removal.

Different change projects will strike a different balance between local improvements of benefit to workgroups and departments and large system-wide structural alterations. This balance will vary according to the programme's principal focus. In our case we were dealing particularly with shop floor and departmental management and with the effectiveness of each group. Our focus was upon coalitions of local interest groups in some conflict with each other within a single works. A wider perspective may be adopted by action researchers working at, say, board of director level, but these researchers will themselves find it difficult successfully to tackle day-to-day operational problems and shop-floor attitudes. In practice, then, each type of study has its own limitations, complementary to its strengths, and really fundamental organisational reconstruction is unlikely.

Factors making for success

Within this general framework of objectives and possible methodological improvements, what else can be said about the specific factors which have a bearing upon the potential success of projects like the ERP? It is in the nature of such projects that they are merely temporary; their objective is to do themselves out of a job. They aim to initiate movement in situations where the self-maintaining aspects of conflict have led to relatively fixed positions of mutual opposition. This forward movement has to be directed towards new and more effective organisational structures and routines.

There are many companies where some 'nudging' process of this kind may be useful. Yet many factors can impede success, and in this section we will consider some of them. They will be illustrated through comparisons between the two departments at Tinsley Park Works where the Employee Relations Project had its most and least noticeable impact: Billet Finishing department and the Melting Shop respectively. Eight factors will be considered.

Initial scope for improvement

Even within a single works it is unusual for relationships to be equally good or bad in all departments and some will have more difficulties than others. Not surprisingly, an Employee Relations Project is likely to be of greater value in a department judged by its members to have more problems than in one where problems are fewer.

Within Tinsley Park Works it was apparent that there was greater initial scope for improvement in Billet Finishing than in the Melting Shop. Several features of this have been considered in Part One, but as an example let us here consider the shop floor and non-supervisory staff answers to the Before and After questionnaire item: 'There is a friendly atmosphere in my department'. The percentages of Melting Shop employees agreeing with this statement before and after the Project were seventy-four and seventy-seven. It may be thought that percentages as high as this are unlikely to be greatly exceeded whatever actions take place. On the other hand the Billet Finishing initial percentage was only forty-nine, clearly offering greater scope for improvement. In the course of the Project the Billet Finishing figure rose to seventy per cent, an encouraging increase up to near the Melting Shop's initial level.

Two points should be made about this. The first is in terms of evaluation: we should not expect equal success in all departments if they differ in their scope for improvement. The second is that there is still value in including those departments with smaller room for improvement within an Employee Relations Project. Not only will there be within-department issues to tackle, but inevitably there will be between-department questions involving other parts of the works. The initial exclusion of one department from the Project would reduce the possibility of dealing successfully with these between-department issues.

Potential for locally determined changes

A second factor influencing the impact of an Employee Relations Project is the potential within a department to carry out changes with the money and resources available. This is partly a question of the complexity of technology (there is less possibility of altering jobs and relationships in departments operating very large and expensive plant) and partly a matter of the resources which a department can itself bring to bear upon the problems it identifies.

The Melting Shop operated through jobs integrated with each other and dependent upon expensive technology, whereas Billet Finishing had more separated jobs in which employees undertook self-paced batch work. In general terms, then, there was more potential for locally-determined changes and innovations in Billet Finishing. (Of course, this says nothing about the need for such changes.)

Continuity of management

The key role of management in furthering the objectives of an Employee Relations Project has been stressed throughout this book [2]. The impact of a change programme is likely to be reduced in departments where the manager who initially accepts responsibility for it moves out. The new incumbent will require time to learn about his department and its members, he is likely to have his own priorities for action, and he will be less familiar with the goals and progress to date of the programme. During the Employee Relations Project the Melting Shop department manager changed, but the management team in Billet Finishing remained stable.

Management resources and time

A fourth point is in terms of the resources and time which members of a management team are able to devote to a change programme (leaving aside for the moment how much they want to devote to it). The commissioning of new plant in the Melting Shop was one factor which required extensive management attention; there was thus in principle less time available for work on the Employee Relations Project. In Billet Finishing, on the other hand, the equipment and processes remained largely unchanged during the course of the Project. The general pattern of departmental priorities relative to resources needed within a programme is clearly one which influences its impact.

Pressure on management for involvement in the programme

Among the factors influencing management's willingness to take up issues arising from project groups is that of outside encouragement and pressure. This might come from senior managers or friends and colleagues or it might come from the researchers. It is not possible to make detailed comparative statements about this feature at Tinsley Park, but there were probably some important differences in the outside encouragement received by different department managers. These no doubt worked in conjunction with other factors identified in this section to influence the impact of the Employee Relations Project.

Managers' personal interest in the programme

This sixth factor is related to the previous three, but may be presented separately. Managers differ among themselves in their wish to undertake projects of this kind. Factors affecting their outlook include several of those just mentioned, but there is also a personal interest and commitment arising from past experience and present view of one's job and department. If a section manager, say, identifies himself with a style of behaviour opposed to meetings with subordinates and opposed to consideration of their views, then the success of an Employee Relations Project within his section will inevitably be limited.

Shop steward and project group leaders' interest

Another aspect of this question is the degree of interest among other central participants in the programme. It is evident that their interest in making the programme work will influence its level of success.

Interest from outside the works

We have repeatedly observed that it is important to enlist the interest of people outside the works. This naturally includes top management, without whose support a project cannot extend into interworks issues. But it may also include less senior managers and shop-floor members within another works, if the two sites are operationally dependent upon each other. The extent to which such external interest is mobilised constitutes an eighth factor influencing the impact of a change programme.

Activities of the researcher

We have examined the action researcher's role on many occasions throughout the book, and it may be helpful at this point to summarise some of our conclusions about issues to be faced and decisions to be taken. For brevity we will do this in the form of somewhat curt prescriptive statements.

1   Take care when negotiating the research contract to raise at an early stage the central questions of objectives, values and resources, and build in enough flexibility to permit constructive responses to new issues and problems as they arise.
2   Recognise that high level 'gatekeepers' are particularly concerned with general strategies and objectives, but that precise working procedures and tactics need to be examined at length with participants 'on the ground'. In all cases ensure that gatekeepers and opinion leaders are kept well informed.
3   Try to attain widespread commitment at the outset but recognise that prior universal enthusiasm is not usually attainable. Accept that the initial basis for commitment will often be the exercise of authority by superiors but that this is the mainspring for much organisational action.
4   Aim for early momentum by generating initial, observable successes that are clearly important to participants.
5   Be prepared for 'creative tension' in the relationship between researcher and organisation, and do not attempt to avoid this by allowing either party to dominate the other.
6   Try to incorporate a range of interlocking processes for change, and when implementing these work upon the factors necessary for success: knowledge, skills, commitment, and time for acceptance of and experimentation

with new ideas. Select an appropriate 'mix' of change procedures in relation to the organisational participants and your own skills and values.

7 Carefully assess the role of survey feedback in an overall programme, and try to build an active and directed system which is capable of examining action requirements in the light of the data that are fed back.

8 Be prepared to make your own independent assessment and recommendations for change, but be clear about the need constructively to handle dependency relationships. Ensure that recommendations are processed through organisational decision-making mechanisms which have adequate power.

9 Be aware of structural limitations and influences on change, so that broader issues are not overlooked. Examine at the outset and subsequently the need for procedures to tackle problems of relationships between sites and between the works and the larger corporate organisation.

10 Ensure that formal systems of relations are not bypassed by the change programme. In unionised settings build upon established union—management systems and attempt to create long-term improvements in the effectiveness of these systems.

11 Ensure that line managers are centrally involved through all levels and functions of the programme. Remember 'Harvey's Law', that the effectiveness of a change programme is inversely proportional to the number of staff specialists involved [3].

12 Identify a model of the evaluation process and plan evaluation procedures from the outset. Think in terms of multi-stage, multi-criteria assessment methods.

13 Be clear about the need to aim towards long-term structures which incorporate features of the change programme on a permanent basis. At the same time do not lose sight of the fact that an Employee Relations Project is itself essentially a temporary mechanism.

14 Encourage, in the short term and in the long term, the establishment of procedures through which the organisation and its parts can monitor their own effectiveness. Self-correcting systems are the goal [4].

As in previous sections we do not want to give the impression that we always 'practised what we preach', for we met a number of these prescriptions less than perfectly. Indeed, our understanding of some of them has been considerably enhanced through our experiences in the Employee Relations Project.

Organisation development

Many of the points covered in this chapter and throughout the book fall within what has become known as 'organisation development', or 'OD' for short. This is a growing discipline whose practitioners are concerned to work within organisations of all kinds (not merely industry) to increase personal, interpersonal and organisational effectiveness. The literature on organisation development is now substantial [5], and the variety of methods, concepts and value systems is sufficient to confuse the beginner and often the more experienced practitioner.

Friedlander has characterised this by suggesting that organisation development has reached 'adolescence', with all the promises and problems which this can bring. He describes 'a strapping youth — eager, energetic, confused, looking for an identity, looking to prove himself, wondering what he will be and do when he grows up, wondering if he ever will' [6].

The uncertainty about the 'identity' of organisation development is illustrated by the wide variety of procedures and objectives which have been espoused. Our own classification of procedures has been presented in chapters 10 and 11, and the model of French and Bell [7] encompasses the following:

1 *Intervention targets.* Goals, formal procedures, organisational structure, work tasks, rules, personnel policy, skills and abilities, communications, role expectations, group interactions, attitudes, group norms and values, group process skills, 'here and now' relationships between people, life styles, past history, personal behaviour styles and defences, unconscious or repressed personal features.

2 *Intervention techniques.* Job enrichment, management by objectives, role analysis, attitude surveys and feedback, interface problem-solving meetings, team building, training in interpersonal skills, T-groups, encounter groups, personal growth laboratories, group psychotherapy.

It is obvious from these lists that no one researcher or group of researchers could ever realistically seek to 'practice organisation development' in its entirety. Choice of approach will depend upon the situation. The Employee Relations Project dealt with only a few of the suggested targets and techniques, primarily those which were less threatening to individuals and the organisation. We were working principally at the interface between shop floor and management, a setting which is quite rare for organisation development studies where the focus is more frequently on managers or professional staff. For our project we felt that methods such as those used in, for example, personal growth laboratories had little to offer.

One helpful perspective on the wide variety of options in organisation development is Friedlander's suggestion [8] that practitioner values may be classified according to their emphasis on 'rationalism', 'pragmatism' and 'existentialism'. Rationalism is in the intellectual tradition of carefully defining ideas, building models and systematically testing them to discover truth. Pragmatism is more concerned with the success of procedures whether or not they fit within preconceived theories or knowledge. The existentialist philosophy is one which stresses the importance of personal feelings and the role of current needs in determining choice; there is less emphasis on objective reality, in that 'reality' is seen to be whatever a person perceives and uses to guide his choices.

	Rationalism	Pragmatism	Existentialism
Purpose:	To discover truth	To improve practice	To experience, choose, commit
Basic activity:	Think (knowledge building)	Do (acting)	Exist (being)
Learning paradigm:	Conceptualise: define: manipulate ideas	Practice: experiment: valid feedback: improvement	Experience: choose: commit
Terms are:	Precisely defined	Tentatively defined	Need not be defined
Meaning emerges from:	Definition (concepts)	Practice (results)	Experience (perception)
Ingredients for learning:	Concepts, assumptions, logic	Practice, experiment, feedback	Awareness and confrontation of one's existence
Locus of knowledge:	The conceptual model	The organisational practice	The individual experience
Reality is:	Objectivity and truth	Workability and practice	Subjective perception
Causes of good communication:	Semantic precision	Consensual listening and understanding	Shared feeling and resonance

Figure 15.1   Friedlander's summary of three value sets in organisation development

Friedlander's summary of these three philosophies in the context of organisation development (Figure 15.1) is helpful in finding one's way around the literature. What particular 'mix' of the three outlooks does an author or researcher represent? Much of the earlier writing in the field placed 'existentialist' emphasis upon personal experiences and growth, yet that type of approach is not one that will suit all organisations and problems.

The 'mix' of the three outlooks adopted during the Employee Relations Project varied from time to time and from person to person, but it will be clear from what has been described that the principal emphasis was of a 'pragmatic' kind. In comparing the events at Tinsley Park Works with those in other successful organisation development exercises [9], readers might find it instructive to identify the pattern of values in each case, as represented by the three principal outlooks described by Friedlander. At the same time comparisons may be made in terms of the change procedures used (see, for example, the profile presented at the end of chapter 11); some procedures are of course more in tune than others with each of the different value systems summarised here.

Social psychology

In addition to wishing to locate this book within the organisation development literature, so do we view it as example of research in social psychology. Nevertheless, despite the book's extensive discussions of interpersonal and intergroup relationships, roles, attitudes and other clearly social psychological concepts, there is a large gap between the methods and ideas examined here and those presented in the orthodox textbooks of social psychology. Our final task is to examine this contrast and the reasons behind it.

This may be undertaken by looking at three major characteristics of academic psychology in order to identify the style and content of research which have been popular in recent decades [10]. These characteristics will each be presented in terms of contrasting poles of a dimension of difference, so that any psychological study may be given a position between one pole and the other.

Individual versus social

This dimension refers to the principal focus of the psychologist's investigation. Does it deal with isolated individuals (for example, in a study of visual perception or reaction times) or does it deal with people in a social situation of some kind? The work of psychologists can clearly range widely between the completely 'individual' and the unequivocally 'social', and no single focus is 'correct' to the exclusion of others.

Mechanistic versus experiential

A 'mechanistic' approach to psychology is one which chooses topics, methods and explanations which highlight the potential of machine (or computer) analogies of the person. Much academic psychology is of this kind, preferring to deal with quantifiable features of behaviour rather than less easily measured feelings and experiences. The latter type of approach (which has some similarity with the 'existential' outlook described above) may be referred to as 'experiential' psychology.

Pure versus applied

The third dimension of academic psychology is in terms of whether an investigation is 'pure' research, originating within the discipline and aiming to answer questions of principal interest to psychologists alone, or whether it is 'applied' in the sense that it examines questions of practical significance beyond merely psychology.

Putting together these three dimensions we can characterise the recent academic psychological orthodoxy as follows:

1 *Individual versus social.* The bulk of post-war academic pscyhology has concerned the 'individual' pole of this dimension.
2 *Mechanistic versus experiential.* The 'mechanistic' outlook has clearly been dominant.
3 *Pure versus applied.* The large majority of academic psychological research has been within the 'pure research' tradition.

Furthermore, it is clear that social psychological researchers themselves have been influenced by the overriding values bearing upon the other two dimensions. That is to say, academic social psychology has been almost exclusively 'mechanistic' and 'pure' in its orientation. The typical study has been conducted in the laboratory with small temporary groups (usually of students), and has required experimental manipulations and tight controls along with an emphasis on precise observation and measurement.

It is not hard to see the reasons for this. Faced with the enormous complexity of everyday society, social psychology has tried to distill the essence of interpersonal processes through natural-science methods in the laboratory. Whilst we do not wish to decry all such investigations, we are very conscious of their limitations. What is now required is a return to the more 'applied' and 'experiential' interests of Lewin, Bartlett and others [11], coupled with the increased sophistication of method and understanding which has been acquired since their pioneering work.

Social psychology will only assume its rightful place in the forefront of the parent discipline by taking its questions, theories and methods into the 'real' world for validation and refinement. This will inevitably involve more attention to the solution of practical problems wherever they occur. Many of these practical issues are to be found at places of work. The social psychological features of organisations are not only of considerable inherent interest, they are also of major importance for personal well-being and self esteem and the national economic situation. However, their investigation is not possible through narrow traditional research designs, and a new research role is required. This has many features which have been important in the neighbouring fields of 'action research' and 'organisation development'.

To approach many practical issues of psychological importance, a 'mechanistic' stance may be neither possible nor desirable, and the social psychologist will have to be prepared to become more closely involved in the processes of change. Indeed, he may sometimes have to play a part in instigating change if he is to have a useful impact upon society. We hope that our account of the Employee Relations Project will prove persuasive to our colleagues in social psychology as well as being helpful to members of work organisations themselves.

Notes

[1] The idea of an 'interworks project' has some similarity with proposals for 'team-building meetings' described in chapter 10, but the concentration on relationships between two separate sites is of special importance here. A fully comprehensive approach would involve two projects, each within a single works, accompanied by an interworks project to tackle issues of relationships. In the case of large companies, the resources required for this comprehensive programme will be greater than are usually available.

[2] Other action researchers have of course made the same point. Discussing her work in the Esso Petroleum Company Ltd., L. Klein writes as follows: 'A situation of frequent management-development moves of key personnel can have two kinds of dysfunctional consequences: the learning of individuals may be inhibited because they do not stay in position long enough to find out how their ideas work out . . . ; and projects themselves may be left incomplete and unevaluated. New people, in turn, want to initiate. It is much less exciting to develop and apply the ideas initiated by someone else. Also, it does not lead to promotion in a climate which values 'innovation'.' (*A Social Scientist in Industry*, Gower Press, Epping, 1976, p. 79.)

[3] In an unusual evaluation of organisation development Harvey compares it to a religious movement ('blessed are they who collaborate') and coins his own law. See J. Harvey, 'Organization development as a religious movement', *Training and Development Journal*, March 1974, pp. 24–7.

[4] This general point has been developed by Argyris and Schon in terms of 'double loop learning' and by Revans in terms of 'autotherapy' of hospital systems. See C. Argyris and D. Schon, *Theory in Practice: Increasing Professional Effectiveness*, Jossey Bass, San Francisco, 1974; and R. W. Revans, *Action Learning in Hospitals*, McGraw-Hill, London, 1976.

[5] See, for example, C. Argyris, *Intervention Theory and Method*, Addison-Wesley, Reading, Massachusetts, 1970; W.L. French and C.H. Bell, *Organiza-*

tion Development, Prentice-Hall, Englewood Cliffs, 1973; J.J. Partin (ed.), *Current Perspectives in Organization Development*, Addison-Wesley, Reading, Massachusetts, 1973; T.E. Stephenson, 'Organization development, a critique', *Journal of Management Studies*, vol. 12, 1975, pp. 249–65; J.M. Thomas and W. Bennis, *The Management of Change and Conflict*, Penguin, Harmondsworth, 1972.

[6]   F. Friedlander, 'OD reaches adolescence: an exploration of its underlying values', *Journal of Applied Behavioral Science*, vol. 12, 1976, pp. 7–21.

[7]   See the book by French and Bell cited in note 5.

[8]   See the article cited in note 6.

[9]   A general review of the impact of OD has been provided by F. Friedlander and L.D. Brown, 'Organization development', *Annual Review of Psychology*, vol. 25, 1974, pp. 313–41. Other useful references to evaluation studies include: D.G. Bowers, 'OD techniques and their results in 23 organizations', *Journal of Applied Behavioral Science*, vol. 9, 1973, pp. 21–43; J.L. Franklin, 'Characteristics of successful and unsuccessful organization development', *Journal of Applied Behavioral Science*, vol. 12, 1976, pp. 471–92; and J. Taylor, 'Experiments in work system design', *Personnel Review*, vol. 6, no. 3, 1977, pp. 21–34.

[10] The themes developed in this section are presented in more detail by P. Warr in 'Towards a more human psychology', *Bulletin of the British Psychological Society*, vol. 26, 1973, pp. 1–8 and 'Aided experiments in social psychology', *Bulletin of the British Psychological Society*, vol. 30, 1977, pp. 2–8.

[11] See, for example, F.C. Bartlett, *Remembering, A Study in Experimental and Social Psychology*, Cambridge University Press, Cambridge, 1932; K. Lewin, 'Frontiers in group dynamics', *Human Relations*, vol. 1, 1947/1948, pp. 5–41 and 143–53.

Index

Action: limitations on 48–49; recommendations 31, 33, 36, 39, 41, 43, 46
Action research 99, 101, 107, 166
Argyris, C 180, 193

Bakke, E.W. 153
Bartlett, F.C. 192, 194
Beer, M. 127
Behrend, M. 168
Bell, C.H. 138, 193, 194
Benne, K.D. 138
Bennis, W.G. 138
Billet Finishing 14
Bird, M. 181
Blau, P. 153
Bowers, D.G. 138, 194
Bricklayers' strike 45, 57, 62
Brown, C.A. 107
Brown, L.D. 138, 194

Chandler, M.K. 153
Change: in behaviour 87; differences in need for 73–75; in employee attitudes 78–83; operational 76–78; retrospective accounts of 83–86; scaling of activities 137–138
Chemers, M.M. 127
Cherns, A.B. 99, 107
Child, J. 153
Chin, R. 138
Clark, A.W. 104, 105, 107
Climate: departmental 115; industrial relations 155–159; organisational 155–156, 167
Colbert, M. 127
Commitment, departmental differences 70–72
Communications: difficulties 121–122; intergroup meeting 112; recommendations 64
Consultative system 59; attitudes towards 60–61
Contract 105
Cooper, C.L. 127

Corporate structure and policy 157
Counselling 110–111

Data feedback 128–129
De Monthoux, P. 107
Differentiation 145–146, 150
Discussion skills 116
Disputes 16, 57, 87–88
Douglas, A 107
Dunnette, M.D. 127
Dyer, L. 168

Educational activities 110
Employee Relations Project: aims 8–9; components 182–183; costs 88–90; factors making for success 184–187; labelling 103; major events 1–2; mechanisms 7–8; opposition to 57–58; origins and introduction of 4–6, 18–24; productivity effects 89–90; stages 18
Evaluation: of change 90–91; effectiveness assessment 175–177; reviews and adjustment 174–175; seven-point plan 169–170; stages of 169–170; strategy choice 172–173; strategy execution 173–174
Existentialism 189
Expectations of success 121–122, 126–127

Fielder, F.E. 127
Fineman, S. 127
Focus 25–27
Fox, A. 107
Franklin, J.L. 194
French, W. 138, 193, 194
Friedlander, F. 138, 191

Gellerman, S. 127
Getting in 97–102
Getting on 102–105
Getting out 105–107
Gowler, D. 181

Publication of: project findings 58–59, 196–107; survey results 53–54

Questionnaire survey: after 20, 79–83; before 20, 74, 80–83; feedback of results 53–55; main project 50, 103; main project response rate 51; main project results 51–53

Rackham, N. 127, 181
Rationalism 189
Ravenscraig survey 6–7
Reality concept 8
Relationships 97–98
Research dimensions 191–192
Researchers' activities and roles 99, 118–119, 125–126, 187–188
Research groups: types of 101
Resources 97–98, 171–172
Revans, R.W. 193
Rigby, A. 153
Role modelling 102

Sayles, L. 153, 168
Schein, E.H. 127
Schon, D. 180, 193
Section Council 23, 24, 60
Sirota, D. 138
Shop stewards 61
Social psychology 191–193
Steering Committee 19, 103: composition 24
Stephenson, G.M. 168
Stephenson, T.E. 194
Stockbridge Works 3, 4, 13
Structures, establishing 136
Success factors in the project 184–187: continuity of management 186; initial scope for improvement 185; interest outside of Works 187;

management resources and time 186; managers' personal interest 186; potential for locally determined changes 185; pressure for managerial involvement 186
Survey feedback: conclusions 135; decision-making 133–134; feedback process 132–133; item layout 131–132; location within change programme 135; management commitment 130–131; outside researchers 134–135; willingness to use results 134
System processes 144–145

Taylor, J. 194
Technological innovations 137
Thomas, J.M. 194
Thomson, A.W.J. 168
Tinsley Park Works 10–18: amenities 15; climate 5, 15–16; hours of work 14; organisation and history 12–14; pay 15
Traffic 14
Training of group leaders 28–29, 110
Trist, E.L. 101, 107
Turnover: of group members 49, 123; of managers 56; of staff 56; of leaders 56–57

Unions 16–17

Values 97–98, 100, 102

Walton, R.E. 168
Warr, P.B. 127, 181, 194
Weber, M. 153
Wolfson, A. 138
Woodward, J. 152
Works Council 17, 60